ANCIENT AND MEDIEVAL ART

CHARIOTEER FROM DELPHI

ANCIENT AND MEDIEVAL ART

A SHORT HISTORY

Margaret Bulley

BRACKEN BOOKS
LONDON

TO

E. H. B.

Ancient and Medieval Art

First published in 1914 by Methuen & Co., London. This revised,
second edition first published in 1926 by Methuen & Co., London

This paperback edition first published in 1996 by Bracken Books,
an imprint of Random House UK Ltd, Random House,
20 Vauxhall Bridge Road, London SW1V 2SA

ISBN 0 09 185050 9

Printed and bound in Guernsey by
The Guernsey Press Co. Ltd

PREFACE

MY warm thanks are due to all who have so kindly helped me in the preparation of this book. A number of publishers and authors have given generous permission for extracts from copyright works to be included in the lessons. In this connection I would like to specially mention Mr John Murray and Messrs Macmillan, who allowed a large number of extracts to be used; Mr John Lane for permission to quote a verse from *The Father of the Forest* by William Watson; M. Fasquelle for leave to include two verses by Gautier from *Emaux et Camées*, published by the Librairie Charpentier et Fasquelle; Mr Theodore Watts-Dunton for permission to include an extract from Swinburne's *Erechtheus*; Mr J. E. Flecker for allowing me to quote part of *The Golden Journey to Samarkand*; and the Controller of His Majesty's Stationery Office for granting permission for the inclusion of an extract from one of the South Kensington Hand-books.

As regards the illustrations, I would like to acknowledge my debt to the following, who so kindly sent me photographs, or gave me permission to have others made from copyright reproductions: to Dr Herzfeld for the photograph of the mosque at Samarra; to Sir A. Evans for the photograph of the "diver" from Knossos; to M. Doucet for the photograph of the head of a Bodhisattva; to

vii

Professor Delbrück for the photograph of Euthedemos I. of Bactria ; to the Rev. Canon Binney for the photograph of Athens ; to Sir William van Horne for permission to reproduce the painting by Han Kan ; to Dr Petrie for the photographs of the " Sheikh-el-Beled " and the somersaulting girl from *The Arts and Crafts of Ancient Egypt* ; also to the Deutsche Orient-Gesellschaft for the photograph of Amenhotep IV. ; to the Kaiserlich Deutsches Archäologisches Institut for permission to reproduce the two heads of Meleager, and to the Abbé Breuil for a similar permission in regard to his water-colour of a bison.

For valuable help and advice I would like to take this opportunity of thanking Mr Laurence Binyon, Mr F. F. L. Birrell, Professor Bosanquet, Professor Baldwin Brown, Sir Martin Conway, Professor Newberry, Mr H. A. Ormerod, Dr Flinders Petrie, and Mr and Mrs Bernard Whishaw, and also Miss Margaret Wroe, who has given me constant help and encouragement, particularly on the educational side of the book.

Owing to the kindness of Miss Charlotte Mason, I have been able to reprint certain passages from an article called *Beauty as an Educational Force*, which was published in the *Parents' Review*.

Above all, my thanks are due to those authorities whose published works serve as a guide to travellers along the hazardous paths of archeology.

M. H. B.

CONTENTS

LIST OF ILLUSTRATIONS

PREFACE TO SECOND EDITION

IF we want men and women to care for art, and to feel that art is something of national importance, we cannot, as usual, do better than to start by interesting the children. Now the natural approach to art for children is through the interest of the subject-matter, as anyone knows who has taken a child to a museum or picture gallery. And as all teaching should be adapted to mental development, a child's interest in art can best be stimulated through the medium of stories which will provide points of contact with the works of art to be enjoyed.

I have experimented at some length with the various methods by which such an interest in art can be aroused. In museums and galleries I first watched the results of allowing children to enjoy themselves in their own way, telling them nothing except in answer to their own questions, and leaving them to explore after their own fashion. Next I told them about certain pictures and sculptures while we looked at them; and lastly I talked to them about what we were going to see before the visit took place, finally casting these talks in the form of stories which were planned to waken an interest in definite works of art so that the children should set off on their expedition in a state of expectancy, with a foretaste of pleasure to come.

There was never any doubt as to which was the most popular method. After a story the children were always agog for the visit, and the more intelligent soon developed the habit of going to museums and galleries by themselves, or dragging with them a reluctant elder sister or parent. It became great fun to go on these visits, almost as exciting as going to the Zoo, and from this interest grew an interest in the look of the houses or buildings we passed in the street. Which looked the best? Which had well-shaped doors and windows? Then the chairs we sat upon, and the china we ate and drank from were inspected and considered. Nothing could be more catholic and undiscriminating than the taste displayed, but this was to be expected. Honest opinions were insisted upon, and every one was made to realize that what mattered was individual observation, thought, and feeling, with the hope that taste would mature with years and with a growing knowledge and love of art.

As to the time when interest in the historic and illustrative side of art can best be supplemented by serious study of design, the fundamental and permanent element in all forms of art, no rule can be laid down, for it depends upon individual development. The questions and comments of each child will generally give the clue to the teacher. I know a small girl of nine who objected to a particularly ugly "art nouveau" villa because it had such "bad manners." When I asked for an explanation of her comment she pointed to each hideous excrescence—bow windows, sham half timber, contorted eaves and balcony—saying, "This is rude, and this and this." A child who could in this way realize a lack of harmony, dignity and control, would be ready for some simple suggestion as to why a fine work of art is beautiful. The subject can best be introduced in connexion with architecture and the applied arts, and later on simple talks as to the relation of art to photography and the difference between the beauty of art and the beauty of nature can be added.

In the first edition of this book the nature of art was

briefly discussed. These paragraphs have not been re-printed in the present edition, not only because they were very incomplete, but also because, since they were written, I have discussed the subject at length in a second book [1] in which passages from the writings of good critics of all ages and countries are collected, and illustrated by many examples of true and counterfeit works of art of all kinds. In this book the teacher can study the question of the permanent element in art, as opposed to the variable elements of subject-matter, archæology, craft, history, etc. The nature of the complete work of art compounded of these various elements will then be more clearly understood.

The question of the appreciation of art for older children is not, however, the concern of this book. The subject of the drawing lesson is also another matter. All the arts have their theoretic and their practical aspects. We take children to hear good music and we also teach them to sing and play. We do all that we can to foster a love of great literature and we encourage them to write themselves. In the visual arts theory and practice should also go hand in hand. As the child grows older its mind should be saturated with the sense of design, while at the same time it should be encouraged, above all things, to express its own personal discovery of beauty. It should realize that it has creative gifts, waiting to be developed, and in its own handwork, drawing, and painting it must realize kindred activities to those that found expression in the objects that it has learnt to enjoy in the galleries and museums. The problem for the creative artist is very different and far harder than it was in the past. There is danger that in familiarizing children with the great art of the world they may be so bewildered that they may abandon the attempt to express their own experience and vision

[1] *Art and Counterfeit.* 15s. net. Methuen.

and may be satisfied with an attempt to reflect the art
of others.   But we cannot praise a cloistered and fugitive
virtue.   In these days children are continually seeing ugly
things around them, and we must provide them with an
alternative influence.   Wise teaching can counteract the
dangers of studying the art of others, and as a child grows
older its instinctive experience must inevitably be steadied
and inspired by the great art of the world, and the best of
modern art.   It was Renoir who said, when asked where
art could best be studied "*Au musée parbleu!*" and an
interest in the museums and galleries will be of the greatest
service to the student in the years to come.

It must also be remembered that only a small proportion of the children who learn drawing will become artists.
If we cannot create works of art ourselves we can harmonize
our own natures through a love of art, and in this love we
can find a source of joy for the rest of our days.

But to return to the historic aspect of art and the stories
in this book.   In these stories man is represented as some
one with an innate love of making beautiful things, and
people are depicted as demanding these things as a matter
of course, because of their beauty and also because of their
various uses.   Art will appear as a normal activity of
normal life, as indeed it should be, answering normal
needs.   But no attempt has been made to differentiate
between varying artistic values.   The child is encouraged
to share the life and general outlook of the times as the
background to the works of art that grew from them.
For both true or counterfeit works of art (or good art and
bad art if preferred) are woven out of the fibres of life, and
if we try to sever the two, art dies, just as the plant dies
when cut away from the soil from which it draws its
nourishment and strength.   The stories are not written
in connexion with works of art in any museum or gallery.

They are also not written to be read aloud. They are given as general schemes or types of lessons to be adapted to objects in particular collections, or to reproductions of works of art when originals cannot be studied. They have all been told to classes of children, and have been modified or enlarged according to the age and development of the different audiences. Their nature has made them somewhat discursive and they had to be considerably abbreviated when told to small children.

Every effort has been made to make the lessons as accurate as possible, but the scope of the book has made it advisable to omit references to authorities, except where the sources of the stories are concerned. The additional matter at the end of each story has been added for use in the compilation of lessons for older boys and girls to whom a lesson in story form would naturally not be given. It is also hoped that it will be of use to the teacher, or to anyone who wants a simple outline of some of the chief phases of art up to the time of the Renaissance.

Certain modern psychologists are warm advocates of the teaching of the history of art in schools, on the grounds that it can both develop and train the emotions, while at the same time providing them with an outlet, without which the health and character of the children will suffer. The well-known words of Charles Darwin can be quoted here, as a fitting conclusion. " Up to the age of thirty, or beyond it, poetry of many kinds gave me great pleasure ; and even as a schoolboy I took intense delight in Shakespeare, especially in the historical plays. I have also said that pictures formerly gave me considerable, and music very great delight. But now for many years I cannot endure to read a line of poetry. I have tried lately to read Shakespeare and found it so intolerably dull that it nauseated me. I have also almost lost my taste for pictures and music. My mind seems to have become a machine for grinding general laws out of large collections of facts; but why it should have caused the atrophy of that part of the brain alone on which the higher tastes depend I cannot conceive. . . . If I had to live my life again, I would have made a rule to read some poetry and to listen to music at least once a week; for perhaps the parts of my brain now atrophied would thus have been kept alive through use. The loss of these tastes is a loss of happiness and may possibly be injurious to the intellect and more probably to the moral character, by enfeebling the emotional part of our nature."

M. H. B.

COMPARATIVE CHRONOLOGICAL CHART (*Illustrating points mentioned in the early lessons*)

EGYPT (Breasted's Chronology).	MESOPOTAMIA — BABYLONIA (Hall's Chronology).	MESOPOTAMIA — ASSYRIA.	CHINA.	THE AEGEAN.	ROME.
B.C.	**B.C.**	**B.C.**	**B.C.**	**B.C.**	**B.C.**
4500. Pre-dynastic kingdoms flourishing. 4241. Introduction of calendar year of 365 days. c. 4000. Fusion of small states into kingdoms of Upper and Lower Egypt.					
3400. Menes, 1st king of United Egypt. 1st Dynasty	c. 3000. Ur Nina. Eannatun.				
2980. Zoser. 2900. Senoferu. 2900. Khufu. 2865. Khafre. } Old Kingdom Dynasties III.-VI.	c. 2750. Shargani-Sharri (Sargon of Akkad) and his son Naram Sin.		c. 2852. Fu-Hsi. First historical Emperor. Legendary origin of Chinese painting. 2700.	2800. Beginning of Early Minoan period. 2600 to 2100. Culmination of Early Minoan period. Burnt city Hissarlik.	
2590. Pepi I. 2475.	c. 2450. Gudea.		2205.	2100 to 1900. Culmination of Middle Minoan period. First climax of Minoan civilization.	
2160.			} Hsia Dynasty.		
2000. Amenemhet I. 2980. Sesostris I. 1980. Amenemhet II. 1938. Sesostris II. 1887. Sesostris III. 1849. Amenemhet III. 1788. } Middle Kingdom Dynasties XI. & XII.	c. 2050. First Babylonian Dynasty.	2000. Rise of Assyria.	1766.		
1580. Ahmose I. 1501 to 1447. Thutmose I., Thutmose III., and Hatshepsut. 1411. Amenhotep III. and Tiy. 1375. Ikhnaton. c. 1390. Harmhab. } Early Empire Dynasty XVIII.			} Shang Dynasty.	c. 1700. Rise of Tiryns and Mycenae. 1500 to 1450. Culmination of Late Minoan period, known as Palace Period. 1350. Supremacy of Tiryns and Mycenae.	
c. 1315. Rameses I. c. 1313. Seti I. c. 1292. Rameses II. c. 1150. } Late Empire Dynasties XIX. and XX.	c. 1250. Babylon conquered by Assyria.	1100. Tiglath Pileser I.	1122.	c. 1200. Sixth city; Hisarlik (Homer's Troy). Period represented by Homeric poems. c. 1000. Dorian Invasion.	c. 1000. Etruscans settle in Italy.
661. Conquest of Egypt by Assyria. Destruction of Thebes. 660. Psamtic I. {Restoration or Saitic period. Dynasty XXVI.	Conquest of Babylonia by Assyria.	745. Ashur-Nasir-pal III. 732. Tiglath Pileser IV. 705. Sargon. Sennacherib. 681. Esarhaddon. 668. Ashur-bani-pal. 606. Fall of Nineveh. Rule of Medes and Persians.	} Chow Dynasty.	750. Rise of classic Greece.	753. } Period of Kings
530. Conquest of Egypt by Greece. 525. Conquest of Egypt by Persia.	605. Nebuchadnezzar II. 539. Persian conquest.			490-479. Victories against Persians. 449. Death of Pericles.	509. } Period of Republic.
	331-330. Conquest of Alexander the Great.		225-206. Beginning of Han Dynasty.	333. Death of Alexander the Great. 146. Greece becomes a Roman Province.	
30. Conquest of Egypt by Rome.					27. Beginning of Empire.

ANCIENT
AND MEDIEVAL ART

LESSON I

PALEOLITHIC ART—THE ANCIENT HUNTERS

PART I.—ELEMENTARY LESSON IN STORY FORM

INTRODUCTION—This is a story about the first artists who
ever lived. They were born so long ago that at that time even
the earth looked different from the earth of to-day, for there
was no sea between England and France, and people could walk on
dry land from France to Africa. So long ago was it that no one
can tell how many thousands of years have passed since then. We
cannot even tell if these men, who lived before history, had a
language as we have. In the story, however, they will be made to
speak as we do.

1. The Cave—It is evening, and a father and mother
and two children are making their way over some rolling
upland country in the north of Spain. They are savage-
looking folk, dressed in a few skins only. Their hair is
long and flowing, and their faces and bare arms are
painted with curious patterns. The father carries a bundle
tied in a skin containing the family's worldly goods, and
he has also a long wooden spear, the end of which is
tipped, not with metal, which is as yet undiscovered, but
with flint, a hard kind of stone. Round his waist an axe
is fastened, also flint-headed. It is getting late, and the
sun is sinking behind the hills, but the travellers do not

seem to be tired. They are strong and muscular, and
the mother seems to be as unconscious of the weight of
her baby as the father is of his burdens. The boy, who
is also armed with a spear, runs backwards and forwards
until a call from his father summons him to return.
"You must keep near me," he says; "how often have I
told you that this hour is a dangerous one. Who knows
how many bears may be concealed in these thickets ; and
listen ! Surely that is the snarling of hyenas ; perhaps
they are stalking us at this minute." The mother holds
her baby more closely, and the father grasps his stone
dagger, but after listening intently for a minute the sounds
die away in the distance and the family resumes its
march.

At last the boy calls out, " See, surely that is the
mouth of the cave ! Smell the smoke of a camp fire, now,
when the wind blows this way ! " They hurry on and
presently arrive at a steep hill-side, in the middle of which
the mouth of the cave is visible. The father enters it,
followed by his wife and son, and the boy coughs, for the
cavern seems half full of smoke. There is a fire burning
on the ground, and round it are seated a group of men,
women, and children, as wild and savage-looking as the
new-comers. On seeing the strangers a man leaps to his
feet, grasping his spear, but recognizing the father he
drops it by his side. "So you are back from your
wanderings," he exclaims. "Are these your wife and
children ?   I suppose you will settle down for a little
now with the rest of us." The father explains that he
has done with wandering with other branches of the tribe
and has come back to the old cave, to live and hunt with
his former friends. A woman squatting on the ground
motions the new-comers to be seated, and they are soon
busy over some pieces of roasted bison and mammoth,

tearing the flesh off the bones with their teeth and fingers, and then breaking the bones with sharp flints and sucking the juicy marrow. The meal over, they roll themselves in warm skins, and, lying round the fire, are soon asleep. At the mouth of the cave one of the hunters keeps watch, ready to raise an alarm should a great cave bear or a tiger try to force a way in during the night.

2. **The Paintings**—The next morning all are astir with the dawn, for the men of the tribe are going on a hunting expedition. The larder is nearly empty, and unless they can kill a bison there will be nothing to eat in the cave. The boy begs his father to let him come too. " I am strong and swift and can take care of myself," he cries ; "you know I can shoot straight too." His father consents, but adds, " I must make my drawing first. I will draw and paint a great fat bison, and then perhaps the animal will be under a spell, and the unseen powers may send me luck, and I may kill him with straight aim and swift spear." He stoops and takes from his bundle three small hollow bones filled with red, yellow, and black powder. Then rubbing two flints together he makes the sparks fly until a small flame is kindled. Lighting a small stone lamp he turns and enters a lower recess to the left of the cave entrance. The boy follows, and with the help of the tiny flame can see that, above his head, the rocky roof is covered with a number of paintings and drawings of bison and other animals. His father now hands him the light and begins to mix his colours with liquid. The boy gives an involuntary shudder, for the place in the dim light seems uncanny and mysterious. He stands very close to his father and watches him, fascinated, as, kneeling with head thrown back, he draws in outline on the low roof the spirited figure of a bison. After smearing a lump of reddish colour on its body with his fingers, he

then takes a brush and deftly finishes the figure, giving the animal a thick dark mane, little bright beady eyes, and delicately executed feet. The boy almost gasps. The creature looks as if it were alive! His father meanwhile is gazing at the figure, moving his arms, and muttering strange words. "Now may the unseen spirit send me this fat bison to-day," he says, and returns with the boy to the outer cave, where preparations for the hunt are in full progress. Soon the stone heads of the spears and daggers are sharpened and the men start off, while the women look after them wistfully, knowing full well the dangers to which they will be exposed.

3. The Hunt—The men and the boy pass down the dew-drenched hill-side, and cautiously enter the thick forest below. Great yews, oaks, and firs throw a dense shade, and leaving the sunshine the hunters plunge into the forest, pushing their way through the undergrowth, while the boy follows closely at their heels, his dark eyes bright and alert. "Let us go by the river and make a pit by the animals' drinking-place," the leader suggests. "In that way we might get a mammoth, and his flesh would provide us with meals for many a long day." So the hunters make a halt by the river at a place where a track is clearly visible among the bushes. They have no spades, but with the aid of flattened and pointed pieces of wood and stone the pit is begun. By nightfall it is completed, and over it the men lay branches of trees and sods of grass. When leaves and earth are sprinkled over this light structure their task is done, and finding an open clearing they light a great fire to frighten away the wild beasts and leaving some of the men to watch, the rest are soon asleep.

The next morning before daybreak the hunters, treading lightly, return to the river-side. The pit is untouched,

PLATE 1

INCISED DRAWING ON REINDEER BONE FROM A CAVE AT LORTET
PALEOLITHIC EPOCH
(From an extended facsimile)

PAINTING OF A BISON FROM THE CAVE AT ALTAMIRA, SPAIN
PALEOLITHIC EPOCH
(From a water-colour by the Abbé Breuil)

but hardly have they examined it before one of the men, laying his ear to the ground, whispers that he can detect the heavy tread of some great animal. " An elephant or a mammoth," he cries ; " the wind blows the other way ; it will suspect nothing ; quick, hide." The men disappear noiselessly among the trees, and the boy, as agile as a young monkey, swings himself up into the branches of a large tree. After a few minutes, which seem like hours, he hears a trampling, and sees an enormous beast pushing its way through the bushes. It is far larger than an elephant, and is covered with a thick, hairy coat of grey. Its mane, which is of a reddish brown, falls nearly to its knees, and two immense ivory tusks curl on either side of its long trunk. The great lumbering beast pauses, looking around it with little beady eyes, as if scenting some disturbance. Then, catching sight of the river, it starts forward again grunting and pulling branches from the young willows as it passes. Suddenly there is a crash. The mammoth has trodden on the branches and turf and is in the pit ! The boy gives a shout of triumph, and the hunters, arriving quickly on the scene, soon put the poor beast out of its pain. That night, by the light of the big camp fire, there is a great feast, and the flesh is cut off the mammoth in readiness to be carried back to the cave. When the meal is over the hunters dance wildly round the fire, shouting and singing, while the flames light up their savage faces, streaming black hair, and their gaily painted limbs. The night is dark, and no moon penetrates the inky blackness of the forest that surrounds the little clearing. Suddenly out of the darkness a roar is heard, and a big tiger springs into the circle of light. In an instant the mad dancing is ended, and all are in deadly peril, until one of the hunters succeeds in placing a spear in the tiger's heart.

The next morning a procession starts homewards, the spoil being partly carried and partly dragged on wooden sledges. The boy still remembers the bison that his father had painted, but the latter only says, "Wait and see, we are not home yet. I may kill it still." Sure enough, on leaving the forest a whole herd of bison is discovered, one of which falls a victim to the father's spear. "So you did not paint him in vain," the boy cries.

4. The Carvings—The next day the hunters rest from their labours. They kill so that they can have food to eat, and, at the moment, they have more than enough. The boy squats by the fire, telling the story of his adventures to his mother. "What was the mammoth like?" she asks. "I have never seen one, for I seldom venture into the forest. The work in the cave takes up all my time, and these beasts must be shy, for they seldom come near one of our homes." "Why, he was very big and shaggy," answers the boy; "he had little eyes, and a trunk, and his tusks were not straight like an elephant's, but were curved —see, like this." He makes a curve in the air with his finger, and then, dissatisfied, seizes a splinter of bone from the floor of the cave, and draws the curved outline of the tusks in the cinder dust at his feet. Pleased with what he has done he suddenly laughs, and adds the outline of the head, and puts a small dot for the eye. His mother, watching him admiringly, calls his father. "See," she says, "he has got your gifts, and can draw too, and why not, when he is your son, and you are the cleverest artist of the whole tribe?" The father is greatly pleased, and begins to improve the occasion and give his son a lesson. Taking a small piece of reindeer's horn, he engraves on it with a pointed flint the outline of the reindeer itself, with its big branching horns. He then gives a small flat stone to the boy. "Try yourself and scratch the figure of a deer on it," he says. "When you get older, and have learnt how to draw and paint and carve animals, then you can barter their images done on small stones, and can get meat and ivory and colour or good spears and daggers in exchange. The men will love to carry the drawings and carvings that you have made, for they may bring them luck in their hunting." So when the snowy owl hooted that night in the darkness, and the hunters lay sleeping, and the tiny cave mouse scuttled about among the bones and the cinders, the boy lay smiling in his sleep, because he had found out that he could draw, and was very happy.

. . . . . .

5. The Cave of Altamira—Thousands of years passed. The climate of Europe changed, and melting snows filled the great rivers, which in their turn overflowed and turned plains and woods into marshes and swamps. Some of the tribes of hunters died out, and others migrated to distant lands. Part of the rock at the cave's entrance fell down and blocked it up completely, so that nobody knew it was there. Again thousands of years passed, nobody knows how many. Then one day some blasting near the cave shook the hill-side, and the rocks sealing the opening fell down, and a tiny entrance was revealed. Not very long after a Spanish nobleman found the opening, and on entering discovered that the floor of the cave was covered with bones of animals, long extinct, and with stone implements and the ashes and bones of an ancient kitchen. One day he came again to hunt on the cavern floor, and brought his little daughter with him. Suddenly he heard her call out, " A bull." On going to find out what she meant, he discovered her in a low part of the cave, pointing to the rocky roof above her. When he looked to see what it was that she had found, he saw clearly in the dim light the painting of a bison (which she took to be a bull), and round it many other figures of bison and other animals, some of them of life size. These were the figures drawn so many thousands of years ago by the ancient hunters, and ever since treasured and preserved by time in the keeping of the earth.

Notes on the Story—All paragraphs but number 5 are naturally imaginary.

PART II.—MATERIAL FOR ADVANCED LESSONS ONLY

Prehistoric Man—The study of prehistoric man was first undertaken scientifically rather less than a hundred years ago. Since that time interest in the subject has grown steadily and rapidly, and a number of able scientists and archeologists have devoted themselves to examining geological strata, and tabulating the results of their discoveries in scientific form. Part of a human skull found in Java in 1890 seems to point to the presence of the " Missing Link," the creature half ape, half man, from which man is descended. Skulls found still more recently near Heidelberg and in Sussex prove that the earliest men were of a very primitive type, with flattened brains and possibly without the power of speech. Part of a skull found in the Neanderthal in Germany is witness to a human type of a somewhat more intellectual stamp, but we have to wait until a later period than this before we find the first artists who, according to the Abbé Breuil, were of an immigrant race which migrated into Europe and succeeded the Neanderthal race of men. These first artists were hunters, men living a precarious life in open camps, finding shelter in rocky caverns, and exposed at all times to the attacks of wild beasts more powerful than they. They had not as yet learnt agriculture or the art of domesticating animals, and metals were unknown to them. Their implements were made of flint, and later of ivory, bone, and horn. In the place of bottles they used skins; pottery was not yet invented. The bones of these ancient hunters, together with those of their quarry and also the works of their hands, were buried during the course of time on river bank and cavern floor, there to lie sealed and undisturbed for tens of thousands of years. Now, in the twentieth century after Christ, the hand of man has laid them bare, and their relation to the geological strata which held them has enabled scientists and archeologists to indicate their position in the annals of time.

The Paleolithic artist is an isolated phenomenon. At the close of the epoch a change in climate again took place, and the increased warmth caused the higher fields of ice and snow to melt. The great rivers overflowed their banks, and plains were turned into vast swamps, while many of the caves were filled with water. The reindeer retreated to higher altitudes, and the ancient hunters were probably partly exterminated. After a great lapse of time we meet a fresh European civilization, that of the Neolithic or Polished Stone Age. Neolithic man had learnt to make pottery, had mastered the science of agriculture, and had learnt to tame and domesticate animals. Rude stone monuments such as Stonehenge and the Dolmens of Brittany reveal him as the possessor of the first architectural impulse, but the power of the sculptor and painter had been lost, and only inferior paintings and carvings have been found. Following the Neolithic Epoch we have the various ages of metal, which comprise, among others, the early civilizations of Egypt, Mesopotamia, and the Ægean.

Although primitive man has long since passed away from the greater part of the world's face, he is still represented by certain savage races, such as the Australian

Aborigines, the Bushmen of S. Africa and the Eskimos. The Tasmanians were even more striking examples of men who had remained at the Early Stone Age state of development, but this race became extinct nearly fifty years ago. It is by observing these primitive peoples that we are helped to gain an understanding of the life of Paleolithic man, for modern research has proved that in many respects the customs and arts of the former are nearly identical with those practised by the latter, and that the thousands of years that separate the past and present-day savages have done little to forward the latter's development.

In order to make clear the place of the first artists in the world's history the following summary may prove useful :—

DIVISIONS OF EARTH'S HISTORY BY GEOLOGICAL STRATA

Primary Epoch—Age of fish, sea-weed and ferns. First appearance of terrestrial vertebrates.

Secondary Epoch—Reptiles highly developed. Birds appear. Numerous early mammalian remains. Ichthyo-saurus, etc.

Tertiary Epoch—Subdivided into four periods : the Eocene, Oligocene, Miocene, and Pliocene. During this incalculably remote age the surface of the earth suffered many changes, and many of the great mountain ranges were formed. At first the northern hemisphere possessed a warm climate ; coral reefs have been found in regions now polar, while palm trees grew in Switzerland. During the later part of the epoch the continent took approxi-mately its present form. During the Tertiary epoch the earth was inhabited by great mammals, such as the mastodon, stegodon, rhinoceros, hippopotamus, the *Elephas antiquus* and the great apes. The existence of man during this epoch is still unproved.

Quaternary Epoch—Subdivided into the Pleistocene and the Holocene periods, in the second of which we are now living. The Great Ice Age occurred during the Pleistocene period, and it is believed to have included four separate glacial epochs in Europe, with intervening periods of heat and luxuriant flora. During the early Pleistocene period no channel divided England and France, and the Irish Sea and German Ocean were fertile plains. The Adriatic Sea was non-existent, and two small inland seas lay where the Mediterranean now separates Europe from Africa. Europe was inhabited by the mammoth, cave bear, soft-nosed rhinoceros, elephant, sabre-toothed tiger, hyena, wild horse, reindeer, stag, etc., etc. The first definite trace of man is found during the Pleistocene period (Java, Sussex, Heidelberg, and Neanderthal skulls). A further classification of the Quaternary Epoch is as follows : (1) Paleolithic, or Early Stone Age (Pleistocene period), and (2) Neolithic, or Later Stone Age, followed by the Bronze, Iron, and Steel Ages. The men of the Pleistocene period are also known as " Drift Men," as they date from the period of drifted strata, originally washed up on ancient river banks or cavern floors. Many of these caverns in which the Drift Men lived are now high up on the slopes of valley or hill-side, while the great rivers that flowed past them have long since dried up or are represented by streams in the valley beds below.

The Origin of Painting and Sculpture—The arts of painting and sculpture are believed to be two-fold in origin. Modern savages paint themselves in order to add to their charms by means of decoration and colour, or else for the purpose of covering themselves with a substance that will serve as a protection against heat or the bites of insects. It is probable that primitive man also painted his skin, and in this way first learnt to mix colours and apply them with effect. The second cause which gave birth to these arts was no doubt found in gesture, used to convey knowledge. A hunter saw a strange wild beast far away in the forest. " What was it like ?" he would be asked on his return. With his finger he would trace its shape in the air, or, squatting on the ground, would try to model it in clay or draw its outline in the mud with his finger or with a pointed stick, as is the habit of the bushmen of to-day. When colours were arranged decoratively, with a feeling for design, for a rhythmic arrangement of line, mass and space : when powers of observation and characterization were clearly shown, the artistic powers of the mind had been brought into play, and we have the beginning of the so-called " fine arts."

There seems little doubt that even at this early age art was connected with religion, or rather with the magical rites which no doubt took its place. The American Indians draw on the rocks the animals that they desire to capture for their food, and if they want wet weather, they make a sketch of rain. Before these drawings they perform incantations and prayers. In a similar way it is probable that the drawings and paintings of animals found in the caves of the ancient hunters were executed for the same purpose. This theory seems all the more reasonable when it is remembered that the cave paintings and drawings are almost invariably executed in some dark or distant part of the cave, where daylight cannot penetrate and artificial light would have to be used. There is always something uncanny and mysterious about a cave, and no doubt the inner recesses of these early habitations of men were regarded as the haunts of supernatural powers. The cave at Font-de-Gaume, which is decorated with over a hundred figures of animals, is so long and narrow that it is more like a passage than a cave, and it could hardly have been used as a dwelling for man. It was probably some form of temple, and it has been remarked that scarcely any implements or relics of a dwelling have been found in its floor deposits. Another fact that points to the superstitious origin of the paintings and drawings is that almost without exception they represent animals suitable for food. Primitive man must have chiefly lived on the flesh of the mammoth, bison, reindeer, stag and horse, and it is these and similar animals that are depicted by hundreds on the walls of the caves. Representations of the savage carnivora, the lion, the sabre-toothed tiger, the hyena, and the cave bear are seldom found. In certain instances the figure of an animal has been represented as transfixed with an arrow, no doubt as an indication of the hunter's desire. In the same way the drawings of animals on small stones, and the small carved figures, may have been considered as some form of token, which when carried by the hunter would serve to give him power over the animal represented. It may be remembered also in this connection that animal worship formed part of the religion of the ancient Egyptians. We cannot tell how much these early works of art owe to utility and how much to the painter or sculptor's delight in the representation of nature and to his natural instinct for self-expression. Although his work was primarily utilitarian in conception, the æsthetic impulse must have played no small part in its production, for among these works we find some that show genuine artistic qualities. It was also obviously owing to these elements, and not to utility, that dagger heads and *batons de commandement* were so elaborately decorated.

Art of the Paleolithic Age—These first works of

art have been found, almost without exception, in the caves and rock shelters in France, Spain, and Belgium. In many instances the infiltration of water charged with lime has sealed the drawings and sculptures on the walls, and also those in the earth, under an impermeable coating of stalagmite, which has preserved them intact during the thousands of years that have passed, and which has been recognized by geologists as a paleolithic deposit. In other places parts of the caves have fallen in, and in this way the entrances have been blocked and the contents hermetically sealed until recent years. The floors of many of the caves have yielded layer after layer of slowly accumulated deposit, each stratum containing implements and artistic remains, and the bones of animals peculiar to a particular stage of human development. For example, in a cave at Pair-non-Pair, in France, seven different layers of occupation were found, each covered with a fairly thick layer of stones and mud, and each quite distinct from the other. When in this way sculptures, drawings, and stone implements have been found in the same stratum with certain combinations of animals' bones, experts are able to gauge, with some certainty, the epoch in which the early artist lived.

A comparison of these objects with bones and stone implements found on the ancient banks of rivers has also been invaluable in solving these problems of archeology. Many of these caves have now been discovered and explored, and the greater number of them have been found singularly undisturbed. Some slight damage has been done in certain instances, probably in the sixteenth century, when search was made for the bones of the mythical unicorn, then considered an antidote to disease. In many cases the drawings and paintings are so faint that only the eye of an expert can discover them ; on the other hand, some are marvellously preserved. Although composition and grouping

PLATE II

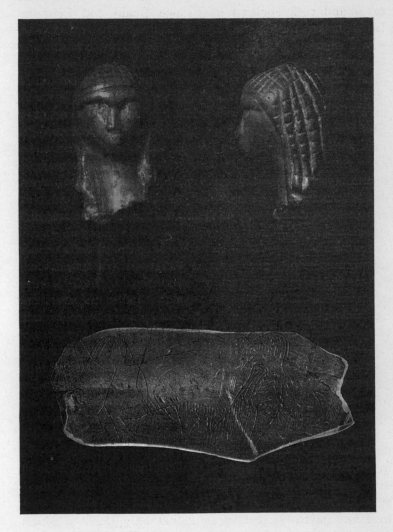

HEAD OF A GIRL FROM BRASSEMPOUY. (MAMMOTH IVORY)
INCISED DRAWING OF A MAMMOTH. (MAMMOTH IVORY)
PALEOLITHIC EPOCH

have hardly ever been attempted in these drawings and paintings, and the figures are rarely conceived in relation to each other, these early works of art show astonishing skill. They are spirited in conception, the drawing is free and direct, and the special characteristics of the animal represented are faithfully observed and reproduced. Not until comparatively modern times do we find again such skill in the delineation of movement. At this remote stage of human history man was more interested in animals than in himself, and Grosse accounts for the realism of Paleolithic art on sociological lines. " Power of observation and skill with the hand are the qualities demanded for primitive naturalistic pictorial art, and the faculty of observation and handiness of execution are at the same time the two indispensable requisites for the primitive hunter's life. Primitive pictorial art, with its peculiar characteristics, thus appears fully comprehensible to us, as an æsthetic exercise of two faculties which the struggle for existence has developed and improved among primitive people."[1]

The earliest works of art are the carvings in relief and in the round, chiefly executed in mammoth and elephant ivory. Following on these come the paintings, and lastly the drawings. Towards the end of the paleolithic epoch, reindeer bone and horn were almost exclusively used for carvings and incised drawings. Although most of the drawings and sculptures represent animals, a number have been found with man as their subject. Among them is a small ivory head of a young girl, marvellously preserved, with hair arranged somewhat in the manner of an early Egyptian (see Plate II.). Of the features the mouth alone is wanting, a trait which has often been observed in the drawings by young children. Some small figurines of women have also been found, most of them

[1] *The Beginnings of Art.* Grosse. New York.

lacking the heads, and some the legs. In no cases, however, are the features of drawings or sculptures clear enough or well enough executed to serve as an illustration of the human type that they represent. Among objects of the late Pleistocene age found in the caves are some curious implements made out of the antlers of reindeer, generally perforated with one or more holes, and often elaborately carved. These *bâtons de commandement*, as the French call them, have been explained in various ways, among them being the following :—(1) For use in killing game ; (2) as arrow straighteners ; (3) as objects of some superstitious practice ; (4) as sceptres, the number of holes perhaps showing the dignity of the chief.

Perhaps the most famous of all the paleolithic works of art are the paintings in the cave of Altamira, near Santander, in northern Spain. Since prehistoric times the entrance to this cavern has been hermetically sealed by a fall of rock which became cemented with stalagmite deposit. During the second half of last century blasting operations in the neighbourhood caused a fresh fall of rock, which caused an opening to be made again into the cave. This opening was shortly afterwards discovered by the Marquis de Sautuola, the owner of the land (see paragraph 5 of the story). A full description of these astonishing paintings was published in 1880, but it was not until 1901 that the scepticism with which they were received began to yield, and fresh discoveries of a similar kind opened the eyes of modern archeologists to the existence of this vigorous and realistic prehistoric work. The recent publication of M. Cartailhac and the Abbé Breuil, *La caverne d'Altamira à Santillane près Santander*, has furnished excellent coloured reproductions of the paintings, and also a full description of the cave. The paintings are executed on the roof of a recess to the left of the cave entrance. The recess is so low that in places the artists must have had to crouch or lie in order to carry them out, and it is also so situated that artificial light must have been necessary in order either to execute them or to see them. The earliest of the drawings are figures outlined in black. Next in date are paintings washed in with red, and then follow some incised drawings, excellent in workmanship. Then come the polychromes, boldly sketched in three colours. The latest of these are the masterpieces of Paleolithic art. The surface of the rock has been carefully prepared for their execution, and earlier drawings or paintings have been washed off, or scraped, to make a place for them. The colours used are black, red, brown, and various shades of yellow, obtained from mineral substances such as iron-ore, etc., ground to powder and kept in small tubes made from the bones of reindeer. (One of these has been found which still contains the pigment.) The outlines of the figures were first sketched in in black paint, and in some instances also emphasized by engraving. Afterwards the colour was smeared on, and lastly the modelling and all details were added with a brush.

Although the cavern of Altamira is the most famous museum of prehistoric art, there are a number of other caves in France and Spain hardly less famous, and every few months fresh discoveries are being reported. In the Grotte des Combarelles, a cave so narrow and low that it is more like a long passage, a complete series of engravings starts about half-way down its length, where the darkness is complete, and continues along either side for a distance of 100 metres. Among the hundred animals represented there are no less than fourteen mammoths.

Many cave engravings and paintings are accompanied by curious and indecipherable signs and marks, and imprints of the human hand are frequently met with. Among the debris of ancient hearths found in the strata of the cave floors, numberless implements in flint, bone, and horn have been discovered, such as arrow heads, daggers, harpoons, a lamp decorated with engravings of reindeer, ivory chisels, bone needles, throwing sticks, etc. Many of these objects are elaborately decorated.

The art of the Paleolithic Age has been so recently revealed, and is at present attracting so much attention, both from the professional and amateur archeologist, that fresh and important discoveries may be expected at any time, and may serve either to add fresh proof to, or else to upset, existing theories. But we must not confuse the great archeological and historic interest of these early works with their ultimate value as art. A work of art must be judged independently of its age or country. Some of these carvings and paintings have undoubted artistic merit but they are only wonderful in relation to their age. As far as the chronology of the period is concerned, and the dates assigned to various works of art, it must be remembered that the estimates of several of the most famous experts differ from each other by many thousands of years. According to the most conservative estimates of the leading specialists, however, the Pleistocene age came to an end some fifteen thousand years ago, while its duration has been estimated by Dr Arthur Keith at four hundred thousand years. The rough estimate of the age of the Altamira cave paintings is generally given as about fifteen thousand years.

LESSONS II AND III

EGYPTIAN ART

PART I.—ELEMENTARY LESSONS IN STORY FORM

FIRST STORY—OLD KINGDOM ART

INTRODUCTION—Thousands and thousands of years passed, nobody knows how many. The face of the earth changed ; land formed where there was sea, and seas dried up. The mammoth disappeared and the great cave bears, and reindeer survived in northern lands only. Men learnt how to tame wild animals and to cultivate the land : they learnt how to make weapons and bowls out of different kinds of metal, instead of only out of stone, and they began to make buildings and statues also. The earliest people to be civilized in this way were the people who lived in Egypt and Babylonia. This is a story about some ancient Egyptians.

1. **Rahotep and Nefert**—Once upon a time, long ago, about three thousand years before the time of Christ, two Egyptians were sitting in an arbour in their garden, not very far from the river Nile. The man was called Rahotep, and he was a general of infantry, and a prince of royal blood. His wife, the Lady Nefert ("The Beautiful"), was clever and shrewd, and loved her babies, who were playing by the fishpond, guarded by two slaves, who stood near to look after them. The children laughed as they played and called each other by their names, which were very different from our names—" Cool-Breeze," " Gold-and-lapis-lazuli," " Little-wild-lion," and " I-have-wanted-you." The day was very hot. No wind stirred in the palm

19

trees, and the sky above was blue and cloudless. A slave stood by his master and mistress, who were playing draughts, and slowly fanned them with a great palm leaf fan to keep them cool. The babies, who, like other babies in that hot country, wore no clothes, splashed in and out of the fishpond, trying, with shouts of laughter, to catch the gold and silver fish. The garden was full of trees—sycamore, fig, palms and vines—and there were lotus flowers and lilies and gay creeping plants. Musicians squatted cross-legged on the ground with their flutes and pipes, and standing by them was a man with a big many-stringed harp. At a signal from Prince Rahotep a slave ran to the players, and the children splashed out of the water and sat round, listening to the low-toned, monotonous Egyptian melodies.

Presently the Lord Rahotep proposed a hunting expedition, and when the day became cooler he set out, accompanied by his wife, and two slaves to row his skiff. The sun was setting, and, as the boat glided out upon the great swamps and marshes by the river Nile, the broad fields of waving wheat and barley were turned to a still deeper gold in the evening light. The houses and the palaces of Memphis stood out sharply in the clear air, and in the distance towered a huge mass of masonry—the giant pyramid that the King was building over his tomb. Great flocks of wild fowl flew out from the reeds, and Rahotep, standing in the bows of his boat, let fly his throw-stick, which his slaves had put in the boat. When he had killed enough wild fowl to replenish the larder, he took a double-pointed fish-spear, and, looking down into the clear water, tried to harpoon two fish at a time. As the twilight fell, the boat was rowed home again, and the Lady Nefert trailed her hand in the cool water. She gathered great white and blue lotus flowers, or water-lilies, but had to beware lest a crocodile should be lurking in the deeper pools. As the skiff was pulled ashore some great boats, rowed by scores of oarsmen, passed by them and anchored at the quays. They were filled with blocks of alabaster, green malachite, lapis-lazuli, copper, and pieces of soft stone, in which ran veins of the bluest turquoise. They had come from the mines in Sinai, and were now unloaded by black slaves, who staggered under the weight of their burdens, and piled them in great heaps on the quays. "To-morrow we must buy some," cried Rahotep. "We must get some beautiful things made for our tomb." They were young and strong and well, but, like all rich Egyptians, they were preparing the tomb where they would eventually lie.

2. The Great King—The next morning Rahotep and Nefert were commanded to pay a visit at the palace. The King was considered to be a god and was worshipped by the people, but the nobles were allowed to see him, and their sons were brought up with his sons. Rahotep and Nefert put on their best clothes, which were very simple. Rahotep wore a short linen kilt secured by a girdle and band, and Nefert a long, closely-fitting sleeveless garment of the finest linen possible, fastened by two bands over her shoulders. Each wore necklaces and collars made of coloured beads, pieces of turquoise, and other stones. They took off the short black wigs which all Egyptians wore, and over their shaven heads put on the long ones, with the hair parted in the middle, which were kept for ceremonial occasions. Rahotep took his long staff, and they set off to the palace. Horses were not known, and the streets were full of asses and oxen. They passed the rough mud hovels where the poor lived, and the houses of the rich, which were built of wood and sun-dried brick, with gay hangings falling over the window

spaces and open doors. The King's palace was built like
the houses of the nobles, but it was far bigger and was
surrounded by brick fortifications and beautiful gardens.
Rahotep and Nefert were known to the guards, who let
them pass, and soon they emerged from the courts, which
were crowded with soldiers armed with long spears, bows
and arrows, and arrived at the great hall of audience.

The hall had very little furniture ; just a few rugs,
chairs, stools, and chests inlaid with ivory, on which were
standing richly carved vases. Crowds of courtiers filled
the room, and servants of the King came and went—
" the Overseer of the Cosmetic Box," " the Overseer of the
Cosmetic Pencil," guardians of the royal wardrobe, per-
fumers, launderers, bleachers, and wig-makers. Marshals
and court chamberlains stood in groups, and saw that all
conformed to the rigid court etiquette which none might
disobey. A marshal advanced to Rahotep and Nefert.
He could not mention the name of the King, who was a
god, so he said to them instead, " I shall let one know
you are here," which was the impersonal way in which
the King had to be mentioned. The King having expressed himself willing to see them, Rahotep and Nefert
advanced before him, and, falling on their faces, kissed
the ground at his feet. A king had once been known to
allow a noble to kiss his foot, but this was an unheard-
of honour, never repeated. Sounds of music were heard,
and Rahotep and Nefert, sitting on one side of the throne,
watched some lithe Egyptian girls who danced before the
King a slow, graceful dance with curious rhythmic movements. The King ordered gifts to be sent to them, and
fruit and wine were brought in and handed to the guests.
The high priest of Ptah, the great god of Memphis, and
patron of all art-workers, was next announced. He was
the King's chief architect, and had come to report upon

the building of the pyramid. The guests withdrew, and Rahotep and Nefert, though much honoured at the friendship of the King, were not sorry to leave court etiquette behind them, and to return to their babies and their cool garden at home.

3. The Tombs—The river Nile was in flood and its waters were overflowing the banks on either side. Not far from the river the King was building his great pyramid. One morning Rahotep and Nefert decided to see how the work was getting on. They were rowed over the flooded fields until they came to the stone causeway, which had been built from the pyramid down to the water. Here they ordered the slaves to stop rowing while they watched the big rafts fastened at the end of the causeway, from which the huge blocks of stone were being removed. The blocks were then slowly dragged up the causeway by hundreds of slaves. When these poor creatures stumbled and fell in their weariness, the overseer's whip was in readiness, and Nefert covered her eyes, for she could not bear to see their sufferings under the scorching sun. She begged Rahotep to come away, and they left their boat, and walked to the base of the great pyramid, which looked like a vast mountain of stone towering above them into the blue sky. In the middle of it, hidden away, was a little room, in which the great King would one day be buried. " The world has never seen such a mighty tomb as this," said Rahotep. " All who come after will know how majestic was our great god the King." A procession of priests passed by on their way to Memphis, and Rahotep was roused from his thoughts and suggested that they should now pay a visit to their own tomb, which was not very far away, in the shadow of the great pyramid.

The tomb was a long, solid red-brick building, in the

centre of which was hollowed out a little chapel, and a
secret chamber built to contain their portrait statues.
Like all the Egyptians, Rahotep and Nefert believed that
when they died their *Kas*, or doubles, would stay on earth
and would want food to eat and a body to return to, and
as they themselves would no longer be there, they had
ordered two stone portrait statues to be executed as like
themselves as the artist could make them, so that each *Ka*
could find its counterfeit to which it could attach itself.
Rahotep and Nefert were very proud when they saw how
well their tomb was progressing, for every rich Egyptian
prepared for his death in this way, as a matter of course.
Some friends passed on the way to visit their tomb, and
the Lady Nefert called to them, and showed them how
the walls of her chapel were being covered with delicate
carvings, cut in low relief out of the stone, and representing scenes from their life.   When their friends were gone,
the husband and wife passed into the secret chamber.
Nefert held a light above her head, and in the uncertain
light two statues could be dimly seen.   They represented
herself and her husband sitting side by side, he in his
short white kilt, she in a finely woven robe and with a
thick wig and necklaces.   The statues were just finished
and the likenesses were excellent.   Rahotep and Nefert
then discussed together the other arrangements that they
had made.   A priest had been engaged who after their
death would supply the food needed by their *Kas* in the
tomb—ten different kinds of meat, five kinds of poultry,
sixteen kinds of bread and cakes, six kinds of wine, four
kinds of beer, eleven kinds of fruit, and many and varied
kinds of sweets also.   Husband and wife then went home
together, feeling that now that their tombs were prepared, they could have free minds with which to enjoy
themselves.

PLATE III

RA-HOTEP AND NEFERT
OLD KINGDOM. C. 2900 B.C.

4. Nearly Five Thousand Years Later—Thousands
of years passed. Empires were built up laboriously, had
their hour of triumph, and faded away into the dim
recesses of time. The English ruled in Egypt, and men
from the great cities of Europe and America searched
among her sands for traces of the life that was past.

One day in winter, some forty years ago, a few workmen were hunting among some rubbish in the desert not
far from the Mêydûm pyramid. Suddenly one of them gave
a cry of surprise. He had found a small slab of stone,
engraved with unknown words, and below it, half hidden
in the sand, a little square door. The news was spread
abroad, and a man was sent by the Government to report
upon the discovery. He recognized the door as an
opening to an ancient *mastaba* or brick tomb of the old
Egyptian kingdom, and skilled workmen were sent to
investigate it. After two days of work spent in clearing
away the sand, a perfectly preserved *mastaba* was exposed
to view. The square opening in the tomb was blocked
by two carefully adjusted stones. When these were
removed, and a ladder was let down, two more stones
were discovered, and then again six others in pairs. What
could be at the end of this carefully barricaded passage?
The stone-mason who was making his way down could
only work very slowly, for the passage was so small
that he had to keep in a horizontal position.

At last the final block of stone gave way, and suddenly
a puff of warm air was felt. Some open space was near.
The stone-mason called for a light, and he was given a
candle and told to go forward. He took a few steps, and
then with a wild cry turned and made his way back along
the passage. He was shaking with terror, and said that
he had seen two live heads glaring at him from out of
the darkness. The other men took lights, and at the end

of the passage found themselves in a little room. Candles were held up high, and by their flickering light two statues could be clearly seen. They were carved and painted and seated side by side—a man and a woman, looking almost as if they were alive. All held their breath. The little chamber might have been prepared yesterday, and yet no foot had trodden there for nearly five thousand years. The veil of the past was lifted and ancient Egypt lived again. In the little chapel in the tomb, paintings and carvings were found, and a table for food. Who were the man and the woman who lived so long ago, before Abraham kept his sheep and Joseph served the proud Egyptian King? An inscription revealed their names— the Lord Rahotep and the Lady Nefert.

SECOND STORY—NEW KINGDOM ART

Introduction—After the deaths of Rahotep and Nefert, hundreds and hundreds of years passed, yet Egypt was still the most powerful nation in the world. To-day we are going to hear more about it. We are going to take three peeps into the past and see the country at the height of its power during the reigns of three great sovereigns.

1. Queen Hatshepsut—The great Queen Hatshepsut is ruler of Egypt. She lives in a town on the banks of the Nile called Thebes. It is filled with great temples and palaces and beautiful gardens. Fleets of boats with great white sails sweep up the river to the quays, bearing treasure and merchandise from foreign lands. The Queen decides that she will build a temple at the foot of the cliffs by the desert, and sends for her architect Senmut. They consult together and choose as a site the base of some great cliffs. The architect draws plans and soon the building begins. It has long colonnades and terraces which gleam white in the scorching sunshine, and behind them are rooms and chapels.

The Queen would like to have some green myrrh trees to plant on the terraces and fill the air with their sweet scent. Where can she get them from? She goes to the temple to ask the god of Thebes, Amen-Ra, and in the dusk of the shrine she thinks she sees the statue of the god bow his head to her and say, " Go to the land of Punt, there you will find all you want." The Queen is full of excitement, and leaving the deep gloom of the temple and the bowing priests, she goes out into the burning sunshine, and returning to her palace, calls her ministers and orders an expedition to be prepared.

Some big ships are got ready, and her ambassador, and many soldiers, slaves, and seamen go on board. Crowds of people stand on the banks as the big sails are hoisted and the great boats are rowed down the river in search of the far-away land. They proceed by river and canals to the Red Sea, and at last sight the land of Punt. There are huts built on piles by the edge of the water, and at the sight of the ships the people swarm to the shores to view the strangers. The chief of the district comes forward with his wife and daughter and addresses the Egyptians in the following words : " Why have ye come hither unto this land, which the people of Egypt know not ? Do ye come down the ways of heaven, or did ye sail upon the sea and upon the waters of God's land ? Or have ye trodden the path of the sun ? " Assured that the Egyptians have come upon a peaceable errand, the people of Punt provide them with a feast of meat, fruit and wine, and then trading begins. The Egyptians offer beads, axes, daggers, bracelets, and wooden chests. In exchange the Puntites give them treasures of every sort, which are piled on the ships. They include thirty-one incense trees placed in baskets, with their roots done up in balls of earth ; ebony, ivory, and " goodly

fragrant woods," eye cosmetics, dog-headed apes, grey-
hounds, gold, silver, and lapis-lazuli, green malachite, panther
skins, ostrich eggs and feathers, and even a live giraffe.

Then with friendly farewells the boats put off to sea
again, and after many weeks come once more in sight of
Thebes. The people crowd the banks in hundreds, eager
for news of the expedition and a sight of the marvellous
treasures. These are unloaded and brought before the
Queen, who inspects them with pride and delight. The
spices and gold are weighed out in great scales, and
Hatshepsut makes as an offering to the gods the thirty-
one living myrrh trees, some eye cosmetic, some throw-
sticks of the Puntites, ebony, electrum for inlay, and a
live southern panther! She also adds 3300 small cattle
to her present, and all these things are taken to the
priests in the temples.

Some days later the Queen goes in her chariot to her
own temple of Der-el-Bahâri, under the cliffs, and there
sees her myrrh trees planted in rows, all green and sweetly
smelling. She calls artists and orders them to carve
pictures of the expedition on the walls inside, and by them
to inscribe its history—and there they remain to this day,
having been safely buried under the sand for thousands
of years until they were recently excavated.

2. **Amenhotep III. and Queen Tiy**—Years pass.
Kings and queens have their day and then are buried
among the western hills. We now come to the time
when two children reign in Egypt. The King is called
Amenhotep III., and he is about twelve years old. His
wife, Queen Tiy, is a little dark-eyed girl of ten, with
merry ways and a keen, intelligent face. They live in a big
palace in Thebes, across the river Nile, and not far from the
hills. Its walls are painted with gaily-coloured frescoes;
on the ceilings flights of birds are represented against a

blue summer sky, and the floors under their feet are inlaid with the gayest of colours and patterns. The little King and his wife sit on gilded thrones, and ambassadors and envoys from Babylonia and Crete and other far-away countries prostrate themselves before them, kissing the ground at their feet, and murmuring to the King, "Thou resemblest Ra," which is the greatest compliment they can pay him, as Ra is the chief Egyptian god. Behind the throne stand the little Queen's father and mother, Yuaa and Tuaa. Yuaa is a very important person. He is one of the chief priests, and the Master of the Horse, and Chariot Captain to the King. It is one of his duties to see that the King's stables are full of the most beautiful horses that Asia can yield. He governs the country for the little King, and is helped by the King's vizier or prime minister, who is also the chief architect, who has the same name as the King—Amenhotep.[1]

The little King and Queen get very tired of sitting still on their thrones and behaving sedately, and they are much happier when they are allowed to run out into the gardens that surround the palace. Here grow beautiful trees, many of them fruit trees bearing pomegranates, figs, and dates, which the children gather ; and here also are beautiful flowers, and strange and curious animals with which they love to play. Often Yuaa and Tuaa sit in the garden with them, and tell them stories of the kings and queens who have gone before them, who are buried in the huge pyramids by the river Nile. Then the dusk falls and the King and Queen get drowsy and are taken off to bed.

When the King and Queen grow older, Amenhotep orders his slaves to dig out a great lake, and fill it with

[1] Worshipped as a god in Ptolemaic times under the name of " Amenhotep, son of Hapi."

water from the Nile, and he also gives Queen Tiy a beautiful gilded boat. In the evenings when the feasting and the dancing are over the Queen loves to escape with a few of her courtiers and sail on the still waters of the lake, while the stars come out overhead and the air is filled with the fragrance of the spice trees growing on the banks. So the short summer nights and the long scorching days pass, and Yuaa and Tuaa grow old and die. They have collected some beautiful furniture for their tomb, and have left orders that food shall be placed there too, because, like all other Egyptians, they think that after their death their doubles will still wander on earth, and so must have necessities provided for them. So Queen Tiy sadly watches her parents' possessions packed up and taken off to the tomb that has been hollowed out on the hill-side. Among other things there are beds, chairs, Yuaa's chariot, legs of mutton, honey, and a beautifully carved toilet box with the names of the King and Queen painted on it in blue and gold, for it is their present.

Amenhotep determines to erect some splendid new buildings by which all shall remember the magnificence of his reign. He calls Amenhotep, his architect, who sets to work at once and draws plans of a great hall and court to be added to the temple of Luxor by the Nile. A great new temple is also designed with two gigantic statues of the King to stand at its entrance.[1] Thousands of slaves are set to work on the buildings, and every day the King and Queen watch the progress of the work with interest and pride. The architect orders huge blocks of stone to be cut out of the mountain side, out of which he fashions a colossal statue of the King. The stone is floated down the river from the quarries on a great ship, and when the day comes when the statue is set up in the temple, all

[1] The so-called "Colossi of Memnon" are all that remain of this temple.

Thebes crowds to see the wonderful sight. For another temple the King orders some lions to be carved out of red granite, for he is a great hunter, and has spent many days in hunting in the desert and the hills.[1]

The King and Queen live for many years, and when Amenhotep dies, his little son reigns in his stead.

The story has a sequel. Early in the year 1905 some diggers were excavating in the Valley of the Kings near Thebes. Under a mound of rubbish they discovered the entrance to a tomb, and exposed to view a flight of steps, leading to a passage half blocked with stones. As it was too late in the evening to explore further, guards were posted on the hill-side, and three people lay down outside the tomb entrance to keep watch under the stars, lest any thief should force his way in. Early next morning the small party of excavators made their way, one by one, down the passage. They passed a bundle of onions thousands of years old, and at the end of the passage came upon a wall plastered with mud, and sealed with a priestly seal. The top of the wall was broken away, and beyond it could be seen glimmering faintly in the dim, uncertain light, the shimmering glint of gold and silver and the ghostly forms of chairs and chests.

A way in was made, and the explorers found themselves standing in a little room, full of furniture of the most beautiful design and colouring. There was no speck of dust; the place might have been vacated only a few days before instead of more than three thousand years ago. Two mummies lay in their wrappings, and painted and gilded cases stood by. Round about were the things that had been placed for their use in the after life; chairs exquisitely carved and gilded; alabaster jars; three beds, carved and gilded, with rush bottoms; a cushion of down

[1] "Lions from Gebel Barkel." Now in the British Museum.

and fine linen ; a chariot that gleamed with crimson, green, and gold ; a jar where honey was still liquid ; joints of meat, each placed in a wooden box ; two pairs of sandals, one old and one new, and a beautifully carved and painted toilet box, inlaid with ivory, on which were carved the names of Amenhotep III. and Queen Tiy.   One of the explorers knelt down by the mummy cases, and by the flickering light of the candle spelt out the names of those for whom the tomb had been prepared.   They were " Yuaa and Tuaa."

   3. Ramses II., the Pharaoh of the Oppression— Again time passes.   Again another Pharaoh is ruling in Egypt.   We see him driving through Thebes in his golden chariot.   Runners before him clear the way.   As he passes through the crowded streets all bow low to the ground— rulers and princes, merchants, freemen, and slaves.   On every side rise great buildings—palaces, avenues of sphinxes, and temples, where white-robed priests pass in and out.   Ramses II., for that is the King's name, stops at the temple of Karnak.   Slaves hold the horses of his chariot, and he passes the bowing priests and goes to visit the great hypostyle hall that is being added to the temple. It is nearly finished.   Toiling slaves move to and fro, and if they stumble under the weight of the heavy stones the lash of the overseer falls across their shoulders, and with groans they struggle to their feet again and work on. The Pharaoh watches unmoved : it is nothing to him that the slaves should suffer.   Thousands of them, Israelites, are labouring in his two store cities in the Delta, where they have to build walls of brick to protect the corn for his armies.   Day after day they press the red Nile mud into moulds and make the bricks.   It is nothing to the King that the Israelites are not provided with the necessary chopped straw, which binds the clay together.

If they cannot do the work without it, they can always be beaten. But help is coming for the oppressed people. Who can finish the story, and tell what happens?

NOTES ON THE STORIES

First Story—The first three paragraphs are imaginary. They are founded on information chiefly derived from Professor Breasted's *History of Egypt*. Paragraph 4 is taken from *Recueil de traveaux relatifs à la philologie et à L'archéologie Egyptiennes et Assyriennes*, vol. iv., pages 69-73, 1884. The tomb of Rahotep and Nefert was discovered in 1871. Critics agree that it probably dates from the reign of Sneferu, at the end of the third dynasty. It is not known whether Nefert was the wife or sister of Rahotep. The names given to the children are genuine Egyptian ones, but of a later date. The list of food to be provided in the tomb also dates from a rather later period.

Second Story. Paragraph 1—The story of the expedition to Punt can be read with every detail in the reliefs of the temple of Der-el-Bahâri. The Queen's sending for Senmut and her visit to see the myrrh trees are imaginary.

Paragraph 2—The first part is imaginary. The details are largely taken from *The Life and Times of Akhnaton*, by Arthur Weigall. The description of the opening of the tomb of Yuaa and Tuaa, in the second part, is taken from an article in the *Century Magazine* of November 1905. As the toilet box is inscribed with the names of the King and Queen, it has been concluded to have been their gift. The ages of the little King and Queen and the order of events in the story are approximate only.

Paragraph 3—The story of the oppression of the Israelites has been introduced to connect the lesson with something that is familiar to the children. It should be left out if the lesson proves too long.

PART II.—MATERIAL FOR ADVANCED LESSONS ONLY

History—The earliest traces of the civilizations of the world are found in the eastern Mediterranean region, in the two great river valleys of the Tigris and Euphrates

and the Nile.   In Egypt the small kingdoms do not fall
within the historic age, which is no doubt due to the fact
that for thousands of years heavy deposits of Nile mud
have accumulated in the Delta, the seat of the earliest
Egyptian civilization, and irrevocably buried its material
remains.   Some idea of the state that this early civilization attained to can be gathered from the fact that these
pre-dynastic Egyptians perfected a form of alphabetic
letters two thousand five hundred years before any other
people, and in the year 4241 B.C. invented the system of
the calendar year of 365 days, which, being dependent on
the sun, was a matter of great difficulty.   So good was
the system that it was introduced into Rome by Julius
Cæsar, and is still in use to-day, over six thousand years
after its invention.

The Egyptians were native African people, with a Semitic
strain.   The nature of the country made them agricul-
turists, for, to quote Herodotus, " Egypt is the gift of the
Nile," and the dry and parched deserts were intersected by
the broad Nile valley, which was rendered extraordinarily
fertile by the annual inundation of the great river.   Here
the people lived, cultivating their crops, hunting and fish-
ing, while the Nile, which dominated their lives, worked
unnoticed upon their minds, and determined to a great
extent their thoughts and beliefs.   Slowly the small states
were absorbed, and the country became two kingdoms :
one the valley to the Delta, and one the Delta itself.
Slowly these " Two Lands " were developed, until, in the
year 3400 B.C., they became one country, when under
Menes, first king of united Egypt, the first royal house, or
dynasty, was established.   Then followed four centuries of
rapid development leading up to the first great period of
Egyptian history known as the " Old Kingdom," or
Pyramid Age.   This was an age of great mental enter-

PLATE IV

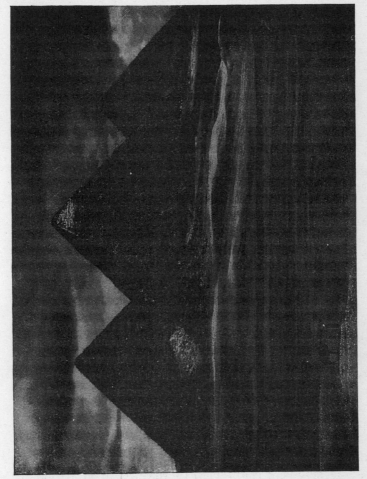

THE PYRAMIDS

prise. Art and mechanics reached a level which was never again surpassed, and trade developed until the great Egyptian ships, some 170 feet long, touched the shores of Phœnicia and penetrated to the coasts of Somaliland.

After the Old Kingdom, an age of decline followed, and a period of foreign invasion, which was succeeded by the next great period of the country's history, known as the "Middle Kingdom." This was the feudal age, and the classic period of Egyptian history and art. Trade was still further developed, particularly in relation to the early Ægean centres, and the foundations of the empire were laid. Then a second period of disorganization and reaction set in. The supremacy of Memphis waned, and its place was gradually taken by the town of Thebes, which was destined to be the centre of Egyptian supremacy until the fall of the empire.

The "New Kingdom" or "Empire," the third and last great period of Egypt's history, was in many ways the most famous and splendid time that the country had known. The great Pharaohs were emperors, rulers of vast dominions, and controllers of what was now, under the kings of the xviiith and xixth dynasties, a military state. Thebes had become the most important city in the world, the centre to which ambassadors and traders from far and near converged. Victorious generals brought thousands of foreign captives from the wars, and they were set to work as slaves upon the beautifying of the city. Much of the loot of war was also expended in this way, and Thebes became famous from one end of the civilized world to the other. The town had spread to such an extent that it not only included the residential quarter of Luxor, but also Karnak, the official seat of Egyptian religion, and the group of ecclesiastical buildings that had grown up near the tombs and temples on the edge of the western desert. Here in the hills beyond the waters of the Nile the royal dead were buried.

Towards the end of the xxth dynasty the age of decadence set in, and the last page of Egyptian history tells the story of a succession of foreign conquests, when one nation after another ruled the land.   There was one period, however, known as the Restoration, when the country regained for a short interval some of its power. This was the Saitic period, when during the years 663-525 B.C. Sais, a town in the Delta, became the centre of a flourishing civilization.

Religion—The dominating factor of ancient Egyptian religion was the belief in a life after death.   However debased the theology of the people became, the belief in immortality was never abandoned, even when most obscured by the doctrines of magic and superstition. " Thou hast departed that thou mightest live " are the words of an ancient Egyptian epitaph, and the death of King Pepi is described as " the day when King Pepi was summoned to life."   A high ethical standard required that conduct on earth should determine future happiness, and this is another proof of the advanced state of Ancient Egyptian civilization.   The people believed that the sun, having completed its daily course through the heavens in a celestial barque, and disappeared in the west, then passed beneath the earth, through a succession of dark and gloomy caverns, until it again reached the light of day, ready to run its course afresh.   In this dark and mysterious nether world dwelt the dead and the gods of the dead.   Here, according to the more advanced theories of the Egyptians, Osiris, judge of the dead, weighed the souls of the departed, helped by forty-two assistant judges, represented by hideous demons.   If the life was held to have been unworthy, the shade was condemned to hunger and thirst and the darkness of the tomb ; if worthy, it might linger near its tomb, or ascend to heaven, to be rowed through the waters that surrounded it to the celestial fields of Yaru, the lentil fields, where it lived in peace and joy.

Egyptian religion was composed of a mass of varying beliefs, many of which were entirely contradictory. The people deified all natural phenomena, which they recognized as regular and persistent. Sun, moon, sky and water were represented under various names as gods and goddesses, and the river and desert, and many birds and beasts, became symbols of a host of deities. The great number of Egyptian gods were attached to local centres, and as these rose and fell in power the popularity and greatness of the deities rose and fell with them. Some of the gods were held to be friendly to man, others antagonistic. Chief of all was Re or Ra, who, according to one of the earliest Egyptian myths, issued from an egg or flower floating on the vast sea which represented the world. From him were descended the eight most famous deities, who, together with him, constituted the " ennead," of which later each temple possessed a local form. It is impossible here to do more than mention one or two of the chief Egyptian gods. Their number was legion, and the study of them is complicated by the fact that many of them appeared under a number of different names and forms. The following are some of the chief among them :—

Re or **Ra,** the sun god. Often represented as a hawk, or as a sun's disk with a hawk's outstretched wings. The supreme god of Egypt. The chief centre of his worship was at Heliopolis.

Seb or **Keb,** the great god of the earth ; present when the heart was weighed before Osiris in the judgment hall.   Represented as a man with a crown and solar disk, upon which is engraved his symbol, the goose.

Nut, the goddess of the sky, the type of woman's love and joy.   Worshipped at Denderah as the cow goddess, Hathor ;   at Bubastes as Bast, the cat goddess, and at Memphis as a lioness, and the goddess of storm and thunder.

Osiris, king of the dead and judge of the nether-world : the symbol of immortality.   The god of the Nile. Centre of worship, Abydos.

Isis, the great goddess of womanhood, often represented as a queen with a head-dress surmounted by horns and a solar disk.   The cow was sacred to her.   Her chief shrine was in the Delta.

Horus, the son of Osiris and Isis.   One of the greatest gods of the dynastic Egypt.   At one time worshipped as two gods, one the hawk god of upper Egypt and identified with Ra, and the other Horus the child, sometimes represented as sitting on a lotus leaf.

Thoth, the god of letters, magic and divine intelligence. Represented with the head of an ibis and associated with a dog-headed ape who was supposed to bring him the results of the judgment of the dead.

Sekhemhet or **Sekhet,** the goddess of the destructive heat of the fire and the sun.   The minister of Ra for the punishment of the wicked.   Represented with the head of a lion surmounted by a solar disk.

Anubis, the jackal god of the nether-world, the god of embalmment.

Ptah, the chief god of Memphis, the patron of all artificers and artists, whose high priest was always the chief artist at court.

Amen or **Ammon,** the chief god of Thebes, who at the time of the city's greatness was identified with Ra, and was known as Amen-Ra. He was generally represented in human form with two tall upright plumes rising above his head, and holding a sceptre as a symbol of life. The goose was sacred to him, and the Thebans believed him to be incarnate in a ram.

Sebek, the crocodile god. Worshipped in the Fayûm. Represented as a crocodile or as a man with a crocodile's head.

Khnemu or **Khunm,** the personification of the creative force. The god of the first cataract. Represented with a ram's head.

The kings or Pharaohs of Egypt were also worshipped as gods and were considered " Sons of Ra," the successors of the sun god. The Horus hawk was one of their most frequent symbols, and also the serpent, which represented the early kingdom of Upper Egypt. During the later phases of Ancient Egyptian civilization, religion became much debased. Belief in magic was universal, and formulæ were collected and buried in the tombs with a view to guiding the deceased in the life hereafter. *The Book of the Dead*, which is a collection of these formulæ, is the most famous example of this kind of literature. Charms were also placed in the tombs, such as certain of the models of scarabs, or sacred beetles. The greater number of them served as seals, but in other instances they were associated with Ra, and were believed to silence the accusing voice of the heart when questioned by the judge. Animal worship was also a persistent feature of Egyptian religion.

Standing out in sharp contrast to the recognized beliefs of the time, came the religious revolution of Ikhnaton, which were largely due to the influence of his parents, and in particular to that of his mother, Queen Tiy. Ikhnaton was a king of lofty and intellectual aims. Caring

little for matters of state, he devoted himself to philosophic and ethical problems, and in the worship of Aton,
whom he identified with the sun god, introduced a fine
and idealistic system of monotheism.   After his death,
however, the old beliefs reasserted themselves, and were
jealously guarded by the priests at Thebes, where Amen-
Ra again ruled supreme.

The Egyptian belief in a life after death created an
elaborate tomb ritual.   The people imagined that every
person possessed a soul, which could take the form of a
bird, lotus flower, serpent, or even crocodile.   Besides this,
each mortal was believed to be accompanied by a *Ka* or
double, which accompanied him through life, and not
only followed him after death, but frequented the place of
his burial.   The Egyptian could not conceive of a future
life without the body, and for this reason each man that
was able prepared a tomb for himself, furnished with all
that was necessary for the maintenance of the *Ka*.   The
Egyptian of the early dynasties prepared a *mastaba* or
solid brick tomb for himself and his family, in which was
concealed the *serdab* or cellar, a secret chamber containing
their likenesses, carved or painted in wood or stone.   To
these counterfeits the *Kas* could then attach themselves,
and so that they should not suffer hunger or thirst, food
and drink was provided for their use, either in the form
of wall paintings, or as usually was the case, the real
material itself.   This was placed in a small chapel in the
tomb, to which the priest and family had access.   It
contained a false door, built at first in the east wall, and
later on in the west for the use of the *Ka*, and its walls were
covered with paintings and sculptures representing scenes
from the life of the owner, and pictures of his slaves and
other possessions, for the *Ka's* use.   Lastly, in a sub-
terranean chamber under the tomb, and approached by a

shaft, the mummy or mummies were deposited.   During
the vith–xiith dynasties the paintings on the walls of
the tomb representing the servants and belongings of
the owner were to a great extent superseded by small
models, provided to supply the needs of the *Ka*.   In the
tombs of this period numberless groups of this kind have
been found, such as regiments of soldiers, servants occupied
with the grinding of corn, boats manned by sailors, etc.,
etc.   In the xviith dynasty we find these models replaced
by small figures known as "respondents" provided for
the same purpose.

The following extract, which forms part of a hymn
in honour of the god Aton, was written by King
Ikhnaton (Amenhotep IV.), who reigned during the
years 1411-1377 B.C.   It shows the height of spiritual
beauty to which the king's conception of religion had
attained :—

"Thy dawning is beautiful in the horizon of heaven,
O living Aton, Beginning of life !
When thou risest in the eastern horizon of heaven
Thou fillest every land with thy beauty . . .

All cattle rest upon their herbage, all trees and plants flourish.
The birds flutter in their marshes, their wings uplifted in adoration
    to thee.
All the sheep dance upon their feet,
All winged things fly ; they live when thou hast shone upon them.

The barques sail up-stream and down-stream alike . . .
The fish in the river leap up before thee,
And thy rays are in the midst of the great sea . . .

When the chick crieth in the egg-shell,
Thou givest him breath therein to preserve him alive . . .
He cometh forth from the egg to chirp with all his might,
He runneth about upon his two feet.

How manifold are thy works !
They are hidden from before us,
O thou sole god, whose power no other possesseth."
(Professor Breasted's translations.) [1]

Art. General Characteristics—Egyptian art is the
best preserved of the earliest arts. We owe our knowledge of it to the dry climate of the country which has
kept the monuments in such an excellent state of preservation, and also to the Egyptian belief in the life after
death, which caused the tombs to be veritable museums
of art. It is an art full of monumental dignity and calm.
The effect of the pyramids and of the great temple is one
of enduring strength and primitive vitality.

The same characteristics are present in the sculpture,
which was governed by the strictest of artistic conventions. An interesting allusion to this is found in the
great Abydos *stela* or memorial tablet of King Neferthotep
(Middle Kingdom). It tells how the King searched for
the old ideals in art. "(Let) me know the god in his
form that I may fashion him as he was formerly, when
they made their statues in their council, in order to establish
their monuments upon earth." Professor Breasted writes,
that from these lines, " it is evident that the gods were
supposed to have held a council in the beginning at which
they determined for all time exactly the form and appearance of each." [2]

One of the most persistent conventions of Egyptian
art was the refusal to represent the human figure, either in
relief or painting, from one point of view. While the
head or lower limbs would be shown in profile, the torso
and eye were painted and carved as squarely facing the
spectator. In the whole course of Egyptian art it is rare
to find figures treated other than in this way, and it is no

[1] *A History of Egypt.* Breasted. Scribner.   [2] *Ibid.*

doubt owing to this, and to the peculiar and unchanging emotional quality of Egyptian art, that the charge of monotony is so frequently brought against it. It must be remembered, however, that this criticism is levelled against three thousand years of the artistic production of one people, and that although their art contains these persistent features and self-imposed limitations, yet it triumphs over them again and again, and constantly rising above the level of everyday artistic production, when a lack of inspiration and vitality is often apparent, we have a series of vigorous works which stand high in the annals of early art. It must also be remembered that artistic convention is a first necessity of decorative art, and that the great sculptured figures of the kings, which formed part of the architectural equipment of the temples, gained in decorative value by their lack of realistic treatment. When these statues are torn from their proper setting and placed in rows in museums they lose much of their true effect. The finest of the Egyptian sculptures, however, were produced when the artist was in closest touch with nature, when the blending of artistic convention, and the close observation of natural forms and character, produced such animated work as the best portrait statues of each great epoch.

Egyptian art was to a great extent utilitarian in character. Each tomb, statue, or carving had a purpose to serve. Masterpieces of statuary were walled up in tombs for the use of the *Ka* and were lost to the sight of man. Paintings and reliefs, in the same way, were only visible to the priest or member of the deceased's family, who had the right to enter the chapel of the *mastaba*. A pyramid was built to symbolize the power of a king. The Egyptians did not regard the creation of ideal beauty as the end and aim of their art. They loved the beauty of nature. We find cups in the shape of lotus buds, and blossom and leaf forming the handle of a spoon ; but these motives were secondary to the utility of the object.

Owing to the climate and the customs of the people, the Egyptian artist was accustomed to the nude, and in all his work the human figure is treated frankly and directly ; but it will be noticed, as Professor Lange has pointed out, that all early statues in the round, until the year 500 B.C., were treated in the following manner, which he calls "the system of frontality." He shows that a figure was always sculptured in such a way that an imaginary line, drawn from the top of the head, straight down through the backbone and continued in a similar direction to the ground, would never curve to either the right or the left. The figure could be made to bend backwards or forwards, because this would not affect the line ; a leg might be advanced or might be bent in a kneeling attitude, but the body or head would never be made to alter in position from the established line of direction. A little latitude was allowed to the position of the arms alone, but only in so far as it did not affect the line of the rest of the figure.

Egyptian temples, and the great tombs, were built of granite, limestone, and sandstone, which were found in large quantities on the mountains and hills that bordered the desert. For the erection of palaces and houses, mud bricks were employed, with the result that these buildings have generally perished. Buildings were coloured in the most brilliant hues. Pillars, reliefs, and sculptures blazed with red, blue and gold, and the reason for this is explained by the science of optics, which show that the more intense the light, the more pleasure the eye takes in colour. It is well known that the nearer we get to the equator, the more brilliantly coloured are the birds and flowers, and this is also true of the works of man. Long ago the Egyptian found out that all details of his architecture became faint and almost undiscernible in the intense clarity and brilliance of the Southern light, and that deep shadows were nearly non-existent. He therefore called colour to his aid, and with its help gave the required variety to the surfaces of his buildings. This use of colour was also employed by other Southern peoples, such as the Babylonians, Assyrians, and Greeks. Another characteristic of Egyptian architecture is its decoration, which was used to reflect the life of the people by means of endless scenes, carved and painted upon its walls, and coloured in the manner described above.

The lesser arts of Egypt developed steadily from earliest times until they reached their most beautiful form at the time of the Empire. Crystal vases, gold and silver vessels, exquisitely chased, glazed and painted tiles, gilded and carved chariots, the finest of linens, bowls ground to translucent thinness, and furniture of the most elegant design were produced in large quantities, and have been preserved to us in the tombs. The temples were inlaid with silver and electrum, and the royal jewels were worth a king's ransom.

CHRONOLOGICAL AND ARTISTIC OUTLINE

(Chronological outline taken from Breasted's *History of Egypt*.)

FIRST PERIOD.—PRE-DYNASTIC TO OLD KINGDOM

Pre-dynastic kingdoms already flourishing 4500 B.C.
Introduction of calendar and earliest fixed date in History, 4241 B.C.

Kingdoms of Upper and Lower Egypt probably
flourishing by 4000 B.C.
Accession of Menes, first king of united Egypt, and
beginning of dynasties, 3400 B.C.
First and second dynasties, eighteen kings ruling at
Thinis, 3400-2980 B.C.

The pre-dynastic Egyptians made mud pottery by
hand, some of which was decorated by rudely drawn
patterns and figures. These vessels were superseded by
others of stone, and woven cloth and reed mats were also
made. During the early dynasties, buildings were made
of brick and interwoven palm sticks. The temples of the
time of King Menes were little more than wooden shrines
with walls of plaited wattle. That stone buildings were
erected by the second half of the second dynasty is
testified to by a fragment of the mortuary text of King
Pepi I. of the sixth dynasty (2625-2475 B.C.), where it
was claimed that in remodelling the temple at Denderah,
he was reproducing the plan of the ancient sanctuary of
pre-dynastic kings of that spot. Sculptors were meanwhile acquiring considerable skill, and some of the tombs
that have been excavated have been found to contain
delicately carved slate palettes for face paint, decorated
with reliefs of men and animals, which are freshly and
vigorously treated, and are also interesting as showing
how at this early date artistic conventions were growing
up. On the other hand, some small figures and other works
of art found at Hieraconpolis are singularly free from
convention, and show direct observation of nature. Perhaps
the most famous work of art of this period is the slate
palette of King Narmer, dating from the first dynasty
and also found at Hieraconpolis.

SECOND PERIOD.—OLD KINGDOM, 2980-2475 B.C.
DYNASTIES THREE TO SIX

Capital : Memphis.

Third dynasty, 2980-2900B.C. Zoser to Sneferu; 80 years. Pyramids at Sakkara and Meydûm.

Fourth dynasty, 2900-2750 B.C. Prosperity of Old Kingdom at its height.

Chief rulers:

 Khufu (Cheops), builder of great pyramid of Gizeh, 2900-2877 B.C.

 Khafre (Chephren), builder of second pyramid of Gizeh, 2869-2774 B.C.

Sixth dynasty. Chief ruler : Pepi I., 2590-2570 B.C.

Egyptian art was firmly established during the Old Kingdom or Pyramid Age. For many hundreds of years the civilization of the country had been steadily developing, and in this way the foundations had been laid for the splendid activities of the fourth dynasty. The step pyramid of Sakkara (the oldest existing stone building) was erected by King Zoser of the third dynasty, and was followed shortly afterwards by the vast and impressive tombs of Sneferu at Mêdûm, and Khufu and Khafre at Gizeh. These pyramids are immortal testimonies to the reverence in which the Egyptians held their king. He was believed to be a god, " the Son of Ra," and no labour or money was spared to provide him with a lasting memorial, which by its vast proportions and strength should testify to his greatness and power. The pyramid of King Khufu (Cheops) is the only one of the so-called " seven wonders of the world " which has come down

to us. The very mass of this gigantic monument
tells of the organization and labour involved in its
erection and the highly developed state to which
mechanics had attained at this time. The pyramid is
built of some 2,300,000 blocks of stone, of an average
weight of two and a half tons each, and its construction
took the labour of a hundred thousand men during
a period of twenty years. Although the pyramids cannot
be described as works of art, so perfect and exact is
their construction that they are the wonder of modern
architects. The king was buried in a tiny chapel hidden
in the heart of the pyramid, and numerous tombs of the
nobles were built in its vicinity. These lesser tombs are
known as *mastabas* (from the Arabic word for a bench),
and although they are of no architectural importance they
are interesting because some of them contain arches of un-
burnt brick, and except in certain early Babylonian tombs
this architectural form was not again employed until the
time of the Romans. The most famous temple of the age
that has been preserved is that of Khafre at Gizeh. It is
a plain and massive building with square pillars and no
trace of decoration, and, like the pyramids, it gives an impression of strength and noble severity.

The sculpture of the Old Kingdom is full of character
and force. The ancient Egyptians were the first people
to put the human body into sculptured form in the
round, and nearly three thousand years before the
time of Christ they were producing figures which for
realistic vitality have seldom, if ever, been surpassed.
The finest of these statues are those which were placed
in the tomb in fulfilment of religious beliefs. The general
form of these figures is only broadly and somewhat
conventionally treated, but the heads are realistic. It
was necessary that they should be exact likenesses of the

PLATE V

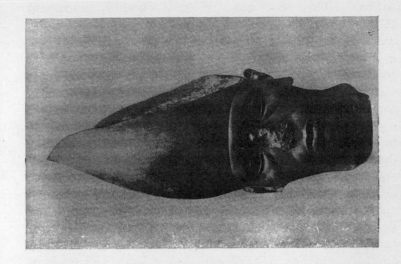

HEAD OF AN UNKNOWN KING
(MIDDLE KINGDOM)

HEAD OF A WOODEN PORTRAIT STATUE, KNOWN AS
THE "SHEIKH-EL-BELED"
(OLD KINGDOM. IVTH DYNASTY)

subjects, and the sculptors responded by producing heads that were brimful of character and vivid with life. To make the statues still more lifelike they were coloured in natural hues, and the eyes were inlaid with rock crystal in copper sockets, but the treatment was never so realistic that the æsthetic qualities of the work were spoilt. Among the most famous of these statues is the figure known as the Sheykh-el Beled and those of Rahotep and Nefert, and the "Seated Scribe" of the Louvre. They appear before us as living people, full of individuality and vital force. Another famous statue of this period is the black diorite seated figure of King Khafre, now in the Cairo Museum. It is impressed with the dignity and majesty that would be worn by "the Son of Ra," and the sculptor shows in it the complete mastery which he had gained over the hard and difficult material used.

The reliefs of the Old Kingdom are exquisitely modelled, and are full of life and freshness. They do not show the realism of the portrait statues, because this was not required by religious motives, but they are more realistic than similar work produced at any later period of Egyptian art. The sculptors of this age even attempted life-sized figures in copper, such as the splendid statue of Pepi I., which is made of metal moulded over a wooden core. In spite of its bad state of preservation the head is excellent, and also the whole pose of the figure.

The paintings of the Pyramid Age were stamped with many of the same vigorous qualities found in other works of art of the same period. Among the most famous of the tomb paintings is that of geese, found in a *mastaba* at Medûm. It shows all the directness and observation of Old Kingdom work at its best. Generally speaking, the remarks previously made as to the reliefs apply equally well to the paintings, for the greater number of the former

were cut in such low relief, and were so gaily coloured,
that they were little more than slightly raised and modelled
drawings.

THIRD PERIOD.—MIDDLE KINGDOM, 2160-1788 B.C.
DYNASTIES ELEVEN AND TWELVE

Residence at Dahshûr, Lisht, and in Fayûm.
Twelfth dynasty, 2000-1788 B.C.   Highest prosperity
of Middle Kingdom.

Chief rulers :

    Amenemhet I., 2000-1970 B.C.
    Sesostris I. (Senusert I.), 1980-1935 B.C.
    Amenemhet II., 1938-1903 B.C.
    Sesostris II. (Senusert II.), 1906-1887 B.C.
    Sesostris III. (Senusert III.), 1887-1849 B.C.
    Amenemhet III., 1849-1801 B.C.

The Old Kingdom fell through internal struggles, and
a period of disorganization set in.   When the Middle
Kingdom was established art, which had been in abeyance,
once more emerged triumphant, and although some of the
strength and the vividness of Old Kingdom art had been
lost, Middle Kingdom art had many important qualities of
its own, and the period has been styled the classic time of
Egyptian art.   The buildings of the period are so frag-
mentary that we can form little idea of the architecture.
The great kings of the twelfth dynasty built many temples,
but they have for the most part perished, while the buildings at Thebes were pulled down, enlarged, or altered out of
all recognition by later kings of the Empire.   Cliff tombs
became more frequent, and although no more portrait statues
were made for the tombs, many vigorous life-like statues

were produced, showing that the Old Kingdom traditions
had not died out, and that the sculptors still had power
to triumph over the bondage of a too stereotyped æsthetic
convention. At the same time statues began to be carved
in colossal form, some forty to fifty feet in height, and the
spirit of imperturbable calm began to make itself felt in
art. The Sphinx of Gizeh may possibly have been made
at this time, although certain critics assign it to the fourth
dynasty.

The reliefs and paintings of the period share many of
the characteristics of the sculpture. Some of the best
paintings that the ancient Egyptians produced, found in a
tomb at Beni Hassan, date from this time. They represent figures of birds and animals, and are as full of life
and vigour as Minoan paintings of similar subjects
executed some three hundred years later.

An interesting insight into the mind of a Middle Kingdom artist is found in the inscription of a funerary tablet
of a sculptor named Mertisen, where he states, " I was an
artist skilled in my art. I knew my art, how to represent
the forms of going forth and returning, so that each limb
may be in its proper place. I knew how the figure of a
man should walk, and the carriage of a woman, the pois-
ing of an arm to bring the hippopotamus low, the going
of the runner." [1]

The downfall of the Middle Kingdom was brought
about by foreign invasions, when the Hyksos, the " shepherds, princes of the desert," who introduced the horse into
Egypt, and who were probably Syrians and Canaanites,
ruled the land. It is thought that Joseph lived during
the reign of one of the last of these foreign kings,
while Abraham and Sara probably lived about the year
1850 B.C.

[1] *The Ancient History of the Near East.* H. R. Hall. Methuen.

FOURTH PERIOD.—NEW KINGDOM OR EMPIRE

(A) *The Early Empire*, 1580-1350 *B.C.*
Dynasty Eighteen

Capital : Thebes.

Chief rulers :

Ahmose I. . . .	1580-1557 B.C.
Thutmose III. (including the rule of Thutmos II. and Hatshepsut) . .	1501-1447 „
Amenhotep III. (Amenophis III.) and Queen Tiy .	1411-1375 „
Ikhnaton (Amenhotep IV.) .	1375-1358 „

(B) *The Late Empire*, c. 1350-1150 *B.C.*
Dynasties Nineteen and Twenty

Capital : Thebes and City of Ramses.

Chief rulers :

	Approximate Dates.
Harmhab . . .	1350-1315 B.C.
Ramses I. . . .	1315-1314 „
Seti I. . . .	1313-1292 „
Ramses II. (The Pharaoh of the Oppression) . .	1292-1225 „

Ahmose I., the first king of the eighteenth dynasty, expelled the hated Hyksos invaders from the land and organized Egypt into a military state. Under Thutmose III. Egypt became the first great Empire in history, and vast wealth was accumulated as the result of successful campaigns abroad and the development of trade. The

Empire reached its greatest glory under Amenhotep III.,
and a period of splendour and luxury began which lasted
until the time of Ramses II., after which time a gradual
decadence set in.   By the year 1150 B.C. the great days
of Egyptian civilization were over.

During the Empire art flourished as never before.
The most famous temples of the age are those at Luxor
and Karnak.   The former was built by Amenhotep III.
on an older foundation, and the long avenue of sphinxes,
which connected it with the temple at Karnak, was also
added by the same king.   The latter temple was enlarged
by Thutmose III., who gave it to a great extent its
present form, but the famous Hypostyle Hall was not
added until the reigns of Ramses I. and Seti II., and its
decoration was only completed by Ramses II.   A striking
feature of these temples is their colonnades, an architectural motive entirely Egyptian in origin.   The columns
are often designed in the old Egyptian form of palm trees,
with the crown of foliage forming the capital, or else as
bundles of papyrus stalks, with the cluster of buds bearing
the weight of the architrave.   The temple usually took the
form of a colonnaded hall, behind which was a series of
small chambers containing furniture and implements for
services.   In the centre of these chambers stood the
shrine of the god, the holy of holies, into which the king
and high priest alone could penetrate.   In front of these
temple buildings was a forecourt, open to the sky, with a
pylon or gateway facing the front of the hall.   There was
also a smaller type of temple, composed of a simple
rectangular *cella*, some thirty or forty feet long, and fourteen high.   It contained a door at either end, and was
surrounded by a portico.   The whole was raised on a
base, which was about a half of the height of the temple
walls.   There is no doubt that this form of building,

which was of beautiful proportions, exercised an influence on Greek architecture.

An immense number of statues were produced during the Empire, many being as fine or finer than those of the Old and Middle Kingdoms. The greatness of the kings was represented by colossal statues of immense dignity, in which realism gave way before symbolism and sheer bulk of material. Little if any attempt was made to record the individual features or character of the kings, which were considered entirely secondary to their majesty. An interesting inscription on the statue of Amenhotep, son of Hapi, the chief architect of Amenhotep III., tells of how he executed two colossal statues of the King. One of these may be the statue still existing in the temple of Karnak. The inscription is all the more interesting because it shows how this famous artist endeavoured to break away from artistic convention and to fight against the influence of his time. The following are some extracts from it :—

" The king's scribe, Amenhotep, triumphant ; . . . I did according to that which he (the king) said, I followed according to the things which he commanded me, I found them excellent things for the future. . . . My lord made me chief of all his works. I established the name of the king for ever, I did not imitate that which had been done before . . . I did according to my desire, executing his likeness in this, his great house (Karnak) with every precious stone, enduring like the heavens ; there was not one who had done it (the like) since the time of the founding of the two lands. I conducted the works of his statue, immense in width, taller than his column. . . . I built an eight-vessel. I brought it (the statue) up-river. It was set up in this great house, enduring as heaven.   My witnesses are ye, ye who shall come after."[1]

The most famous of the colossi representing Amenhotep III. are the so-called " Colossi of Memnon," which were erected on either side of the mortuary temple of the King. Although the temple itself has perished, the colossi still stand, immense and solitary, on the plain. The figure of Queen Tiy is seen by the foot of one of the statues. It is possible that these colossi are also the work of the same famous sculptor.

The reliefs of the new kingdom are executed with delicacy and precision. Although the conventional formulæ are strong in them, a spirit of emotion and gaiety has crept in also, which reflects the life of the times, and the foreign influences brought to bear on the art of the Empire through the growth of trade, and the presence of foreign craftsmen in the court. The tombs became personal monuments to the deceased, and were filled with scenes from his life, and imaginary pictures of life in the next world. Deeply incised reliefs were introduced for the first time and became a special feature of the period. Painting reached a very high level during the Empire, and many fine examples are preserved in the tombs. It was found to be a cheaper form of interior decoration than sculpture, and more adapted to the light and graceful treatment of designs in vogue at the time, and we find in it the same animation that is shown in the reliefs.

There is one striking moment in the history of the Empire which demands special mention here, on account of the individual stamp which it left upon the life of the time. This was the short period when important religious and artistic reforms were brought about by Amenhotep III.,

[1] *Ancient Records of Egypt*, translated by Breasted.   University of Chicago Press.

Queen Tiy and their son Ikhnaton. The credit of
these reforms has been generally given to Ikhnaton, but
a careful study of the works of art and inscriptions that
date from his parents' reign will prove that the mental
and artistic vigour of the age was largely due to the influence of the mother and father, and that the beliefs of
the son were but a further development of the ideas of
the parents. Queen Tiy, who was a woman of unusual
gifts and force of character, helped to control the affairs
of state after the death of her husband, during the early
years of her son's reign, and there is no doubt that she
exercised a profound influence upon the sensitive and
imaginative youth.

Ikhnaton was not only a poet and a philosopher, but
he made war upon the state religion, and instituted a
lofty monotheism in its place. He also extended his
reforms to artistic matters. The young King had been
used to the well-executed and naturalistic frescoes which
decorated the walls of his parents' palace, but he determined that his artists must forsake all old conventions
and return to the observation of nature. So much must
he have had the matter at heart that his chief sculptor,
Bek, appended to his title the words "whom the king
himself taught." The result of these resolves was that
the art of Ikhnaton's reign often reached a high
level, although it also frequently lacked the necessary
artistic control. The King and his relations were represented by statues and portrait busts which are obviously
striking likenesses, and the reliefs show an honest, if
somewhat clumsy, attempt to find their inspiration in
nature. One of the best examples of these is in the
museum at Berlin, and shows the Queen presenting flowers
to the King; while in painting, we have as examples of
this freshly realized art the portrait of the King's little

PLATE VI

PAINTING OF A GIRL, SOMERSAULTING
(LATE EMPIRE)

HEAD OF AMENHOTEP IV (IKHNATON)
1375-1358 B.C. (EMPIRE)

daughters, in which even the effect of *chiaroscuro* has been attempted—an attempt which after this date was not again repeated until Greek times nearly a thousand years later. The excavation of Ikhnaton's palace at Tell-el-Armana has also revealed how the king employed the realistic painting of natural objects for its scheme of decoration. Flights of birds are represented against a blue sky on the ceiling, while the pavements show fish and water plants, floating about in blue waters. Unfortunately, after the death of Ikhnaton, art again came under the control of the priests, and steadily lost in vigour and inspiration.

FIFTH PERIOD.—THE RESTORATION OR SAITIC PERIOD, 663-525 B.C. DYNASTY TWENTY-SIX

Chief ruler :

Psamtic I. . . 660-525 B.C.

During the Restoration, which was a short period of great prosperity, a renaissance in art and literature set in. The Egypt of Psamtic, however, was a new Egypt, changed from the Egypt of olden days, and with a lowered vitality. The art of the Restoration was in consequence largely a deliberate return to old types and conventions. New temples were modelled on old designs, and new sculptures were, to a great extent, echoes of the sculpture of the past. In spite of this reversion to old types, a certain freedom crept into the work, and in some instances the old conventional canons of art were frankly cast aside, and less stereotyped and more original works of art were executed. A school of portrait sculpture also grew up, which produced some splendid heads, full of character and observation, the best being worthy to be ranked with the early portrait busts of Greece and Rome.

Egyptian Chronology—Dr Petrie's system of Egyptian chronology differs considerably from that of Professor Breasted, who follows the Berlin system. From the beginning of the Empire onwards, the two systems are almost identical, but the following dates are given by Dr Petrie for the early periods [1] :—

First dynasty, Menes, c. 4777 B.C.

Dynasties III. to VI. [Old Kingdom], c. 4212-3335 B.C.

Dynasties XI. and XII. [Middle Kingdom], c. 2985-2565 B.C.

EXTRACT

Hymn to the Nile (xixth Dynasty) [2]

Hail to thee, O Nile !
Thou showest thyself in this land,
Coming in peace, giving life to Egypt ; . . .
Overflowing the gardens created by Ra,
Giving life to all animals ;
Watering the land without ceasing . . .
Bringer of food, great lord of provisions,
Creator of all good things ! . . .
The inundation comes, (then) cometh rejoicing,
Every heart exulteth . . .
The hymn is addressed to thee with the harp,
It is played with a skilful hand to thee. . . .
O inundation of the Nile, offerings are made to thee,
Oxen are slain to thee,
Great festivals are kept for thee. . . .
Shine forth, shine forth, O Nile, shine forth,
Giving life to men by his oxen ;
Giving life to oxen by the pastures !
Shine forth in glory, O Nile.

---

[1] *A History of Egypt.* Methuen.
[2] *Records of the Past.* Published by Samuel Bagster.

LESSON IV

BABYLONIAN AND ASSYRIAN ART

PART I.—ELEMENTARY LESSON IN STORY FORM

INTRODUCTION.—Last Lesson.—This is the story of the people who conquered Egypt when her great days were over. The King whom you will hear about lived rather more than six hundred years before the time of Christ.

1. **Ashur-bani-pal at Nineveh**—Ashur-bani-pal, the great King of Assyria, is living and ruling in his palace in Nineveh. It is the most famous city in the world. Built up above the River Tigris on great terraces and substructures of enormous breadth, it covers miles of land and is ringed in by walls so broad that two chariots can drive abreast on them. The city swarms with people of every nationality; foreign slaves and captives; soldiers with their leathern coats and huge shields and spears; merchants "whose number is greater than the stars of heaven"; sorcerers, magicians, astronomers, priests, and country people with fruit and corn to sell. On every hand are signs of riches and luxury. The gold, silver, and inlay on the walls and doors of the temples gleam in the sunlight, and the merchants tempt the passers-by with silks, perfumes, gold, jewels, and green and purple Tyrian dyes. The men are strong, thick-set, and fierce looking, mighty warriors returning from distant wars. "Their horses are swifter than the leopards, and they are more fierce than the evening wolves; and their horsemen bear

themselves proudly ; yea, their horsemen come from afar :
they fly as the eagle that hasteth to devour.   Their faces
are set as the east wind, and they gather captives as the
sand."   With cries and shouts the chariots dash past.

"The chariots rage in the streets,
They jostle one against another in the broad ways,
The appearance of them is like torches,
They run like the lightnings."

The city is crowned by the great palace of the King,
with its courts and gardens and many storied temple.   At
its gates huge human-headed and winged bulls, carved in
stone, keep silent guard.   They are sacred images of the
gods and no evil spirit may pass them by.   Inside the
big court people come and go, but in the King's own
rooms all is ordered and quiet.   Servants, slaves, and
marshals pass noiselessly to and fro, for the King is read-
ing in his library and has given orders that none must
disturb him.   He is ill at ease and full of fears.   Last
night there was an eclipse of the moon.   Its clear pale
light had been swallowed up in darkness and the land
had been plunged in black shadow.   What could it mean ?
How had the country offended against its gods ?   The
King walks restlessly to and fro.   Sometimes he sinks
back into his golden chair and signals to a scribe to read
to him the story of his victories.   The books are tablets
of clay on which letters have been scratched with a stylus
while the tablet was still unbaked.   There are thousands
of them, neatly arranged on shelves and carefully
catalogued, and each bearing the royal stamp of the King
and the palace.   They tell of the history and wars of the
country, of its old legends and poems, of birds, animals,
and insects, of astrology and theology, of magic and
mathematics.   Some give lists of spoil and plunder.

Some are inscribed with lists of omens and portents and their meanings.

The King commands a scribe to read him one of the latter tablets, and the scribe begins: "When a piebald dog entereth a palace that palace will make peace with its foes. When a yellow dog entereth a palace there will be destruction in the gates thereof." The King abruptly stops him and sends a slave to inquire if a yellow dog has been seen. He then commands a second scribe to write down a prayer at his dictation. A damp clay tablet is fetched, and the King repeats a prayer to the god of thunder and storm who he thinks is responsible for the eclipse. (Extract *A*.) The tablet is then taken away to be baked, after which it will be returned to the library and stored in one of the shelves. At this moment a diversion is made by the arrival of some soldiers, who bring with them copies of some rare tablets from the palace library at Babylon. This town has been conquered by Assyria and Ashur-bani-pal, who is always eager to add to his own library, has ordered scribes to undertake the work. He listens with much interest to the ancient poems, which he has always wanted to possess, and himself superintends the arrangement of the new tablets on the shelves. The library is a very precious place adjoining the temple, and under the especial protection of the gods. As the hour is late the King retires to bed, for he has arranged to start off early the next morning on a hunting expedition.

2. **The Palace of Ashur-nasir-pal. The Hunt—** Early the next morning all is bustle and excitement. Stores and provisions are packed up and tied on to big camels; the soldiers of the royal guard polish up their bright shields and spear heads, and the King's chariot, harnessed to two splendid horses with gorgeous trappings,

is brought round to the great gate of the palace. King Ashur-bani-pal is dressed in a long robe with heavy fringes and a high mitre-shaped head-dress, and by his side he wears a dagger, inlaid with gold and ivory. He mounts the chariot, and two slaves stand behind him with fly-flaps which they wave to and fro. The King takes the reins and the horses break into a gallop. The people crowd the streets on either side, and bow low as the King passes. The foot soldiers, horses, and camels follow, and the whole procession leaves the town by one of the great gates, and passing through the big suburbs that surround the city, reaches the open country.

The day is brilliantly fine, and the great River Tigris sweeps by its banks, broad and sparkling in the sunshine. The early morning air is fresh and cool, and the King forgets his fears of the night before, and looks back proudly at the splendid town behind him, with the sun gleaming from its battlements and from the golden dome of the great temple which shines like a ball of flame. By night the town of Calah is reached, and all enter the courtyard of the palace, which was built more than two hundred years before by Ashur-nasir-pal, a former King of Assyria. Ashur-bani-pal is very fond of the palace, for it is filled with sculptures and inscriptions telling of the great deeds of his ancestors. He feasts that night in the large hall, which is decorated with reliefs of winged gods and a frieze of a lion hunt. The King decides that if he has good hunting the next day he, too, will call in sculptors, and order reliefs to be carved in his palace in Nineveh in celebration of the day.

Next morning the King again rises early, and at sunrise has started off across the plain in his chariot. A large parasol shelters him from the sun, and a coachman drives the chariot in order that the King's hands may be free

for the hunt.   Nobles and princes accompany him, and
behind their chariots follow soldiers and servants, and
mules and horses bearing a tent and provisions.   The
plain is covered with a carpet of wild flowers ; birds are
singing ; frightened hares leap away through the grass,
and partridges rise from underneath the horses' feet.
Gazelles bound off and are lost to sight, and wild asses
set off at a gallop towards the distant hills.   Some of the
horsemen pursue the game, but the King turns neither to
right nor to left, as he is watching for lions.   At last a
river is reached.   A strong boat has been provided for
the King and his chariot, but the horses and mules plunge
in and swim over, and the soldiers, who carry specially
prepared skins, inflate them, and with their aid are able to
cross in safety.

A halt is called and the tent is pitched.   Here the
King rests during the fiercest heat of the day, while
servants light a fire and a meal is prepared.   A country-
man now arrives at the camp with the information that
two large lions have been seen in some wooded slopes to
the north.   The King is roused, and hastily mounts his
horse.   He is armed with bow, arrows, and a spear, and
is soon galloping over the grassy plain.   Huntsmen
scatter to right and to left, and soon an auroch, or wild
ox, runs snorting from some bushes.   Ashur-bani-pal
starts off in pursuit, and so swift is his horse that he has
soon overtaken the animal, and drawing alongside he
kills it with his dagger.   But where are the lions ?   The
huntsmen are still beating the thickets when suddenly
with a low growl, two great tawny coloured beasts creep
out and make off in the direction of the river.   In the
twinkling of an eye the King's horse is turned, and he
starts off in pursuit.   The baying of the hounds rouses
the lions to fury, and they turn and leap at the King and

the noble who follows him.   Ashur-bani-pal raises his
spear, and so sure is his aim that the largest of the great
beasts rolls dead at his feet, while the second is killed by
the arrows of his attendants.   The lions are carried back
in triumph to the camp, and are laid at the foot of a
small altar.   Two priests stand to right and left of them,
playing a hymn of victory upon their harps.   The King
advances, followed by the bearers of his parasol and fly-
flap, and his Vizier hands him a golden cup of sacra-
mental wine.   This the King tastes, and then pours the
wine over the spoil, at the same time thanking the gods
and goddesses for their aid in the hunt.

The next day the King has still further adventures.
He follows another lion into the marshes, but the horse
that he is riding stumbles in the mud and reeds, and in
the excitement of the moment Ashur-bani-pal leaps to
the ground and follows the great beast into the bushes
where it has taken refuge.   Here it turns, and rising on
its hind legs prepares to spring on him, but before it has
time the King has closed on it and has seized it by the
ear, and plunged his spear into its heart.   The lion is
dragged into a boat which has hardly been pushed off
from the shore when a second lion, already wounded,
springs from the bank into the water, and with a savage
roar makes for one of the rowers.   Its fate is settled by
an arrow from the King, and it is hauled into the boat
and rowed back to the camp.

When the King returns to Nineveh a few days later he
summons his sculptors to appear before him, and commands them to carve reliefs representing the lion hunt,
of which he gives a detailed description.   He orders the
sculptured slabs to be placed round the walls of his great
hall, and dictates the following words to be engraved
above them : " I, Ashur-bani-pal, King of peoples, King

PLATE VII

ASHUR-BANI-PAL HUNTING. RELIEF FROM THE PALACE AT NINEVEH
(668-626 B.C.)

COLOSSAL LION INSCRIBED WITH THE NAME OF ASHUR-NASIR-PAL
(885-860 B.C.)
FROM THE TEMPLE AT CALAH (NIMRÛD)

of Assyria, alone on foot, in my majesty, I seized a lion
of the desert by the ear ; and by the mercy of Ashur and
Ishtar, Queen of battles, I pierced it . . . with my lance,
with mine own hands."

3. The Fall of Thebes—There is great excitement
in Nineveh. News has been brought by a messenger, dusty
and travel-stained, that the proud city of Thebes has
been sacked by the Assyrian troops, and that Egypt
has been conquered. The victorious generals are even
now on their way home, and will shortly deliver the spoils
of war to the King. Great are the rejoicings in the town,
and when the first detachment of the victorious army
reaches the town, the whole of the population turns out to
meet it, and, with singing and jubilation, the fierce-looking
soldiers with their cruel hard faces " set like the east
wind," are welcomed to their homes again.

The generals of the army are conducted to the palace
where the King is waiting for them in pride and impatience. He is seated on his gilded throne, and has put
on his most magnificent robe for the occasion. It is a
state costume heavily fringed, woven with figures of the
gods in gold and crimson and blue, and ornamented down
the centre with a scene of the King killing a lion. Ashur-
bani-pal has powdered his face, and his perfumed hair
and beard are combed and arranged in heavy curls which
fall over his shoulders and chest. Earrings hang in his
ears and jewels round his neck and by his side is a great
sword. The members of the court are grouped round
the throne, and a murmur of excitement passes from one
to another as the generals are announced and prostrate
themselves before the King, kissing the ground at his feet.
Following them are many slaves, who stagger under heavy
loads. They contain some of the booty from Thebes, and
the eyes of the King light up with greed as the treasure

is poured at his feet—gold, ivory, and precious stones,
electrum torn from the walls and doors of the temples,
delicate carvings, gold and silver cups from the royal
palaces of the Pharaohs, and rich stuffs and spices of
every kind. The King makes a sign to the nobles who
crowd round, fingering, touching, and examining, with
their hard faces untroubled by any thought of the poor
Egyptians, vanquished and sad, with their beautiful town
on the Nile, captured and looted. They do not mind if
many of the Egyptians have been tortured and massacred,
and others taken into slavery.

As this is a day of national rejoicing, the palace gates
are thrown open, and according to custom all may enter
and feast. Brilliantly coloured stuffs are stretched over
the great open courtyard, and thousands of men, women,
and children crowd in. Hurrying slaves pass to and fro
bearing food and wine from the royal kitchens, and fruit,
loaves, and joints of every sort disappear like snow in
thaw. In the meantime the Queen wishes to have some
share in the festivity, and gathering her courage together,
she sends an invitation to the King, begging him to
honour her with his presence that evening. She lives in
a separate part of the palace, round which the King has
laid out beautiful gardens full of palms and cypresses, and
fruit trees, and flowers of every kind. Here the Queen
awaits him, and reposing on a golden couch in the shade
of a trellised arbour, he drinks wine with her from a
golden bowl, and tells her of the great victories. Musicians
play on golden harps, and fountains throw their glistening
showers into the scented evening air.

But the King is not happy. Again his old fears
possess him. He feels ill and restless, and leaving the
Queen directly the meal is over, he goes to the royal
library and asks that the tablet should be brought to him

on which is written a magic cure in which he has great belief. The scribe reads it to him. " Mix six different kinds of wood ; pound them with a piece of serpent ; add some wine and raw meat ; then form a paste of the mixture and let the patient swallow it." The King believes this to be an infallible cure for all ills, and he orders it to be prepared for him at once. He wanders about the palace, and finally turns his steps to the temple, and penetrates into the inner shrine where he and the high priest alone may enter. He stands before the figure of the god which can be seen faintly by the dim light of the flickering candles. This shrine is the Assyrian holy of holies. Honey was spread on the ground when it was built, and the very bricks that enclosed it in were blessed by the gods.

Leaving the shrine, Ashur-bani-pal ascends the great tower of the temple. Here the royal astrologers keep watch over the night, their eyes fixed on the stars above. The King tries to find consolation in their prophecies, but in vain. Below him lies the great city, looking dim and ghostly in the moonlight. The river rushes below its walls, swift and unheeding. From the court of the palace the sounds of revelry and music float up into the night air, and by the light of hundreds of torches the moving figures of the people can be seen, dancing, carousing, coming and going unceasingly. Keeping guard over them stand the great sculptured bulls, silent and inscrutable. Ashur-bani-pal is the King of Assyria, the mightiest empire on earth, and this day his triumph is complete, but his heart is heavy within him, and the certainty of disaster hangs over him like a black cloud. He repeats again the prayer that is now inscribed on a tablet in his library, but the gods of Assyria cannot prevent her doom. Not in the reign of Ashur-bani-pal, but some twenty years later, enemies from the north and south descend upon the country. The proud towns of Nineveh and Babylon give way before them, and are burnt and razed to the ground, and the rule of the Medes and Persians begins. (Extracts *B* and *C*.)

4. The Excavations—At the beginning of the last century people began to interest themselves in certain great mounds which stood up above the rivers and plains of Mesopotamia. Here the Babylonians and Assyrians had lived and triumphed and fallen, thousands of years ago. Would it be possible to make excavations in these mounds and see if they hid within their depths traces of the great civilizations of the past? A Frenchman, M. Botta, made the first important attempt, and laid bare an ancient Assyrian palace at Khorsabad, and the treasures he found in it were sent to the Louvre. Then Austin Henry Layard, an Englishman, began to dig. A peasant had told him that there were many things to be found in a great mound near his home, so Mr Layard procured a raft and, accompanied by a friend and one servant, proceeded down the River Tigris until he came to the place. Near the ruins a miserable hovel was found, and the explorers prepared to spend the night there.

" I had slept little during the night," Layard wrote afterwards. " The hovel in which we had taken shelter, and its inmates, did not invite slumber ; but such scenes and companions were not new to me. They could have been forgotten had my brain been less excited. Hopes long cherished were now to be realized. Visions of palaces underground, of gigantic monsters and sculptured figures and endless inscriptions floated before me. After forming plan after plan for removing the earth and extricating these treasures, I fancied myself wandering in a maze of chambers from which I could find no outlet.

Then again all was reburied, and I was standing on a grass-covered mound. Exhausted, I was at length sinking into sleep when, hearing the voice of Awad, I rose from my carpet and joined him outside the hovel. The day had already dawned ; he had returned with six Arabs, who agreed for a small sum to work under my direction. The lofty cone and broad mound of Nimrūd broke like a distant mountain on the morning sky."

The efforts of Layard were crowned with success. Trenches were sunk into the mound ; the site of the ancient city of Calāh was laid bare, and a wealth of treasure was brought to light—great figures of winged bulls with human heads, friezes representing lion hunts, in fact all the glories of the palace of Ashur-nasir-pal. A strong cart was made, and, with immense difficulty, the figures of the bulls were lowered on to it and pulled by scores of men to the river, where they were dispatched by rafts to the sea, and taken by ships to London. Encouraged by the success of his efforts, Layard next started excavations on the great mound which tradition held to be the site of Nineveh. Here the capital of the Assyrian kings was discovered, and, although the town had been ravaged by fire and war, the ruins still contained many relics of its ancient splendour. Among the things that were found in the palace of Ashur-bani-pal were the carved reliefs of his lion hunt ; the colossal figures of the gods, and hundreds of the tablets from his library. All these treasures are now in London in the British Museum, while far away in distant Mesopotamia corn is waving on the mounds that covered them, and blue bee-eaters dart in and out of the deserted pits.

Notes on the Story—Paragraphs 1, 2, and 3 are imaginary. The matter in them is largely drawn from the bas reliefs and inscriptions themselves. The books of the Old Testament give many vivid pictures of Assyrian life. Among the mass of modern books dealing with the subject *Life in Ancient Egypt and Assyria* by Professor Maspero, has been constantly referred to for details of the daily life of the people. A good description of Nineveh is given in Principal George Adam Smith's *Book of the Twelve Prophets*.

PART II.—MATERIAL FOR ADVANCED LESSONS ONLY

History—(a) **Babylonia**—During the fourth millennium B.C., when the kingdoms of Upper and Lower Egypt were flourishing in the valley of the Nile, a second nation was growing up in the fertile plains of the Tigris and Euphrates rivers in Mesopotamia. The primitive civilization of this country was due to people known as Sumerians, who had come from the hills, and who founded the early cities of Eridu, Nippur, and Erech, and invented the pictorial system of writing which developed later into the cuneiform characters. To the Sumerians were joined a people of Semitic race; a gradual mingling of both races took place; and Sumer, or South Babylonia, and Akkad, or North Babylonia, became one country. The small local states and city kingdoms which flourished during the years 3000-2000 B.C. were governed by *patesi* or hereditary priest-kings, who were also high priests of the local gods. Most of the earliest objects of Sumerian art that have been found date from the reign of Ur-Nina, who made the town of Lagash the capital of Babylonia, and reigned there at some period between the years 3000-2800 B.C. He founded a dynasty, and his reign was followed shortly afterwards by that of Eannatun, who is famous by reason of his sculptured memorial tablet known as the Stele of the Vultures, now in the Louvre. The reigns of Shargani-Sharri, known as Sargon of Akkad (*c.* 2750-2700 B.C.), and his son Naram Sin, are also known to us through works of art, the most important being the well-known

stele of the latter ruler, also in the Louvre, in which he is
depicted as leading his soldiers in battle. Two hundred
years followed of which we have little or no knowledge
until, about the year 2450 B.C., we come to the reign of
Gudea, also a *patesi* of Lagash, who, to judge by the
result of excavations, was a keen patron of art.

About the year 2300 B.C. the country was conquered
by a fresh Semitic race, who raised the town of Babylon
to the position of the capital. They appointed Marduk,
whom they identified with Bel, or Enlil, of Nippur, as king
of the gods, and established the first Babylonian dynasty
about the year 2050 B.C. Another important element in
the population was that of the Kalda or Chaldeans, who
lived in the marshes at the mouth of the Euphrates, and
at one time gave their name to the whole population, by
reason of the reign of a Kalda prince at Babylon. The
Kassites were another tribe which invaded the country,
and at one time ruled there, and they also left their mark
upon the people. So in this way the Babylonians were a
mixed race, with a many-sided civilization due to the
various elements which gave it birth.

(b) Assyria—The rise of Assyria, the northern part
of Babylonia, took place during the years 2100 to 2000
B.C., and about the year 1700 B.C. the country asserted
its independence and became a separate kingdom with
Ashur as its capital. About the year 1250 B.C. Assyria
conquered Babylon, but it was not until the reign of
Tiglath-Pileser I. (1100 B.C.) that the country began an
important campaign of foreign conquests. The great days
of Assyria date from the years 800-600 B.C. when the
Assyrian Empire was the greatest power in the Near
East. Egypt was at her feet; the trade of the world
flowed through her great cities, where the merchants,
to quote the prophet Nahum, were "more in number

than the stars in heaven." The glories of Nineveh and and Babylon and the tale of their luxury and wickedness have been sung by the Israelite prophets, and although the Assyrians were not perhaps more cruel than other nations, their monuments and inscriptions tell of incredible brutality. The city of Nineveh was some three miles long and one mile broad. It contained beautiful parks, gardens, and splendid palaces and temples, and was capable of holding a population of 30,000 persons. It was enclosed by double walls, which were completed in the year 694 B.C., and which were named " The Wall that Terrified the Foe " and " The Wall whose Splendour Overthrows the Enemy." Beyond the walls stretched great suburbs and a network of smaller towns on the plain, and the circumference of this greater Nineveh was described by the prophet Jonah as " a three days' journey," which would be equivalent to about sixty miles. The whole mass of this vast population was held together by the greed of gain, and grew rich with the profits of trade and the loot of city and country-side.

In the year 606 B.C. Assyria was attacked by all the nations whom she had oppressed. Nineveh was taken after a terrible siege, and before two years had passed the Empire had fallen and the rule of the Medes and Persians was established.

Babylonia, however, remained independent and flourished for nearly seventy years. Nebuchadrezzar II. (605-562 B.C.) was the most famous of these later Babylonian kings, and he did much to restore the fallen glories of his capital. In the book of Daniel we get a description of Belshazzar, one of his successors, and of the civilization of the time ; but its prosperity was not to endure for the country fell before the attacks of the Persians. The following are some of the chief Assyrian kings :—

Ashur-nasir-pal III., 885-860 B.C. Lays foundations of Empire. Conquers Babylonia. A great art patron. Moves capital of Assyria from Ashur to Calah (Nimrûd), where he builds a great palace.

Tiglath Pileser IV., 745-727 B.C. Founds Sargonide dynasty. Reconquers Babylonia, which had revolted, and extends Assyrian empire on every hand.

Sargon, 722-705 B.C. A great art patron. Builds a royal palace at Dûr-Sharrukîn (Khorsabad), near Nineveh.

Sennacherib, 705-681 B.C. Rebuilds Nineveh (Kouyunjik) and erects a royal palace there. Destroys Babylon.

Esarhaddon, 681-668 B.C. (Ahasuerus) Rebuilds Babylon. Builds a palace at Calah (Nimrûd).

Ashur-bani-pal, 668-626 B.C. Assyrian Empire at the height of its fame. Great age of civilization and art, and glory of Nineveh. Conquest of Egypt and destruction of Thebes, 661.

Religion—Mesopotamian religion was composed of two elements, the beliefs of the early Sumerians and of the Semites. The Sumerians worshipped natural phenomena, the lightning, thunder, heat, and darkness, which they conceived in the form of spirits. They also believed that every man had a " *zi* " or separate spirit of his own which corresponded to the " *ka* " or double of the " Egyptians." The Semites conceived their chief god as the Lord of Heaven and earth, in whose image man had been created. His visible form was the sun, and his powers were used both for good and evil, for bringing to birth and for scorching and withering. The spirits of the Sumerians were feared as powers for evil to be exorcised by magicians and sorcerers. As the two races amalgamated Semitic influence caused the chief of the Sumerian spirits to be raised to the position of gods, with priests and temples dedicated to their service. The

Assyrians took their religion from the Babylonians, with the difference that they deified their country in the form of the god **Ashur**, whom they placed above all the other gods in power and majesty.   The following are some of the chief among the Babylonian gods :—

Anu.   Earliest and greatest of Babylonian gods, lord of heaven and father of the gods.   Centre of worship, Erech.   Symbol, a column.

En-lil.   The second great Babylonian god, the lord of earth.   Centre of worship, Nippur.   Afterwards identified with **Bel, Baal, Marduk,** or **Merodach** the sun god, and chief deity of the city of Babylon.   He was also considered the god of battle.   Symbol, a shape like a horned hat on a column.

Ea or **Enki.**   The god of the deep and third of the Babylonian gods.   The giver of wisdom and the god of creation.   Centre of worship, Eridu, which in former days, before the retreating of the sea, stood on the shores of the Persian Gulf.   Symbol, a ram's head on a column set on a rectangular throne, beneath which lies the fish-tailed capricorn.   Ea has sometimes been identified with **Oannes,** the god represented as half-man, half-fish.

Nabu or **Nebu,** son of Marduk, and the messenger of the gods.   The god of fate and astronomy.   Centre of worship, Borsippa (Bors Nimrūd), the tradition site of the tower of Babel.

Adad or **Ramman.**   The god of storm and thunder, also of war, associated with the flood.   Symbol, a lightning bolt.

Nergal.   God of the dead and ruler over the lower regions ; also god of war and of the chase.   He represented the midday heat of the sun and was identified with the planet Mars.   Symbol, a lion-headed column.

Sin or **En-zu,** the moon god.   Centre of worship, Ur. Symbol, a crescent.

Shamash, the sun god, and god of healing and beneficent power.   The great judge of the universe.

Ishta (Astarte or Ashteroth).   The goddess of love and of the evening star.   Earliest seat of her worship at Erech.   Identified with the planet Venus.

There were also hosts of lesser gods, and evil beings such as **Timat,** the dragon, symbolizing the powers of chaos and darkness.   **Gilgamish** was a heroic figure of Babylonian legend.   He has sometimes been identified with the mythical Nimrod, the mighty hunter, and is frequently represented in art.   The **Shedi** and **Lamassi** were colossal beings, half-god, half-animal, which, carved in stone, guarded the approaches of temple and palace from the powers of malign spirits.   Among the latter ghouls, the spirit "Headache" was one of the most alarming and deadly, and also the Spirit of the West Wind which left fever and drought in its wake.   The number of these evil spirits was legion, and endless were the spells and incantations provided to repulse their attack.

The Babylonians had a sad and gloomy belief as to the life after death.   They imagined that deep down in the crust of the earth was a great cavern, and here, in Hades, mortals dwelt after death, guarded by seven warders at its seven gates.   They were clothed in feathers like great birds, and their only food was dust.   The name given to this gloomy region was *arallu*, "the land without return."   The dead were regarded as nearer to the gods than to mortals, and could answer questions through the necromancers and sorcerers.   The gods, on the other hand, were only to be approached through the official channel of the priests.

Owing to the marshy condition of the soil, comparatively few Babylonian and Assyrian graves have been discovered. It is thought by some that the people cremated their dead, but if so the custom has not been mentioned on any of the inscriptions that have been discovered. Tombs were built of brick, and in them food, drink, and sometimes furniture were placed for the benefits of the "kis" or doubles. Sometimes these tombs contained many rooms, but in spite of this, very little importance was attached to them and to tomb art in general. Tombs were built on consecrated ground near the chief temple of the district, and as the space was limited, when the sun-dried bricks crumbled away and nothing remained of them but mounds of dust and rubbish, fresh tombs were built upon the old sites. Some of the old cemeteries that have been discovered reveal in this way the different strata of past ages, while to this day many of the peoples of Western Asia bring their dead to be buried in the sacred Temple enclosures, the well-springs of their ancient religion. The official religion was different in many of its aspects from that believed in by the people, which was of a much degraded type. Whereas the general mass of the stars was worshipped by the uneducated classes, in educated circles certain of them only were identified with the different gods. Again, the lower classes resorted to the worship of multitudinous spirits, and to the witchcraft of sorcerers and magicians, while in certain literary circles monotheism was believed in. The Penitential Psalms, forming part of the Babylonian Bible, and dating from long before the time of Abraham, show great dignity and beauty of thought and belief. Here are three fragments from them.

"God my creator, take hold of my arms ! Direct the breath of my mouth, my hands direct, O Lord of light.

" Lord, let not Thy servant sink ! Amidst the tumultuous waters
take hold of his hand !

" He who fears not his God will be cut off even like a reed.
He who knows not his goddess, his bodily strength will waste
away ; like to a star of heaven, his splendour will pale; he will
vanish to the waters of the night."

Architecture—The buildings of the Babylonians were
made of brick, as there was very little stone to be had in
their marshy and low-lying country.   The clay from the
banks of the great rivers, when moulded, was either dried
in the sun or baked in kilns.   When stone had to be used
it was brought from a distance and was generally of a hard
volcanic kind, such as basalt or diorite.   Great brick platforms were used as foundations for buildings to raise them
above the marshy ground.   The bricks were generally laid
when still soft, and were frequently stamped with the King's
name and an inscription.   They were cemented together
first with mud and in later days with clay mixed with a
little water and sometimes with straw.   The Assyrians
followed Babylonian traditions in building, as in everything else, and although drier and firmer ground often
rendered platforms unnecessary, the people continued to
build them as foundations for temples and palaces.   In
the same way bricks were universally used, although the
country possessed a fair supply of limestone and alabaster.
The latter materials were employed in decoration, and
served to line walls and make pavements and sometimes
columns and plinths.   Wood was brought from a distance
for pillars and roofs, although the latter are thought to
have been frequently vaulted and made of brick.   Many
bas-reliefs represent buildings as surmounted by a series
of small domes, and they also show, as an almost invariable
feature of Mesopotamian architecture, a parapet with a
crenelated edge as the decoration to a flat roof.   Walls
were of great thickness.   In Sargon's palace at Khorsabad

the inner ones measure from twelve to twenty-eight feet in width, and this has been mentioned in support of the theory of domed roofs which would necessitate strong walls.

Babylonian and Assyrian temples have been discovered in a worse state of preservation than that of the palaces. The earliest were probably built with only one or two stages, but later seven of these were frequently erected above the artificial platform on which the temple stood. These *ziggurats* or staged towers were built "to reach the heavens," and as kings were sometimes buried in them, some archæologists have drawn a parallel between them and the Egyptian pyramids. The temples, which were enclosed by massive walls, contained chambers for the priests' treasure, houses, granaries, and enclosures for the sacrificial victims. Hidden in their inmost recess, or sometimes erected on the highest stage of the tower, was the holy of holies, containing the golden table, mercy seat, altar, and statue of the god. The very ground on which the temple was built was holy, having been consecrated with libations of honey, oil, and wine.

A contemporary description of one of these temples is given by Tiglath-Pileser I. (1100 B.C.), who, when he repaired the temple of Anu-Adad (founded *circa* 1140 B.C.), recorded his act in the following words :—

" In the beginning of my government, Anu and Adad, the great gods, my lords, who love my priestly dignity, demanded of me the restoration of this their sacred dwelling. I made bricks, and I cleared the ground until I reached the artificial flat terrace upon which the old temple had been built. I laid its foundations upon the solid rock ; I built it from foundation to roof larger and grander than before, and erected also two great temple towers, fitting ornaments of their great divinities. The

PLATE VIII

EXCAVATIONS AT BABYLON
THE GATE OF THE GODDESS ISHTAR. CITY OF NEBUCHADNEZZAR II. (B.C. 605-562)
(The figures of dragons and bulls in glazed terra-cotta are sacred symbols of the gods

splendid temple, a brilliant and magnificent dwelling, the habitation of their joys, the house for their delight, shining as bright as the stars on heaven's firmament, and richly decorated with ornaments through the skill of my artists, I planned, devised, and thought out, built and completed. I made its interior brilliant like the dome of the heavens ; decorated its walls like the splendour of the rising stars ; and made it grand with resplendent brilliancy. I reared its temple towers to heaven and completed its roof with burnt brick ; located therein the upper terrace containing the chambers of their great divinities ; and led into its interior Anu and Adad the great gods, and made them dwell in this, their lofty home, thus gladdening the heart of their great divinities . . ." [1]

The famous "hanging gardens" of Babylon were built upon terraces supported by pillars and arches, and formed one of the most distinctive features of the palaces. It is noticeable that while in Egypt the temples were the buildings of the greatest grandeur, in Babylonia and Assyria the position is reversed, and the palaces were the most splendid monuments.

Sculpture—The earliest sculptures that have been found are Sumerian in origin, and date from the reigns of Ur-Nina and Eannatun. They are primitive and interesting in type and bold in design, but it is not until the reign of Naram Sin that much technical advancement is shown. The most famous monument of this reign is the stele of the king, now in the Louvre, which represents figures full of vigour, and comparatively free from convention. About two hundred and fifty years later, during the reign of Gudea, priest-king of Lagash, a great deal of sculpture in the round was produced, work which shows

[1] Harper's translation from Handcock's *Mesopotamian Archæology*, published by Mr Philip Lee Warner.

80 ANCIENT AND MEDIEVAL ART

the influence of Egyptian art, and which is often clumsy, but which is also full of interest, and frequently reveals considerable originality and force. After the time of Gudea a long period of artistic stagnation seems to have set in, and hardly any works of art have been found until we come to the time of the great days of Assyria.

The most famous examples of Assyrian sculpture date from the three hundred years before the fall of the Empire, and the greater number of them have been found in the palaces of Ashur-nasir-pal at Nineveh and Nimrûd (Calah), of Sargon at Dûr-Sharrukîn (Khorsabad), and of Ashur-bani-pal, also at Nineveh. The favourite form of Assyrian sculpture was the bas-relief, a method which was particularly well adapted to the soft limestone and alabaster found in the hills. While the Babylonians plastered the walls and covered them with frescoes, or adorned them with moulded terra-cotta decorations, the Assyrians lined their halls and temples with carved slabs on which the deeds and triumphs of the kings were set forth. Even the colossal figures of Genii, half bull, half human, which guarded the doors of temple and palace and were called the *Shedi* and *Lamassi* were, to a certain extent, great bas-reliefs and not completely sculpture in the round.

The following description of some of these famous sculptures formed part of an inscription of King Esarhaddon. "The Shedi and Lamassi are propitious, are the guardians of my royal promenade and the rejoicers of my heart; may they ever watch over the palace and never quit its walls. . . . I caused doors to be made in cypress, which has a good smell, and I had them adorned with gold and silver, and fixed in the doorways. Right and left of these doorways I caused Shedi and Lamassi of stone to be set up. They are placed there to repulse the wicked."

Just as the Sphinx of the Egyptians expressed intelligence and strength, so these great sculptures represented the mind and brain of man, the physical force of the bull and the swiftness of an eagle's wings. They are highly conventionalized and splendid in design, and the sense of calm and tranquil majesty in which they are wrapped is still potent, even when the sculptures stand in the crowded galleries of museums. They also present a curious feature which is common to Ninevite art alone. In order that they should look complete when seen from either the front or the side, they were given a fifth leg, a device which may also be noticed in the magnificent figure of a lion, formerly in the temple of Ashur-nasir-pal at Calah (Nimrûd), and now in the British Museum (see Plate VII.).

Equally famous are the series of bas-reliefs representing the gods and sovereigns, and the wars and sport of the Assyrian kings. The growth and development of these reliefs can be traced in the Assyrian rooms of the British Museum, from the bold, vigorous work of Ashur-nasir-pal, both fine and archaic in design, to the delicate and spirited productions of Ashur-bani-pal's reign, which are full of observation, but lack the force of the earlier work. In all these reliefs the artistic conventions of the Assyrians are apparent, such as the expression of strength by enormous and exaggerated muscles and a sameness of face, common to all the figures. When the reliefs are closely examined it will be seen that no attempt has been made to differentiate the faces of the various characters represented, and that even the King's features are exact facsimiles of those of his servants, soldiers, and nobles.

The exaggeration of the muscles has led to an interesting comparison of Egyptian and Assyrian sculpture

by M. Perrot. "The Egyptian sculptor simplifies the
forms of nature, and sums them up, as it were, in an
abbreviated abstract ; the Assyrian renders them more
at length and in detail. The former seems to see the
human body through a fine veil, which hides from his
view all accidents of surface and all unessential features,
so as to leave visible nothing but the main outlines and
the general effect of the contour. On the other hand,
the Assyrian sculptor appears to study nature through
a magnifying glass ; he emphasizes the things that the
Egyptian refines away ; he observes and exaggerates." [1]

The perspective of the reliefs is very elementary, but
the feeling for movement and animation displayed in
them is excellent, particularly in the case of the lions,
which have been most sympathetically studied. The
Assyrians, unlike the Egyptians, were unaccustomed to
the nude, and this fact naturally affected their sculpture
for the worse, particularly in the case of work in the
round, which they seem hardly ever to have attempted.

Interesting references to Assyrian sculpture are found
in the following description of the palace of Sargon
at Khorsabad, which formed part of an inscription in the
great hall :—

"I built in the town some palaces covered with the
skin of the sea calf, and of sandal wood, ebony, the wood
of the mastic tree, cedar, cypress, wild pistachio-nut tree,
a palace of incomparable splendour as the seat of my
royalty. . . . I bordered the doors of pine and mastic
wood with bronze garnitures. . . . I made a spiral staircase. . . . Between the doors I placed eight double lions;
over them I sculptured artistically a crown of beasts of the
fields, a bird in stone of the mountains. I drew upon me

[1] Translation quoted from *A Grammar of Greek Art.* P. Gardner.
Macmillan.

the admiration of the people of all countries. From the beginning to the end I walked worshipping the god Assur, and following the custom of wise men I built palaces, I amassed treasures. . . . I invoked in the midst of them Assur, the father of the gods. I presented vessels of glass, things in chased silver, ivory, valuable jewels, and immense presents in great quantities. I exhibited sculptured idols, double and winged. . . . May Assur, the father of the gods, bless these palaces by giving to his images a spontaneous splendour. . . . May the sculptured bull, the protector and god who imparts perfection, dwell, in day and in night time in his presence, and never stir from this threshold." [1]

Painting, Enamelled Terra-cotta, etc.—Painting formed the chief decoration of Babylonian buildings, the brick walls of which were covered with white or light-coloured plaster for the sake of coolness. On this surface simple decorations or elaborate frescoes were painted, to satisfy the people's love of gay colour, paintings such as those alluded to in the Book of Ezekiel, " men pourtrayed upon the wall, the images of the Chaldeans, pourtrayed with vermilion, with dyed turbans upon their heads, all of them princes to look upon, after the likeness of the Babylonians." The Assyrians, although using bas-reliefs as their favourite form of decoration, also employed fresco painting, but unfortunately very few examples of the art, either Babylonian or Assyrian, have been preserved. The walls of the palace at Nimrûd were covered with elaborate examples, but they all crumbled away on being exposed to the air. The colours used were chiefly royal blue and yellow, while red, green, and black were less popular. They were seldom used in imitation of nature, but were employed for purely decorative effect.

[1] *Records of the Past.* S. Bagster.

Many of the bas-reliefs show traces of colour, and old inscriptions and travellers' tales speak of the brilliance of the decorations, particularly those of the ziggurats, which had each successive stage painted with a different planetary colour, and which in the brilliant sunlight must have looked dazzling in the extreme.

Herodotus gives an account of the painting of the walls of Ecbatana, the chief city of the Medes. As they copied the art of the Assyrians in every detail, this description can in all probability be applied to the famous cities of Mesopotamia. It runs as follows : " The Medes built the city now called Agbatana, the walls of which are of great size and strength, rising in circles one within the other. The number of the circles is seven, the royal palace and the treasuries standing within the last. The circuit of the outer wall is very nearly the same as that of Athens. Of this wall the battlements are white, of the next black, of the third scarlet, of the fourth blue, of the fifth orange ; all these are coloured with paint ; the two last respectively with silver and gold." [1]

Another favourite form of architectural decoration with the Babylonians was that of glazed terra-cotta. The tiles or small bricks were moulded by hand, and the designs that ornamented them were then coloured and covered with a coat of glaze. They were then baked in an oven and fitted together, and many of the friezes that have been discovered testify to the excellence of this branch of art (see Plate VIII.). The ceilings, walls, and doorways of the palaces and temples were also inlaid with rare and costly woods, and sometimes with plates of gold and other precious metals, and were incrusted with ivory and even precious stones. Textiles of rich and elaborate design were produced, and are witnessed to by

[1] Rawlinson's translation. Murray.

the robes represented in the bas-reliefs. The furniture in the palaces was inlaid with ivory, ebony, and precious metals, and many of the seats and couches had legs carved in the form of the legs of oxen. The Assyrians used glass and porcelain, and although it is not known when their manufacture was introduced, it is probable that transparent glass was first invented in the reign of Sargon. They also produced the most elaborate vessels of gold, bronze, and silver, frequent mention of which is made in the prophetic books of the Old Testament.

Seals—The seal-cylinder was a Babylonian invention. As the houses had no locks, doors were sealed with clay for safety, and every man carried a seal with which to impress the wet material. These seals were exactly like small garden rollers in form, and had a piece of wire inserted through the centre to form the handle. On them were engraved mythological or historic scenes, which were imprinted on the clay when the rollers were passed over it. The oldest of the seals were made of shell or white marble, and later various stones were employed, and sometimes lapis-lazuli. The designs of the most ancient of them furnish some of the earliest examples of Babylonian art.

Persian Art—Persian art was founded upon the art of the Babylonians and Assyrians and was also influenced by the art of the Greeks and Egyptians. The Persian Empire, which was the most vast of the ancient Oriental empires, lasted for less than two hundred years, and with its downfall the ancient Persian art of the Achæmenid dynasty came to an end. The Persians were simple hardy people of small culture, and when they found themselves the rulers of wide dominions they adopted the current artistic styles of their new subjects, blending one with another until a brilliant and eclectic style of their own was produced.   The great halls of the royal palaces at Susa and Persepolis were modelled on the design of the Egyptian halls with their many columns, while the bas-reliefs and human headed bulls that formed their decorations were copied from the Assyrian and Babylonian sculptures.   From the Ionian Greeks the Persians copied the flat wooden roofs of their buildings and various architectural refinements, but certain of the capitals of their columns were an invention of their own and consisted of the fore-parts of two bulls, or unicorns, placed back to back with their front legs doubled back beneath them. The Persians also brought the art of glazed and enamelled bricks to great perfection, and well-preserved examples of friezes executed in this method have been excavated. At the fall of the Persian empire the people of Mesopotamia reverted to their own old art forms, and vaulted and domed roofs were once more used to surmount buildings.   Later Persian art of the Sassanid period will be touched upon in Lesson XI.

EXTRACTS

A

"O Ramman (the god of thunder and storm) the prince of heaven and earth, at whose command mankind was created, speak thou the word and let the gods take their stand by thee.   Plead thou my cause and grant me a favourable judgment.   For I, Ashur-bani-pal, am thy servant . . . I make my petition unto thee because of the evil which followeth the eclipse of the moon and the hostility of the powers of heaven, and evil portents are in my palace and my land, and because evil bewitchment . . . and iniquity . . . are in my body ; and because an evil spectre is bound unto me.   Accept thou the lifting up of my hand, give heed unto my prayer, set me free from the spell which bindeth me, do away with my sin and let there be averted any evil whatsoever which threateneth my life. Let a good spirit be ever at my head. Let me live by thy command! Let me bow down and extol thy greatness!"[1]

B

THE DOOM OF NINEVEH

(a) *From the Book of the prophet Zephaniah; (b) from the Book of the prophet Nahum.*

(a) "The Lord will . . . stretch out His hand against the North and destroy Assyria; and will make Nineveh a desolation and dry like the wilderness. And herds shall lie down in the midst of her, all the beasts of the nations; both the pelican and the porcupine shall lodge in the chapiters thereof; their voice shall sing in the windows; desolation shall be in the thresholds. This is the joyous city that dwelt carelessly, that said in her heart I am, and there is none else beside me. Now she is become a desolation, a place for the beasts to lie down in. Everyone that passeth her by shall hiss and wag his hand."

(b) " Take ye the spoil of silver,
    Take the spoil of gold,
For there is none end of the store,
    The glory of all pleasant furniture.

She is empty and void and waste,
    And the heart melteth and the knees smite together,
And anguish is in all loins,
    And the faces of them all are waxed pale . . .

Nineveh is laid waste, who shall bemoan her?
Whence shall I seek comforters for thee? . . .

All thy fortresses shall be like fig trees with the first ripe figs;
If they be shaken
They fall into the mouth of the eater. . . .

---

[1] *Guide to the Babylonian and Assyrian Antiquities.* British Museum Trustees.

Thy crowned are as the locusts and thy marshals as swarms of
   grasshoppers
Which camp in the hedges in the cold day,
But when the sun arises they flee away,
   And the place is not known where they are.

Thy shepherds slumber, O King of Assyria,
   Thy worthies are at rest ;
Thy people are scattered upon the mountains,
   And there is none to gather them.

There is no assuaging of thy hurt ;
   Thy wound is grievous ;
All that hear the bruit of thee clap hands over thee,
   For upon whom hath not thy wickedness passed continually ?"

C

THE DOOM OF BABYLON

From the thirteenth chapter of Isaiah.

". . . and Babylon
   The glories of kingdoms,
   The beauty of the Chaldeans' pride,
   Shall be as when God overthrew Sodom and Gomorrah.

It shall never be inhabited
   Neither shall it be dwelt in from generation to generation ;
   Neither shall the Arabian pitch his tent there,
   Neither shall the shepherds make their flocks to lie down there

But wild beasts of the desert shall lie there ;
   And the houses shall be full of doleful creatures ;
   And ostriches shall dwell there,
   And satyrs shall dance there,

And wolves shall cry in their castles,
   And jackals in their pleasant places,
   And her time is near to come,
   And her days shall not be prolonged."

D

Description of the false gods of Babylonia and Assyria.

From the sixth chapter of the Book of the prophet Baruch.[1]

" Now ye shall see in Babylon gods of silver and of gold and of wood, borne upon shoulders which cause the nation to fear. . . .

" As for their tongue it is polished by the workmen, and they themselves are gilded and laid over with silver ; yet they are but false and cannot speak. . . .

" Yet these gods cannot save themselves from rust and moths, though they be covered with purple raiment.

" They wipe their faces because of the dust of the temple, when there is much upon them.

" And he that cannot put to death one that offendeth him, holdeth a sceptre, as though he were a judge of the country.

" He hath also in his hand, a dagger and an axe, but cannot deliver himself from war and thieves. . . .

" Their faces are blackened through the smoke that cometh out of the temple.

" Upon their bodies and heads sit bats, swallows, and birds and the cats also. . . .

" They are borne upon shoulders, having no feet, whereby they declare unto men that they be nothing worth. . . .

" If they fall to the ground at any time they cannot rise up again of themselves, neither if one set them upright can they move of themselves. . . .

" They can save no man from death, neither deliver the weak from the mighty.

" They cannot restore a blind man to his sight, nor help any man in his distress. . . .

" They are made of carpenters and goldsmiths ; they can be nothing else than the workmen will have them to be. . . .

" For as a scarecrow in a garden of cucumbers keepeth

---

[1] Tell the children that in some of the temples that have been excavated, little blind passages have been found behind the shrines in the holy of holies. Here the priest could hide and work unseen the miracles of the gods.

nothing, so are their gods of wood and laid over with silver and gold.

"And likewise their gods of wood and laid over with silver and gold are like to a white thorn in an orchard, that every bird sitteth upon. . . .

"Better then is the just man that hath none idols, for he shall be far from reproach.'

LESSON V

CHINESE ART

INTRODUCTION.—Who were the first peoples who learnt to write and make laws, and to build and paint? After the Egyptians and Babylonians the next people to be civilized were the Chinese. We hear of them first when the pyramids were being built. This is a story about a great Chinese painter, who lived, however, long after Rahotep and Nefert, Queen Hatshepsut and Queen Tiy, and Ashur-bani-pal of Assyria.

1. **Youth**—Once upon a time there was a boy called Wu-Tao-Tzu. He lived in a big town in China, far away on the other side of the world. The Emperor lived there too, in a great palace, but the part of the town in which Wu lived was dirty and crowded, for his mother and father were dead, and no one cared very much for him, and he had no money. Sometimes he would lodge in one house, sometimes another family would take him in ; more often still he would curl up and sleep under the shadow of a big roof, or leave the town and find shelter under some friendly tree. He loved the beauty of nature, and would lie awake spellbound by the white beauty of the moonlight and the dark pools of shadow beneath the trees. The flowers were so beautiful that they would bring tears to his eyes, and when the dawn broke, and the little birds twittered, and the long grasses bent under their weight of dew, and the sun burnt in the blue skies

he would forget all his troubles, and sing and whistle with delight.

Sometimes he had to dig in the rice fields until his back and arms ached, and sometimes he had to help to carry wood or bricks for building, or else to do housework, and clean and scrub. How he hated it all! When he was very unhappy he would creep away and slip into the big temple near by. There in the dusk was a great statue of Buddha, the god whom the Chinese worshipped. It sat cross-legged, an inscrutable smile upon its lips, lost in thought. But what Wu loved most of all were the pictures painted on the temple walls. He was never tired of gazing at them, at the great dragons and savage-looking tigers, and the figures of men and women, with their pale faces, and long almond-shaped Chinese eyes.

One day, when Wu paid his morning visit to the temple, he saw a Buddhist priest drawing on one of the walls. Wu squatted on the ground by his side, and watched him, entranced, his bright dark eyes riveted on him as he worked, until the priest became conscious of him, and laid down his brush. "So you like painting?" he asked him. "Yes, indeed," Wu answered, "I love it more than anything else, and I want to be a painter like you, when I grow up," he added eagerly. The priest was amused at the boy's interest. "Here is a brush," he said, "dip it into the ink, and show what you can do." Wu took the brush, and thought for a minute; then, trembling with excitement, he made a few rapid strokes on the piece of paper that the priest had given him. The painter watched him, amazed. Wu had drawn a spray of blossom, suggesting, with a few lines only, all the beauty of its delicate growth and exquisite leaves and petals; even the fragrance of the spring seemed to lurk in the drawing. The painter asked him who had taught him to draw, and

Wu answered that nobody had taught him, but that he had watched painters when they worked, and that he loved all the flowers and trees and animals, and often tried to draw them. The priest told Wu to come again the next day, and after that many lessons followed, until Wu began to paint so well that the people began to talk of him, and to take an interest in his work.

One day a wonderful thing happened. Who should come to Wu but a messenger from the Emperor himself. He brought a summons commanding the boy to come to the palace, as the famous ruler of the country had heard of his skill, and wanted to see what the boy could do. Wu went in fear and trembling, and prostrated himsel. before the throne, for he was terrified at all the magnificence that surrounded him. He need not have been afraid, however, for the Emperor was a great lover of art, and was so pleased with the boy's extraordinary gifts that he there and then took Wu into his service. His ragged clothes were taken away, and, well fed and dressed, he began his life at the palace, together with a regular training in art.

2. Symbolic and Landscape Painting—Wu grew up to be a very great painter. Never before in China had there been an artist of such genius. His fame travelled far and wide over the land. The Emperor was determined that his palace should be decorated by Wu, and one day he called him. "I want you to cover the walls with frescoes," he said; "think out your own subjects and begin the work at once." Wu worked with extraordinary speed, and never hesitated. He decided to paint dragons and tigers in the first great hall. In China a dragon represented spiritual power, mystery and change, and a tiger meant physical power and force. What better inspiration could Wu have? Getting a pile of brushes, and mixing his ink, he began to draw in the outlines with a brush. He made his dragons so awful and mysterious that the people who watched him held their breath. The strange beasts seemed to curl and twist, half lost in cloud, while the tigers were so fierce and savage that all shrank back trembling. " His fingers must be guided by a god," the people murmured, lost in wonder.

Another day the Emperor again sent for Wu. " I have heard of the beauty of the great Chi-a-ling river," he said. " I long to see what it is like, and for this reason you shall travel there and paint it for me, and bring me back the pictures." Nothing could be more delightful to Wu, for he loved the beauty of nature even more passionately than he did when he was a boy. He set off on his journey, and soon the face of the country changed ; the hills became wild and rocky, with woods clinging to the steep slopes. At last one day the low and distant roar of waters told him that the journey's end would soon be reached. Wu left his servants and horses behind him, and, pushing down the wooded slopes of a ravine, he saw the great river at last through the trees. Parting the tangled undergrowth, and skirting the big boulders and rocks, he found himself on the river banks. With a sound like dull thunder the water rushed over the rocky bed, and hurling itself over a sharp fall of rock, was half lost to sight in a cloud of spray. A little rainbow hung trembling in the misty air, and trees drenched in sunlight and dripping with myriad sparkling drops, bent over the water's edge. High above a hawk circled, and across the river the mountains rose ridge upon ridge against the blue sky. Wu stood spellbound, drawing deep breaths of delight. Hour after hour he stood there motionless, drinking in the beauty of the scene, lost in awe and wonder. Day after day he lingered by the river until the time came when he must return. When he

PLATE IX

A. BARBARIAN HUNTING
CHINESE PAINTING OF THE T'ANG DYNASTY, ATTRIBUTED TO HAN KAN
(A contemporary of Wu-Tao-Tzu)

reached the palace once more, the Emperor exclaimed, in anger and surprise, " But where are your paintings ?" "I have them all in my heart," Wu answered, and, going into one of the palace halls, he proceeded to cover the walls with marvellous paintings, until the river and mountains lived again in all their beauty before the Emperor.

Religious Paintings—One day Wu thought that he would paint a picture in the temple showing the torments that await evil-doers. He painted the place where he thought that they would go to when they died, and the things that they would have to suffer, and when the painting was done the people were allowed to see it. Many of the townspeople crowded in, among them the butchers and fishmongers. Now, these men were not honest, for they cheated the people who bought goods from them, so when they saw the dreadful scene that Wu had painted, they were filled with terror, and, rushing back to their shops, they hastily collected their belongings and departed, vowing that they would give up their trades at once rather than face the results of evil-doing, as Wu had pictured it. Wu, however, did not only paint terrifying pictures in the temples. He painted one picture, which was perhaps the finest that China had ever seen. It showed the god Buddha leaving this world, where he first lived as a mortal. He was shaded by a great tree, and his face was calm and full of mystery, but those around him were distracted with grief at his death. Kings, princes, priests, warriors wailed and rent themselves, while even the animals, the tigers, lions and elephants rolled in sorrow upon the ground. In the air the birds cried shrilly with grief, and the angels lamented above. This picture became so famous that for hundreds of years afterwards, all the painters who followed took it for their model.

The End of Wu-Tao-Tzu—The end of Wu is lost in legend. Strange tales are told of him. One day he went to a Buddhist monastery to paint a picture for the monks, but instead of receiving the great man politely, they were rude to him. What did Wu do? He said nothing, but painted a donkey on the wall. It was so lifelike that it looked as if it could move and bray, and when the monks came into the room next morning, lo and behold! the donkey had kicked the wall to pieces and had vanished in the night. Even more strange is the last story about Wu. He painted a most beautiful landscape on one of the palace walls. When it was finished he covered it with a curtain, and then requested the Emperor to come and see it. The ruler was filled with astonishment at its beauty, for it showed great forests and mountains, with birds in flight across the sky above. "Look in the cave at the foot of the mountain," said Wu, "there dwells a spirit." He clapped his hands, and at once the door at the entrance of the cave flew open. "The interior is beautiful beyond words; permit me to show you the way," added Wu. He passed into the cave, and the door closed after him; the painting faded away and Wu was seen no more.

Notes on the Story—The story of Wu-Tao-Tzu is imaginary, but is founded on the account of the painter's life given in Professor Giles' *Introduction to the History of Chinese Pictorial Art.* The legendary life of the painter that is given there no doubt incorporates a certain amount of truth, for Wu-Tao-Tzu is the greatest of all Chinese painters, and his name is still a household word in China. The only one of the main incidents in the story that is not founded on legend, is the account of the boy watching the priest and being taught by him. Wu-Tao-Tzu was born at the beginning of the eighth century A.D., near the capital of Lo Yang, and from the first was celebrated for his "imaginative realism and tremendous powers of conception." It is not certain if any of his paintings exist to-day. There are seven or eight examples of work which are considered to be old or contemporary copies of his pictures, and one or two among them are accepted as genuine by a number of Japanese critics. Reproductions of most of them can be seen in the pages of the *Kokka* and the *Select Relics*, although in most instances the originals are now very worn and indistinct. Professor Fenollosa, writing of Wu-Tao-Tzu under his Japanese name of Godoshi, says that there is "a certain primal and universal energy in Godoshi's design which has hardly ever been surpassed in the whole range of the world's art."

Type of Question for this Lesson—What would a Chinese child think of the appearance of an English child? (Illustrate by the story of the Chinese girl, who, when shown a drawing by Du Maurier, asked: "Are they really as ugly as that?") Show examples of Chinese and European painting, and help the children to realize the different ideals that they represent—the Chinese dislike of *chiaroscuro*, and their intense reverence for nature. Quote the following story, given by Dr Bushell:—"When Lord Macartney came to the court of the same Emperor . . . bringing with him several pictures from George III., the Mandarins in waiting were again shocked by the shadows, and they asked gravely if the originals of the portraits really had one side of their face darker than the other: the shaded nose was a great defect to their eyes, and some of them believed that it had come there accidentally." How have Chinese and Japanese art influenced English art? (Whistler's paintings, willow pattern plates, etc.).

PART II.—MATERIAL FOR ADVANCED LESSONS ONLY

Early Civilization and General Characteristics of Chinese Art—Asiatic civilization reached its highest development in China, the classic land of the East. The history of the country begins about the year 2500 B.C., and the first legendary emperor, Fu-Hsi, is believed by the Chinese to have reigned during the years 2852-2738 B.C. Many traces of this early civilization must lie buried near the Yellow and the Wei rivers, where the earliest settlements existed, but the Chinese are distrustful of excavations, and such early bronzes and carvings as have been brought to light have been found during the

construction of canals or owing to the changes effected
by alterations in the rivers' course.

The civilization of China and that of the countries that
surrounded it acted and reacted upon each other, and the
influence of Babylonia, Persia, India, and Greece is clearly
discernible in Chinese art. In the year 200 B.C. the
Chinese opened trade routes, and communication was
established with Western Asia and afterwards with Rome.
After the conquests of Alexander, who died in Babylon
in 323 B.C., the traditions of Greek art were spread far
and wide. Far away from their native shores, Greek
artists demonstrated their beliefs, and in many places in
the East, Greek art took root, and flourished in modified
forms for hundreds of years. China did not escape this
influence, but its ancient arts were more subtly modified
during a period when India became one of the chief forces
in the ancient world. The strongest influence of India on
China followed the adoption of Buddhism, although it did
not make itself felt with any great force until the third or
fourth century A.D. Indian art has always been secondary
in importance to the national literature and philosophy.
Its painting, sculpture, and architecture are, on the whole,
over elaborate and lacking in design. These arts have
been under the constant influence of foreign art, and it was
Buddhist art stamped with Greek influence that the country
passed on to China. An example of the manner in which
these Eastern civilizations met is furnished by Dr Stein.
He tells how in exploring some ruined cities in Khotan,
a region in Chinese Turkestan, he found police notices
which were written in Chinese, in a form of Sanskrit
(Indian) lettering, and sealed with a Greek seal. These
cities were abandoned in the eighth century, and have
been buried in the sand until their excavation a few
years ago.

In spite of the outside influences that have in this way left their stamp on Chinese art, it remained from the first an original art, which transfused foreign ideas with the fire and strength of its own genius. The Chinese have excelled both in painting and in sculpture although their architecture has never reached an equally high level and cannot rank with that of the West.

It is only in recent years that the importance of Chinese art has been realized in Europe. The Chinese have made no effort to establish its fame among Europeans, being profoundly indifferent to their opinion, and we owe most of the knowledge that we possess to the researches of travellers and collectors, and in particular to the Japanese, whose publications on Eastern ait have found widespread appreciation in Europe.

Religion—Although in the earliest times the Chinese seemed to have believed in a simple monotheism, their religion soon changed. Ancestor-worship was introduced, and in later days we find three separate beliefs controlling the thought of the people, and leaving a deep impression upon their art. They are as follows :

1. **The Doctrine of Confucius**—Confucius was born in China about the year 550 B.C. and died in 478 B.C. His theory of life was one of advanced socialism. Social harmony was the end for which he strove, and his preaching urged every man to sink his individuality and work for common ends. He believed greatly in art as a popular teacher, and directed the artists' energies to the glorification of the state by means of historical paintings and sculptured portraits of famous men, whose deeds all should emulate. In this way art produced under the influence of Confucianism wás of a secular character, reflecting social ideals which were in complete opposition to

those advocated by the second great leader of Chinese thought, Lao Tzu.

2. The Doctrine of Lao Tzu—Lao Tzu, a Chinese mystic, was born in the year 580 B.C. and died in 530 B.C. He advocated an individualistic philosophy and a life of contemplation and communion with nature. By these means only could human individuality be realized and developed. His followers revolted from outside control and authority, and preferred the freedom of an undisturbed life with nature. This creed, full of mysticism and imagination, appealed with force to the Chinese temperament, and had a profound influence on painting and literature. The terms Laoism and Taoism have been given to the doctrines of Lao Tzu, but in the latter cult the mystical beliefs were so lost in superstition and magical rites, that it could be called, more truthfully, a separate belief.

3. The Doctrines of Buddha—Sakyamuni, the Buddha, or Enlightened One, was an Indian prince, who was born in the sixth century B.C. He gave up his worldly possessions and lived the life of an ascetic, only to find that the cause of all evil was due to the individual will to live. After his death his doctrines were joyfully accepted by the people, who found in Buddhism an inspiring and mystical faith. The new belief spread rapidly, but it was not until the year 65 A.D. that the Chinese Emperor sent a mission of eighteen men to India to inquire into its doctrines. The envoys returned, bringing with them two Indian monks and Buddhist writings and images. A Buddhist temple was built at Lo Yang, the Chinese capital at that time, and the new religion had soon taken a firm hold. There was much in the teaching of Lao Tzu which was also common to Buddhism, and this may have helped to cause the ready acceptance of the new creed.

The Zen doctrine of contemplation, which was one branch of Buddhist thought, preached the same spirit of communion with nature and the losing of human individuality in the vast and spiritual realm of the universe. The new religion taught that the life of the world was of no value, and that all that mattered was the achievement of the after-life when in Nirvana the soul should be one with eternity. These Buddhist beliefs, when fully accepted and realized, coloured the whole subsequent art of China, and became its chief inspiration, having the same relation to it that Christianity had to Western art at the time of the Middle Ages.

Dr Bushell gives the following outline of the five favourite representations of Sakyamuni, the historical Buddha [1] :—

1. His birth. An infant standing erect upon a lotus-thalamus, pointing upward to heaven.

2. Sakya returning from the mountains. Of ascetic aspect, with beard and shaven poll, attired in flowing garments and holding his hands in a position of prayer. The ear lobes are enlarged as a sign of wisdom, and the brow bears the *urna*, a luminous mark that distinguishes a Buddha or a Bodhisattva.

3. The all-wise Sakya. A Buddha seated cross-legged upon a lotus throne . . . the right hand generally raised in the mystic preaching pose.

4. The Nirvana. A recumbent figure upon a raised bench, with the head pillowed upon a lotus.

5. In the Sakyamuni Trinity. Either erect, or seated in the attitude of prayer, with the alms bowl in his hands, between his spiritual sons, the Bodhisattvas Manjusri and Samantabhadra, the three forming a mystic triad.

[1] *Handbook of Chinese Art.* South Kensington Museum.

The following religious and symbolic subjects are common in Chinese art :—

Bodhisattva—A Bodhisattva was a sacred being destined to become a Buddha. A Bodhisattva, in the spiritual body, could be represented in art in any form.

Kwan-yin or **Kwannon**—The Buddhist goddess of mercy and loving-kindness, often represented with a child. She is also known as the Mother of Waters, the protectress of all travelling by sea. The place she takes in the East is somewhat similar to that given to the Virgin in the West, without of course the divine connection. It was only about the twelfth century A.D. that the idea of the Kwan-yin took a female form. She is generally represented as a seated figure, often lost in meditation.

Arhats—The Arhats, or eighteen immediate disciples of Buddha, are called Lohans by the Chinese and Rakans by the Japanese. They are favourite subjects in Chinese and Japanese art, and are usually represented as solitary figures, lost in contemplation, haunting wild and desolate regions, and guarded by a lion, tiger, or some other protective emblem. An Arhat is conceived as a figure representative of moral and intellectual power and grandeur.

Demonic Figures—Demonic figures in Buddhist art are generally representative of the guardians of the material universe of Buddha.

Rishi—The Rishi, or wizards of the mountains, are figures of Taoist legend, and although somewhat similar in conception to the Buddhist Arhats, are of a gayer and more fantastic character. They are human beings who have withdrawn completely from the world, given up all forms of sustenance, except those of fruits and dew, and who have attained immortality and an ethereal existence by means of certain mystic rites. They are generally represented with some emblem such as a stork, plum, pine, tortoise, or bamboo, and are often carried on the backs of storks or are mounted on some curious and imaginary beast.

The Dragon and the Tiger—The dragon is one of the most familiar symbols in Chinese art. It represents the power of the spirit, of infinity, and of aspiration and change. The tiger, on the other hand, is symbolic of material and temporal power, and it is only when it is painted in natural colours, instead of ink, that it represents the actual animal. In the words of Mr Santiyama, " In their (the Chinese) tiger and dragon pictures they portray the ceaseless conflict of the material forces with the infinite, the tiger roaring his incessant challenge to the unknown terror of the spirit."

Chinese Dynasties—The reigns of the Chinese Emperors have been grouped together into dynasties, which also have given their names to the great art periods. The following are the most important :—

EARLY PERIODS TO 618 A.D.

1. **Shang Dynasty (B.C. 1766-1122)**—There is little historic record left of this dynasty, which was an age of advancement and of growth in art. Early pottery was made at this time and also bronzes, while the first definite mention of portraiture dates from this dynasty.

2. **Chow (or Chou) Dynasty (B.C. 1122-255)**— Bronzes still the chief form of artistic industry. Many fine specimens date from this period.

3. **Han Dynasty (B.C. 206-A.D. 221)**—The first great period of Chinese culture. Trade routes established. Influence of Lao Tzu. Great age in literature.

c. **B.C. 100-A.D. 50.**—Period of Græco-Bactrian influence

on art.   Porcelain probably invented during this dynasty. Growth of pictorial art.

4. T'ang Dynasty (A.D. 618-907)—Under the T'ang dynasty the Empire was at the height of its prosperity and its dominions reached their utmost limit. China was in close touch with India ; Buddhism was firmly established, and the greatness of the period was reflected in the art, which was full of power, dignity and nobility.   Landscape painting was divided into two schools, that of the North and the South.   The former was noted for a vigorous realism, in character with the grandeur and wildness of northern scenery : the latter was distinguished by a more romantic style, in harmony with the more picturesque landscape of the South, and was marked by a greater disdain of fact.   During the second half of the dynasty painting took definite rank before sculpture as the more important art.   The culmination of the T'ang period was reached under the reign of the Emperor Genso at Singanfu (713-755 A.D.).   Mr Binyon has called him the Lorenzo de' Medici of China, for he was as great and discriminating a patron of the arts as was the great Italian of the Renaissance.   Under the rule of Genso, the Chinese court became even a greater and more famous centre of culture than were the courts of the Caliphs of Damascus and Baghdad, surpassing them in splendour and magnificence.

5. Sung Dynasty (A.D. 960-1280)—During this dynasty the Empire, which had been previously broken up by wars, was again united, although diminished in extent.   It was a splendid age of freedom, second only to the T'ang dynasty for the beauty of its art and literature.   The painters of the day were dominated by the Zen theory of contemplation, and the exquisite delicacy of the flower paintings has never been equalled.   Their colouring was unsurpassed, and although their paintings had not the same force as those of the T'ang dynasty, they were more lyric in character. The height of Sung genius was reached during the years 1195-1224. Two years later Northern China was taken by Ghengis Khan, the Mongol, and in 1264 Kublai Khan, his descendant (made famous by Coleridge), established his capital at Pekin. The Sung capital of Hang-Chow, although under Mongol rule, retained its Chinese characteristics and culture, and in the journal of Marco Polo, the Venetian, we are able to read a vivid description of the times. With the end of the Sung dynasty the first signs of the decay of Chinese genius were apparent.

6. **Yuan (or Mongol) Dynasty (A.D. 1280-1368)**—This dynasty was established by Kublai Khan. It continued the Sung traditions, which were encouraged by the Mongol rulers, who were intelligent patrons of Chinese art. Fine works of art were produced, although the level of artistic production was considerably lowered.

7. **Ming Dynasty (A.D. 1368-1644)**—The Mongols were expelled in 1368, and under the first Ming Emperor Chinese rule was again established. Although the period opened with magnificence, the glories of the Sung dynasty had faded, and art began to show signs of over-elaboration and love of ornament. There was a change of mood, and mystical subjects became less popular than scenes of court life. The ink sketch was succeeded by a love of rich colour, and genre painting was introduced. At the same time, although much fine work was done, the conservatism of the Chinese began to tell upon an art that was losing the inspiration of former beliefs, and traditional methods began to take a somewhat stereotyped form. In 1644, when the Empire was weakened and in danger, it called the Manchus, or tribes of wild herdsmen, to its aid.

They had long raided the Chinese frontiers, and having made an entry in this way they came to stay, soon conquering the Chinese, and forcing them to wear a pigtail as a sign of submission. The Ching or Manchu dynasty, which succeeded the Ming dynasty, lasted until 1912, and has witnessed the steady decline of Chinese artistic power.

Chinese Painting—The origin of Chinese painting is ascribed by legend to the year 2700 B.C., while in the year 1326 B.C., a definite mention of portraiture is made. There is very little record of art, however, until the second and third century B.C., when more frequent mention is made of it, and when the hair-brush was invented. In the second century A.D. the names of individual painters begin to appear, and during the sixth century the artist Hsieh Ho formulated a criticism of painting in six canons.

The earliest painting known to exist (although there may be others of equal, or greater, age, hidden away in Eastern collections) is that in the British Museum by Ku-kai-chi, who lived in the fourth century A.D. This wonderful and mature painting alone is enough to prove that the art was at the time no new growth. From the beginning painting was closely associated with caligraphy, or hand-writing, which was also considered a fine art, requiring the utmost skill and individuality on the part of the writer. It was this training that helped to develop the painters' feeling for virile line, which is such a fine characteristic of their best work. " The spirit lies in the point of the brush " is one of the old Chinese sayings.

Early paintings were largely executed in ink, in monochrome, and were associated in design with the hand-writing that described them. During the last dynasties the use of colour became popular, particularly in pictures relating to the Buddhist religion, which were coloured until they glowed with the richest of Eastern tints. Before the first century A.D. paper was the favourite material for pictures, and wooden panels were also used. We read, too, of great frescoes decorating the walls of the palaces and public buildings, all of which, alas, have since disappeared. Silk, however, soon grew to be the favourite material, and, as a medium, served to develop direct and delicate methods of painting.

Chinese paintings are generally in the form of *Kakemonos* or hanging pictures, with a wooden roller at the top and bottom, to make them fall flatly, or else *Makimonos* or scrolls, often of great length. A Chinese artist followed traditional methods of painting and preferred for his subjects those which had been hallowed for centuries by literature and established custom. It never occurred to him to attempt an exact imitation of nature. His art was above all suggestive, and his highest aspiration was the hope of expressing infinity. It was soaked in the atmosphere of his religion, and reflected his national poetry. Painters were frequently literary men also by profession, and the old Chinese saying, " a picture is a voiceless poem," reflects the Chinese ideal. A picture was most prized when it suggested a poetic idea in this way, and breathed forth some lofty sentiment. Buddhist precepts led to an intense and reverent love of nature, as opposed to the Western ideal of the glory of man. The Chinese lacked that scientific curiosity and passion for knowledge which stamped the Europe of the Renaissance, and their self-imposed limitations and artistic conventions, which despised elaborate *chiaroscuro* and realistic modelling, were perfectly adapted to the lyric temper of their art, and served to add to its greatness. On the

other hand, there are Western achievements which the
Chinese have never equalled, but it is of little use to
weigh the art of the East with that of the West, and
wiser to accept them both as splendid expressions of
differing ideals.

The Chinese, largely by reason of their religious beliefs,
excelled as painters of landscape and flowers, and hundreds
of years before Western races had reached an appreciation
of their beauties, the Chinese had established schools of
landscape painting in different parts of the country.   But,
in the words of Mr Laurence Binyon :

" It is something deeper than innocent delight, which
forms these schools of painting, . . . we do not feel that the
artist is portraying something external to himself, that
he is caressing the happiness and soothing joy offered
him in the pleasant places of the earth, or ever studying
with wonder and delight the miraculous works of nature.
But the words of the air have become his desires, and the
clouds his wandering thoughts ; the mountain peaks are
his lonely aspirations, and the torrents his liberated
energies.   Flowers opening their secret hearts to the light
and trembling to the breeze's touch seem to be unfolding
the mystery of his own human heart, the mystery of those
intuitions and emotions, which are too deep and too shy
for speech. . . . It is not the man's earthly surroundings,
tamed to his desires, that inspires the artist ; but the
universe in its wholeness and its freedom has become his
spiritual home." [1]

The joy of a Chinese artist in his art is well expressed by
an artist of the fifth century : " To gaze upon the clouds of
autumn, a soaring exultation of the soul ; to feel the spring
breeze stirring wild exultant thoughts ; what is there in the
possession of gold and gems to compare with delights like

[1] *The Flight of the Dragon.* L. Binyon. Murray.

PLATE X

TIGER
SUNG DYNASTY

HEAD OF A BODHISATTVA
(BETWEEN 386-549 A.D.)

these ? and then to unroll the portfolio and spread the silk, and to transfer to it the glories of flood and fell, the green forest, the blowing winds, the white water of the rushing cascade, as with a turn of the hand a divine influence descends upon the scene. . . . These are the joys of painting."

There are many old poems that illustrate the people's feeling for nature. One recounts how a poor pilgrim, passing along a road shaded by blossoming trees, stopped the ringing of his bell, in fear lest the vibration should cause a single petal to fall. Another tells that a poor girl on going to draw water from a well, found that in the night a convolvulus had twined itself round the well rope and bucket. Rather than tear or displace such beauty, she left the plant undisturbed, and drew her water from some other source. Mr Binyon also quotes a very beautiful old Chinese poem, of the Sung period, as an example of the same reverence. It runs as follows : " It is midnight ; all is silent in the house ; the water clock has stopped. But I am unable to sleep, because of the beauty of the trembling shapes of the spring flowers, thrown by the moon upon the blind."

Sculpture—Until recent times the Chinese have shown scant interest in their own sculpture, and it is only in the last twelve to fifteen years that its importance has been realized in the West. For the first time remote sites and temples have been visited by Europeans and Americans, and fine examples of statues and bas-reliefs have been acquired.

Some of these statues are of extreme beauty, and a growing realization of both Chinese sculpture and painting has led to profound modifications of European art theory.

We know, as yet, but little of the origins of Chinese sculpture. Realistic carvings of animals appear to date back to very early times, while during the Wei and T'ang dynasties magnificent sculpture was produced, particularly such figures as those executed for Buddhist temples. Many bas-reliefs and engraved stone stelai were also executed during the Han dynasty. Early sculpture, although betraying both Indian and Greek influence, is essentially the product of the Chinese genius, and reminds us of the words of an early pilgrim, who recorded that in the sixth century Chinese sculpture was of a distinct national type. During the Tang dynasty very fine work continued to be produced, including colossal stone statues of Buddha, while dating from a later period we have the great stone figures that guard the approaches to the Ming tombs near Pekin. These are some of the most famous sculptures in China, although they are infinitely less great than some of the more inaccessible statues that are hidden away in the temples. These latter statues, which most frequently represent the Buddha or the Goddess of Mercy, are often of great beauty and dignity, and are marked by an expression of calm and gentle inscrutability. After the middle of the fifteenth century a love of profuse ornament put an end to the production of the finest sculpture. The Chinese were extremely fond of carving smaller objects in hard substances, such as jade, rock crystal, hard wood, and horn. These objects are generally grotesque in character, and are exquisite in workmanship and design.

Architecture—The Chinese have never been great as architects. A certain quality of picturesqueness and lack of restraint has hindered their work from reaching a high level. There are no buildings left standing that date from before the eleventh century A.D., and the fact that buildings are made from light and perishable materials no doubt accounts for the scarcity of ruins. It has been suggested by M. Paléologue that the reason for this preference for light materials is to be found in the Chinese indifference to earthly posterity. Early records prove that contemporary Chinese architecture is still the same in essentials as that of the fourth and fifth centuries B.C. The most common form in building is the *Ting*, which consists of a large and massive roof supported by a number of wooden columns. The walls are formed by filling in the space between the columns with stone and brick. The roof, which is always the most important part of a Chinese building, is often a double or a triple one, with elaborately carved ridges and eaves, and is often covered with gay tiles. Another favourite architectural form is that of the *Pail-lou*, an elaborate stone or wooden archway, generally built with a tiled roof, and erected only by official consent in commemoration of some famous person. A third typical Chinese building is the *T'ai* or stone tower, also known as pagoda. It is an octagonal structure with thirteen stories, and probably owes its proportions to the same symbolic idea that suggested the Gothic spire, although in this instance the symbolism would refer to the Buddhist creed. The great wall is one of the most famous examples of Chinese building. It marks the boundaries of four northern provinces, and following the windings, is 1500 miles in length. It was begun in the third century B.C., repaired in the fifteenth century A.D., and was extended some 300 miles in the sixteenth century. It generally measures from 20 to 30 feet in height, and its towers, which come at intervals of about 200 yards, are some 40 feet high. It measures 15 to 25 feet in breadth at its base.

Bronzes—Bronzes are the oldest form of Chinese art. Vessels of this material were made for the service of prehistoric religions, and the same shapes are produced to this day. The oldest existing specimens were taken at the sack of the Summer Palace at Pekin, and date from the Shang and Chow dynasties. The art reached its climax about the year 500 B.C., but from the beginning, fine specimens attained, to quote Dr Bushell, " a certain savage, monumental grandeur."

Porcelain and Pottery—Porcelain was invented in China, as is testified by the term by which it is generally described. The manufacture was probably first introduced during the Han dynasty and soon became famous, being exported in later years to both Eastern and Western markets. Chinese porcelain of the best periods is the highest achievement of ceramic art, and beside the supreme beauty of its design and colour the porcelain of other countries can only take a second place. Chinese pottery is hardly less famous than the porcelain. Some of the finest specimens represent splendidly modelled figures of gods, men, and animals, and these, in their way, are also unequalled. The earliest examples of Chinese pottery, which date from the time of the early bronzes, are strongly reminiscent of the latter in form and design. Pottery was frequently used in China as a form of architectural decoration.

Japanese Art—Japanese art, which until recently has been more generally known and appreciated in Europe than Chinese art, is largely due to the Chinese genius. The Japanese had much original artistic power of their own, but it was probably not until 552 A.D., when Buddhism reached the island shores, incorporated in Chinese forms of art, that Japanese primitive art began. Thus from the beginning, the genius of these island people took colour and form from the great art of their neighbours, and until the present day the art of China has been the chief inspiration of that of Japan. There is no space here in which to give any description or classification of the great art of Japan, and all who want particulars, or who wish to give a second lesson on it alone, should refer to the pages of Mr Binyon and Professor Fenollosa.

EXTRACTS

Description of the Imperial palace of Kublai Khan (written about the year 1275 A.D. by Marco Polo, the Venetian).[1]

" You must know that for three months of the year the Great Kaan resides in the capital city of Cathay. . . . In that city stands his great palace and now I will tell you what it is like.

" It is enclosed all round by a great wall forming a square, each side of which is a mile in length . . . it is also very thick and a good ten paces in height, whitewashed and loopholed all round. . . . Inside this wall there is a second. . . . In the middle of this enclosure is the Lord's Great Palace, and I will tell you what it is like.

" You must know that it is the greatest Palace that ever was. The palace itself has no upper story but is all on the ground floor. . . . the roof is very lofty and the walls of the Palace are all covered with gold and silver. They are also adorned with representations of dragons (sculptured and gilt), beasts and birds, knights and idols and sundry other subjects, and on the ceiling too you see nothing but gold and silver and painting. On each of these four sides there is a great marble staircase leading to the top of the marble wall and forming the approach to the palace.

" The hall of the palace is so large that it could easily dine 6000 people ; and it is quite a marvel to see how many rooms there are besides. The building is altogether so vast and so rich and so beautiful that no man on earth could design anything superior to it. The outside of the roof also is covered with vermilion and yellow and green and blue and other hues, which are fixed with a varnish so fine and exquisite that they shine like chrystal, and lend a resplendent lustre to the palace, as seen for a great way round. The roof is made too with so much strength that it is fit to last for ever.

---

[1] *The Book of Marco Polo, the Venetian*, translated by Sir H. Yule. Murray.

"Between the two walls of the enclosure which I have described there are fine parks and beautiful trees bearing a variety of fruit. There are beasts also of sundry kinds, such as white stags and fallow deer, gazelles and roebucks and fine squirrels of various sorts, with numbers also of that animal that gives the musk, and all manner of other beautiful creatures, insomuch that the whole place is full of them . . . and the Great Kaan has caused this beautiful prospect to be formed for the comfort and solace and delectation of his heart."

LESSON VI

ÆGEAN ART

(ALSO KNOWN AS MYCENÆAN ART)

PART I.—ELEMENTARY LESSON IN STORY FORM

There is no story that will interest children more readily in Ægean art than the old Greek myth of Theseus and the Minotaur. It is true that there is nothing about art in it, but if told briefly, and the stress laid on the subsequent history of the excavations at Knossos, the artistic element will be amply supplied. As the story has been told, once and for all, by Charles Kingsley in *The Heroes*, it will not be repeated here. The book is, or should be, in every school-room or school library, or can be purchased for 6d. from Messrs Gowan & Gray of Glasgow. The following is an outline of the form the lesson should take.

INTRODUCTION—Thousands of years ago, when Queen Hatshepsut was reigning in Egypt, and sending her ships to the land of Punt in search of spices and ostrich feathers and myrrh trees, another race of people was living on the shores and islands of the Ægean Sea. This is an old story that tells about some of them; nobody knows how much of it is true.

1. Theseus and the sword. The journey to his father's court.
2. The journey to Crete, the island of King Minos.
3. Theseus defies King Minos and is imprisoned.
4. Theseus, freed by Ariadne, kills the Minotaur, and the joyful return to Greece.

   .   .   .   .   .   .

5. The Excavations—Thousands of years passed. Still fathers told to their children the story of Theseus and the Minotaur. People began to wonder if any of it was true; if there had been a King Minos, who kept a great

115

bull, and if Theseus and Ariadne had ever really lived, and
if a great palace had existed on the island of Crete.   If
there were such civilized people living then, thousands of
years ago, had they invented a system of writing as the
Egyptians and Babylonians had done?   One day Sir
Arthur Evans, an English archeologist, was working in
the museum at Athens.   This was his discovery, told in
his own words :

"While hunting out ancient engraved stones at Athens,
I came upon some three and four sided seals, showing on
each of their faces, groups of hieroglyphic and linear signs,
distinct from the Egyptian and Hittite, but evidently
representing some form of script.   On enquiry I learnt
that these seals had been found in Crete.   A clue was in
my hands, and, like Theseus, I resolved to follow it, if
possible, to the inmost recesses of the Labyrinth."

Sir Arthur Evans then went to Crete, and from 1894
onwards explored the island, and made a series of excavations.   About four miles from Candia, the chief town,
there is a beautiful valley and sloping hill-side, and on
this hill-side several great blocks of stone could be seen
half buried in the ground.   People had noticed these
stones before, but the owners of the land did not want to
sell it, and the people of the island were also at war with
the Turks, and had no time to help foreigners and make
it easy for them to start their excavations.   At last, however, Crete was at rest again : the war was over, and in
1895 Sir Arthur Evans was able to buy part of the land
in which the grey stones lay buried.   Nearly a hundred
men were engaged to dig and were set to work on the
green hill-side.   What did they find?   Was there nothing
hidden there after all?   Were there only a few stones, or
was there something more?   There was treasure untold !
A vast palace was laid bare.   Its roof and most of its

PLATE XI

EXCAVATED STORE CHAMBER. PALACE OF KNOSSOS, CRETE

high walls had long since crumbled away, but its foundations were there. Room after room was opened up; many were decorated with frescoes, hidden in some instances only a few inches below the surface of the earth. Others contained long rows of great stone jars, for wheat and other necessities. Under the floor of one of these magazines a row of smaller stone jars was found, lined with lead, and carefully hidden as a storage for treasure. Another room was obviously a bath-room, and contained two perfectly preserved and beautifully moulded terra-cotta baths, one being quite small, and evidently made for a little child. "Walls were shortly uncovered, decorated with flowering plants and running water, while on each side of the door-way of a small inner room stood guardian griffins with peacocks' plumes, in the same flowery landscape. Round the walls ran low stone benches, and between those on the north side, separated by a small interval, and raised on a stone base, rose a gypsum throne with a high back and originally covered with decorated designs. . . . Here truly was the council chamber of a Mycenæan King or Sovereign Lady."

In other rooms numbers of tablets were found, inscribed in an unknown script, the writing that had been the object of Sir Arthur Evans' search, and which no one yet has learnt to read. In the portico of the entrance to the great court there were the remains of a big fresco of a man fighting a bull, and by the northern gate the half-crumbled relief of a second great bull was found. One day a splendid fresco of a youth carrying a great cup was laid bare (see Plate XII.). "The colours were almost as brilliant as when first laid down over 3000 years ago," wrote Sir Arthur Evans. "For the first time the true portraiture of a man of this mysterious Mycenæan race rises before us. The flesh tint, following perhaps the Egyptian

precedent, is of a deep reddish brown. The limbs are
finely moulded, though the waist, as usual in Mycenæan
fashion, is tightly drawn in by a silver-mounted girdle,
giving great relief to the hips. The profile of the face is
pure and almost classically Greek. . . . There was something very impressive in this vision of brilliant youth, and
of male beauty, recalled after so long an interval to our
upper air, from what had been till yesterday a forgotten
world. Even our untutored Cretan workmen felt the
spell and fascination. They indeed regarded the discovery
of such a painting in the bosom of the earth as nothing
less than miraculous, and saw in it the *ikon* of a Saint ! "

The whole story of the excavations is indeed a marvellous one. They revealed an advanced civilization, cut off
in its bloom, for traces of burning on every hand, and
charred wooden beams and pillars, proved that this great
palace, covering nearly six acres, had been destroyed
with violence, and its site left desolate. " For three
thousand years or more not a tree had been planted there ;
over a part of the area not even a ploughshare had been
passed." The story of Theseus was to a great extent
proved. The famous king of the dynasty of Minos had
indeed lived in his palace at Knossos, and ruled over vast
dominions. If so much of the story is true we can
no doubt believe also that his daughter lived with him,
and danced in the *choros*, or dancing ground, "wrought
in broad Knossos for fair-haired Ariadne" (Homer).
She may even be represented in one of the frescoes,
showing the ladies of the court, and the dancing girls.
Theseus too can be imagined as a valiant young
Mycenæan, fighting perhaps with a great and savage bull,
kept in the palace by command of the King. The old
frescoes prove to us that bull-fighting was constantly
practised in those days, and the various representations

of bulls found at Knossos point to the fact that they were
kept there. Perhaps there was a savage bull which was
so much dreaded that in time a legend grew up as to its
terrible appearance and human head. On the ancient
gems of this period, figures of a bull, half human, half
animal, are sometimes engraved. Sir Arthur Evans
himself says that "the legend of Athenian persons
devoured by the Minotaur preserves a real tradition of
these cruel sports." The palace contained such numbers
of small rooms and winding passages, that no wonder it
was considered a maze or labyrinth. We can imagine
Greek settlers in the island after the fall of the palace,
wandering in and out of the desolate rooms, half ruined
and burnt, haunted by owls and bats. We can imagine
them scanning the frescoes now barely visible, then perhaps
in their freshness, showing the youthful figures of Theseus
and Ariadne, and the great fight with the bull. We can
hear the story passing from lip to lip, until now, in our
own day, the triumphs of archeology have proved it to be
not only possible, but to a large extent probable. In the
words of Donne :—

> Thou art so true that thoughts of thee suffice
> To make dreams true, and fables histories.

Notes on the Story—For further details, see Part. II. of this Lesson.
The quotations are taken from Sir Arthur Evans' account of his discoveries published in *The English Review*, 1901, vol. 2, Murray.

As an additional, or alternative, story illustrative of Ægean art, a
story from the *Iliad* could be taken, leading up to illustrations of the
excavations at Mycenæ and Hissarlik (Troy), and of the objects of art
found there.

PART II.—MATERIAL FOR ADVANCED LESSONS ONLY

Ægean Civilization—The pre-Hellenic civilization
which flourished on the shores and islands of the Ægean

during the first, second, and third millennia before Christ, had three chief centres—the island of Crete, the towns of Mycenæ and Tiryns, on the Greek mainland, and Troy, on the north-west promontory of Asia Minor. Recent archeological research has proved that the earliest seat of this civilization was in Crete and the more southerly islands of the Ægean, and from there spread to the main-land, and even to distant parts of the Mediterranean. The knowledge of the use of bronze reached Crete about the year 3000 B.C., and put an end to the Neolithic or Late Stone Age civilization that had preceded it. From this date ·Ægean culture developed rapidly, until it came to an abrupt end about the year 1000 B.C., probably owing to the Dorian invasions. It was essentially the civilization of a seafaring people. The Ægeans were famous as traders, and their fleets touched far distant shores. A Chinese axehead of white jadite, found in the second city of Troy, has been dated as prior to 2000 B.C., and, accord-ing to Sir Arthur Evans, a bowl found at Knossos was made in Egypt at the beginning of the Fourth Dynasty or Pyramid Age (c. 2800 B.C.); in pre-Mycenæan island graves, objects in ivory and pieces of glass have been found which could only have come from Egypt. After the year 1600 B.C. intercourse with Egypt became very close. In the tomb of Senmut, the architect of Queen Hatshepsut, at Thebes (see Lesson III.), a fresco has been found which shows men of a foreign nation bearing an offering of great vases, and by the figures the words, "Princes of the Isles in the midst of the Great Green Sea." One of them is designated as a "Prince of the Keftiu," the latter word being now generally identified with the sea Empire of Knossos. It is interesting to see that in this fresco one of the men bears a big vase, decorated with two bulls' heads. The Egyptian artist has also carefully represented the typical narrow waists of the strangers, which are invariable characteristics of the Minoans.

Ægean Archeology—The story of Ægean archeology is a veritable fairy tale. Before the year 1870 the only proofs of the wonderful pre-Hellenic civilization described in the Homeric poems were some old walls, a gate, and a tomb at Mycenæ, and a few vases and other objects, scattered and neglected in various museums. These were all supposed to belong to Homeric times, or to early heroic beginnings of purely Hellenic civilization. The first man to disprove these vague theories was a German, Henry Schliemann. He was born in a small town in North Germany in the year 1822. As a child he was fascinated by old myths and stories, and firmly believed that in a pond behind his father's house a maiden was hidden, who arose from the waters each night, holding a silver bowl. His faith was also firm concerning the legend that vast treasures were hidden in the earth in a small hill near by his home, surrounded by a ditch. The excavations at Pompeii and Herculaneum were at that time arousing the interest of all, and had their share in exciting the boy's imagination, and a still further stimulus was given by the story of the Homeric poems, which his father repeated to him. The boy could not believe that the great fortifications of Troy had disappeared, and, in spite of his father's assurance that no trace of them could be found, he felt convinced to the contrary, and replied, " Father, if such walls once existed, they cannot possibly have been destroyed ; vast ruins of them must still remain, but they are hidden beneath the dust of ages." From that moment the boy decided that he would excavate these walls before he died.

Troubles fell upon the family, and, after only a short period at school, Henry Schliemann had to earn his living

as a grocer's boy.   One evening a drunken miller came to
the shop, who apparently had some knowledge of Homer.
Dr Schliemann has described the scene as follows :
" That evening he recited to us about a hundred lines of
the poet, observing the rhythmic cadence of the verses. . . .
Although I did not understand a syllable, the melodious
sounds of the words made a deep impression upon me,
and I wept bitter tears over my unhappy fate.   Three
times over did I get him to repeat to me those divine verses,
rewarding his trouble with three glasses of whiskey, which
I bought with the few pence that made up my whole
wealth.   From that moment I never ceased to pray to
God that by His Grace I might yet have the happiness of
learning Greek."   After this time the boy's fortunes
suffered many changes, but, owing to his great intelligence
and capacity for learning languages, he rapidly bettered
his position, and by the year 1863 he was his own
master, with enough money to start on the realization
of his cherished schemes.   For two or three years he
travelled extensively, and then spent some years in Paris
in the study of archeology.   In 1868 he paid his first
visit to Greece, and in 1871 the first sod was cut on the
hill of Hissarlik, the spot which, contrary to generally
held opinions, he had identified with the site of Troy.

At first he suffered many disappointments, but nothing
could shake his determination, and in 1873 the faith of a
lifetime was rewarded by the first of his many discoveries,
namely the laying bare of a great wall and gateway, and
the discovery of a vast treasure.   This consisted of
numbers of gold and silver vessels and ornaments, including a diadem composed of more than 16,000 rings and
leaves ; axes, daggers, and objects of every kind.   From
that day excavations were carried on steadily and were continued after Dr Schliemann's death, in 1890, by his friend

and helper, Dr Dörpfeld. In all, the remains of not one, but nine cities were laid bare, the first dating from the sub-Neolithic Age, and the ninth from Hellenic times. Each separate stratum revealed a different stage of civilization, and yielded different objects to prove its age. The second city (counting from the bottom stratum upwards) was charred and burnt, and showed many signs of war and siege. It was this "Burnt City," containing the treasure, that was at first identified by Dr Schliemann as Homeric Troy. In the meantime this indefatigable archeologist turned his attention to the Greek mainland. Again, in defiance of the current beliefs of scholars, Schliemann was determined that Pausanias, the ancient Greek traveller, was right in saying that the murdered King Agamemnon was buried with his kindred, not without the walls of Mycenæ, but within their shelter. He started digging, therefore, just within the walls and near the Lion Gate, and by great good luck shortly uncovered a circle of slabs of stone. Continuing his excavations, five rock-hewn shaft graves were discovered, containing skeletons of men, women, and children, and another horde of gold and silver vases and ornaments, arms, and objects of art, etc., which proved the graves to be those of wealthy princes, if not of the far-famed Agamemnon himself.

Shortly after Dr Schliemann's death there was fresh evidence forthcoming, which proved conclusively that the sixth city at Troy was the fabled city of Homer. It was discovered to be two and a half times larger in area than the Burnt City, and to be surrounded by massive walls, which agreed more or less exactly with the Homeric description. The discoveries of archeology had now confirmed the main lines of the Homeric tradition. The home of the Atridæ, the "Princes rich in gold," had been found at Mycenæ and Tiryns on the

mainland, while across the sea, Troy, the great and
proud city which was conquered by the United Greeks,
led by the princes of Mycenæ, was excavated and
identified. But a further problem remained unsolved.
Who were the people who had lived in the second or Burnt
City of Troy during the years 2500-2000 B.C. ? What
was this earlier and greater civilization, which at the time
of Homer was but a memory ? Where was its mainspring
and centre hidden ? Excavations at Tiryns and Vaphio
on the Greek mainland bore fresh witness to the arts of
these early people. At Mycenæ a tomb had been
excavated containing daggers with wonderfully inlaid
blades, and at Tiryns a palace had been discovered
decorated with wall paintings, one showing an acrobat or
hunter, leaping over a galloping bull, a vivid fresco full
of power and movement, unlike anything known before.
At Vaphio, near Sparta, two golden cups had been un-
earthed, since famous as the most accomplished achievements of Mycenæan art. For many years the thoughts of
archeologists had turned towards Crete. Schliemann
himself in the early eighties had wished to excavate
there, in the hope of discovering " the original home of
Mycenæan civilization," but his plan was frustrated by
various difficulties, and finally by internal disturbances.
The great discovery was reserved for Sir Arthur Evans,
and has been described in Part I. of this Lesson.

Ægean Religion—The chief Ægean divinity was
the " Great Mother," the goddess who survived in
Hellenic times as Rhea, the mother of the Gods, or as
Hera, the wife of Zeus. This Great Mother was the
nature goddess, symbolic of the productiveness of the
earth, and with her as a secondary deity, Zeus, her son
or spouse, seems to have been associated. The " Great
Mother " is sometimes represented with doves, and some-

times with snakes, as symbols of her connection with the air and the earth. The bull, which was regarded as royal and sacred, was the chief of sacrificial animals, and was most commonly offered up to her : it was also frequently represented in religious ritual held in her honour. It seems probable that the Kings, like the Pharaohs of Egypt, were the high priests of Ægean religion, and superintended the rites of the sanctuary, contained in the palace buildings. In the earliest years rocks, pillars, trees and the double axe, symbolic of power, were held as objects of worship, and it was only during the later periods that the divine principle was given a human form. It seems probable that the dead were objects of some form of worship, and further, ornaments, weapons, and other objects were placed in the tombs to supply the needs of the next life. The tombs themselves were of two main types : shaft tombs, or chambers cut in the rock, such as the royal tombs at Mycenæ, or Beehive tombs, vaulted and domed structures, such as the best preserved tomb outside the walls of Mycenæ, which measures nearly 50 feet in diameter. In the earliest burials the bodies were laid in oblong graves lined with slabs, or more rarely in earthenware jars.

Ægean Art. Chronological Outline and General Characteristics—The Ægean, or Mycenæan, civilization was developed from an earlier neolithic civilization, and was itself succeeded by the transitional period represented by the Homeric poems, which, according to the most probable view, depict in the main the age subsequent to the break-up of the Mycenæan civilization and previous to the so-called "Dorian invasion" (c. 1000 B.C.). Ægean art had its first centre in Crete. The term *Minoan*, derived from Minos, has been given to the people, art, and civilization of this island, to differentiate

them from those of the coasts and other islands of the
Ægean area. Minoan civilization has been divided by
Sir Arthur Evans into three periods, each period being
subdivided into three divisions representing the rise,
culmination, and decline of its arts. The following is
a chronological table based on that given by Mr and
Mrs Hawes [1] :—

Early Minoan Period.	1st E.M.P., 2800-2600 B.C.	Beginning of Bronze Age, Knossos.
	2nd E.M.P., 2600-2400 B.C.	Second or "Burnt City," Hissarlik. Ornaments and stone vases found in tombs at Mochlos in Eastern Crete.
	3rd E.M.P., 2400-2200 B.C.	Pottery deposits in different sites.
Middle Minoan Period.	1st M.M.P., 2200-2100 B.C.	Early palaces of Knossos and Phæstos built.
	2nd M.M.P., 2100-1900 B.C.	First climax of Minoan civilization at Knossos and Phæstos. Very good pottery deposits. Good examples of lesser arts produced on small islands near Crete. Destruction of earlier palace of Knossos.
	3rd M.M.P., 1900-1700 B.C.	Later palace at Knossos. First villa at Aghia Triada. Town at Gournia.
Late Minoan Period.	1st L.M.P., 1700-1500 B.C.	Height of prosperity at Aghia Triada (1st palace), Gournia, etc. Minoan art good and spontaneous. Many fine frescoes executed. Shaft graves, Mycenæ.
	2nd L.M.P., 1500-1450 B.C. (so called Palace Period)	Golden age in Crete. Later palace at Knossos remodelled. Fall of country towns such as Gournia, etc. Growth of Mycenæ, Tiryns, and other mainland capitals.
	3rd L.M.P., 1450-1200 B.C.	c. 1450. Fall of Knossos followed by partial re-occupation. c. 1350-1200. Steady decline in prosperity and art throughout Crete. Supremacy transferred to mainland capitals of Tiryns and Mycenæ. Sixth city, Troy.

[1] *Crete, the Forerunner of Greece.* Harper.

Ægean art preserved its originality until the end, in spite of the foreign influences introduced by trade. It is thought that many of the elaborate works found in the Greek mainland, such as the frescoes and sword blades and the Vaphio cups, are the work of Minoan artists, and even if this is not the case, there is no doubt that the chief artistic impulse of the Ægean spread from Crete. Ægean art is full of spontaneous vigour and movement but it lacks a fine tradition of design, and although it is often very effective it entirely fails to reach the dignity, strength, and noble impressiveness of the art of Egypt. There is no evidence that the Ægeans ever tried to produce large sculptures in the round, or works of art of monumental character. Their choice lay rather in delicate reliefs, inlay and carvings. Their frescoes, when discovered, created a new epoch in the history of painting ; their faience and goldsmiths' work showed the same freedom and spontaneity, while their painted vases, decorated with sea creatures of every sort, are often beautiful, and clearly stamp the creators as sons of a sea power. One of the chief characteristics of the human figure, as represented in Minoan art, is the small wasp-like waist, evidently artificial in character. This fashion must have been a long-established custom, both for men and women, for it is always reflected in the sculptures, and the Egyptian artist has not failed to notice it when representing the guests from the Island in the Green Sea. The result, in the case of the women's figures, is that they look strangely modern, rather than beautiful. At the time of the golden age in Crete, the palace of Knossos was a veritable school of art. Large colonies of craftsmen lived within its walls, supplying not only the needs of the royal family, but also no doubt the demands of rich princes on the Greek mainland. After the overthrow of Knossos Ægean art declined. The Minoan traditions were carried out in decadent and imitative forms at the artistic centres of the mainland, until foreign invasion brought Ægean art to an abrupt standstill.

Architecture—" The dwellers on the sea coast began to grow richer and live in a more settled manner ; and some of them, finding their wealth increase beyond their expectations, surrounded their towns with walls." [1]   This is Thucydides' account of the building of the great walls of Mycenæ, Tiryns, and other towns on the Greek mainland, by the princes that governed them.   These walls are among the oldest examples of Mycenæan architecture still standing, and are often described as Cyclopean walls, a title given to them by the Greeks, who believed them to be the work of the Cyclopes, giants of antiquity.   They are made of enormous blocks of stone, roughly hewn into irregular shapes, and sometimes measuring 18 or 20 feet in length.   The walls are interrupted at intervals by massive square towers and big gates, the most famous of the latter being the " Lion Gate " at Mycenæ.   The walls, towers, and galleries of the acropolis of Tiryns are particularly fine, and enclose three successive terraces on the hill-side.   Galleries and chambers are hollowed in the thickness of some of the walls, which also enclose the royal palace.   No Ægean temples have been discovered, and it is believed that these were contained in the palaces, where the King or ruler held the office of high priest. The palaces in Crete were probably slight in structure, the walls being of wood, clay, and rubble, on a solid stone foundation, which no doubt accounts for the fact that in almost all instances only their foundations have been discovered.   Wood was used in large quantities for

---

[1] Jowett's translation.   Oxford University Press.

building. Columns were made both in wood and stone, and tapered from a broader top to a slighter base, a form peculiar to Ægean architecture. The origin of the later Greek, Doric, and Ionic capitals is found in those which surmount these early Mycenæan pillars. After the year 2000 B.C. the Minoan palaces consisted of several stories, and in the late palace of Knossos at one point as many as four were erected. The palaces were generally of one of two types. Either they were composed of a mass of small rooms and passages grouped round a central court, or else, as on the mainland, their principal feature was a big hall or *megaron*, isolated from the rest of the building, and containing a central hearth surrounded by pillars, the room being entered by a vestibule on the short side of the hall. When a palace was built with a *megaron*, it seldom had a central court, and the rest of its rooms formed a separate block. It is noticeable that the palaces of Crete have no fortifications, a fact that bears silent witness to the supremacy of Minoan sea power. Excavations in the island have revealed, besides the palace at Knossos, a fine palace at Phæstos, a royal villa at Aghia Triadha, and a town at Gournia.

Painting—Minoan painting was largely fostered by the fact that the clay and rubble walls of the palaces had to be covered with plaster, and then decorated, in order to make them outwardly attractive. The earliest wall painting that has been preserved is a fragment of a fresco of the Middle Minoan period, from the earlier palace at Knossos, before its reconstruction, and shows a boy gathering crocuses. It is executed with a charming freshness and grace, and is a worthy forerunner to the maturer paintings of the Palace Period that followed it, such as the cupbearer, court ladies, dancing girl, and bull fight, from Knossos; the cat hunting a pheasant,

from Aghia Triadha, and the bull fight from Tiryns.   Sir
Arthur Evans has described the Knossian ladies as
follows : " At a glance we recognize Court ladies in
elaborate toilette.   They are fresh from the coiffeur's
hands with hair *frisé* and curled about the head and
shoulders, and falling down the back in long separate
tresses.   They wear high puffed sleeves, joined across
the lower part of the neck by a narrow cross band, but
otherwise the bosom and the whole upper part of the
body appears to be bare.   Their waists are extraordinarily
slender, and the lower parts of their bodies are clad in a
flounced robe with indications of embroidered bands."

Another example of Minoan painting, chiefly interesting
for the light it sheds on contemporary customs, is the
decoration of a large sarcophagus of soft limestone, found
at Aghia Triadha and representing religious ceremonies.
Painted vases also reached a very high standard in Crete.
The designs, which show an extraordinary freedom of
style, most frequently represent plants, sea-weeds and sea
creatures such as the nautilus, cuttle-fish and star-fish,
and coral and shells.   They are quite unlike any other
early vase paintings that are known.

Sculpture, Reliefs, Goldsmith's Work, etc.—Works
of art found in the same stratum show a great difference
of quality, and this points to the fact that the best
artists worked for the Court, and only second-class works
of art were distributed among the general populace.
The earliest work of sculpture on Greek soil is the famous
" Lion Gate " at Mycenæ, where the two great beasts
are represented as guarding a sacred pillar.   In Crete no
large piece of sculpture has been discovered, but a great
number of works of art in plaster, ivory, faience, gold,
silver, and other metals, and also the engravings on gems,
prove how excellent were these early craftsmen, and what

PLATE XII

SMALL IVORY FIGURE OF A MAN, POSSIBLY DIVING, OR
LEAPING OVER A BULL
FROM KNOSSOS. LATE MINOAN PERIOD

FRESCO OF A CUP BEARER. FROM KNOSSOS
LATE MINOAN PERIOD

complete control they must have had over their material. Among the most famous of the Ægean reliefs, inlays, and carvings are the following :—

1. An ivory figurine of a youth diving, or leaping, found at Knossos, in the women's quarter, together with archives and objects of value. Full of an extraordinary life and vigour (see Plate XII.). With this figure was also found a small head in ivory.

2 and 3. Two groups in faience of a wild goat suckling her kids, and a cow and her calf, charming and naturalistic groups, found in a treasure chest buried beneath the floor of a room near the throne-room at Knossos, and probably forming part of the fittings of a shrine.

4. A faience figure of the "Great Goddess" found in the same spot. The figure, which is in the round, and is about 13 inches high, represents the divinity as a very modern figure, with a small waist, and wearing an embroidered and laced jacket and a full flounced skirt. Two snakes twine round her and she holds their heads in either hand. Probably a representation of the goddess in her fiercer form.

5 and 6. Two black stone vases from Aghia Triadha, one conical, measuring nearly 18 inches, and covered with reliefs representing boxing contests and bull fights ; the other smaller, and decorated with a procession of either harvesters or perhaps warriors.

7 and 8. Two gold cups found in a tomb at Vaphio, near Sparta. These famous drinking vessels show in re-poussé work the favourite design of bulls. On one cup a bull is being snared, while on the other the scene is more peaceful in character. The figures of the men are less realistic than those of the animals.

9 and 10. Two bronze daggers with blades ornamented with scenes of a lion hunt, inlaid with gold and silver.

Realistic figures excellently designed to fit the space. From one of the graves at Mycenæ.

11. A bull's head in black steatite from Knossos.

Knossos and Minos—" I suspect," says Professor Meyer, " that Minos was a name like Pharaoh or Cæsar, given to all Cretan Kings of a certain type." Which of these rulers was Minos, the father of Ariadne, we cannot tell, for the Greek Minos legend is twofold in character. On one hand the King is presented to us as the friend of Zeus, communing with him in his Cretan cave in the mountains. He is the founder of a great sea empire, and is described by Thucydides as " the first person known to us who established a navy," and by Homer as the great and wise law-giver, who promoted the cause of justice in his dominions, established the legal " Code of Minos," the source of all subsequent legislation, and who, after his death, was appointed to be judge of the dead in Hades. On the other hand Minos is revealed to us as the cruel King, the Master of the Minotaur, who each year sacrifices men and maidens to its fury. This Minos, according to Professor Ridgeway, is " Minos the destroyer, under whose rule the luxury and splendour of Knossos came to its sudden and violent end."

Archeology, if unsuccessful in revealing the exact personality of Minos, " or whatever historical person is covered by that name," has done much to clear up the mystery of the Labyrinth and the bull. With reference to the palace, its discoverer says: " There can be little remaining doubt that this vast edifice, which in a broad historic sense we are justified in calling the ' Palace of Minos,' is one and the same as the traditional ' Labyrinth.' A great part of the ground plan itself, with its long corridors and repeated succession of rambling galleries, its tortuous passages and spacious

underground conduit, its bewildering system of small
chambers, does, in fact, present many of the characteristics
of a maze." Sir Arthur Evans has also advanced the
theory that the labyrinth may have derived its name
from the *labrys* or double axe, which is repeatedly engraved
on the stones of the building, and which was a sacred
symbol of the Minoans. Other experts, however, are
inclined to believe that these symbols were only used as
masons' marks.

The works of art that have been discovered are an
ample proof of the Minoan practice of bull-baiting, and
also reveal the fact that toreadors were of both sexes.
" It is highly probable," writes Mr Burrows, "that the
toreadors were slaves, or captives won as spoil, if not as
tribute, from lands over the sea. Each Minoa may have
had to send its quota to the Imperial capital. It is
difficult to explain otherwise the fact that girls as well as
youths played their part in the ring ; and the Athenian
tradition that both sexes were sent as tribute can hardly
be a coincidence. That there were attempts to escape
that failed, who can doubt ? That there was one that
succeeded was a story which, if not true, was at least
ben trovato. As the memories of those man-destroying
bulls 'preserved' by the king for palace sport were
coloured by the man-beast form of art, so the horrors of
captivity seemed real again to after generations, when
they stumbled through the long corridors and deep
basements of the palace." [1]

[1] *The Discoveries in Crete.* Murray.

EXTRACTS

Description of the Palace of Alcinous, from the " Odyssey." [1]

" Meanwhile Odysseus went to the famous palace of Alcinous, and his heart was full of many thoughts, as he stood there, or ever he had reached the threshold of bronze. For there was a gleam as it were of sun or moon through the high-roofed hall of great-hearted Alcinous. Brazen were the walls which ran this way and that from the threshold to the inmost chamber, and round them was a frieze of blue, and golden were the doors, that closed in the good house. Silver were the door-posts that were set on the brazen threshold, and silver the lintel thereupon, and the hook of the door was of gold. And on either side stood golden hounds and silver, which Hephaistos wrought by his cunning to guard the palace of great-hearted Alcinous, being free from death and age all their days. And within were seats arrayed against the wall, this way and that, from the threshold even unto the inmost chamber, and thereon were spread light coverings, finely woven, the handiwork of women. . . . Yea, and there were youths fashioned in gold, standing on firm set bases, with flaming torches in their hands, giving light through the night to the feasters in the palace. . . . And without the courtyard, hard by the door is a great garden . . . and there grow tall trees, blossoming pear trees and pomegranates and apple trees with bright fruit, and sweet figs and olives in their bloom."

---

[1] Translated Butcher and Lang. Macmillan.

LESSONS VII AND VIII

GREEK ART

PART I.—ELEMENTARY LESSONS IN STORY FORM

INTRODUCTION—Rather more than a hundred years after the death of Ashur-bani-pal the people living in Greece grew to be very famous. They were the descendants of the Ægeans of whom you have heard. What do you remember about them? The Greeks, their descendants, were perhaps the greatest artists that the world has ever known, and many of them were splendid-looking men and great athletes. This is a story about one of them.

1. **Agias**—In a town above the flowery plains of Thessaly, not long after the Persians had been driven out of the country, there lived a man called Agias. He was young and strong and handsome, and the best athlete in the whole state. Like all other Greeks of good family, he had been taught that a man must have a well-trained body as well as a well-trained mind and character, and from his earliest years he had practised running and jumping and wrestling. He knew, too, that if he were called upon to defend his country, it would be his duty to be strong and in good training and ready to suffer hardship and exposure.

Agias had entered for many athletic games and competitions, and had already been a victor eight times; but there was one thing above all that he longed for. No Thessalonian had ever won the *Pankration*, or wrestling contests at Olympia. Now the Olympic games were the most famous in all Greece, and if he could

135

only win in these, he would bring great honour to his town and state. So early in the mornings Agias would be up and out on the hill-side, running for miles in the wind or rain or under the burning sun, until he grew still more hardy and strong. He would also practise wrestling with his friends, until there was not one of them whom he could not throw. Each day people would watch him, and would say one to another, " Agias will bring us all glory soon ; if he works hard and earnestly, never sparing himself, he will yet live to be an Olympic Victor and an honour to his state."

At last the time of the festival drew near. One morning when Agias was stretched out on the grass, resting after a hard round of wrestling, he heard in the distance the sound of a trumpet. He started to his feet, his heart beating. It must be the heralds who had come from Olympia to proclaim to all the Greek states the sacred truce, and bid them all welcome to the festival. During the truce no state might war against another, and all might come and go to the games in safety. There was no event in all Greece that was more sacred, because the festival was held in honour of Zeus, the chief of all the gods. The heralds came in sight round the corner of the hill-side. They wore white tunics and crowns of olive, and bore in their hands long heralds' staves. The townspeople flocked to welcome them ; the gates were thrown open, and they were eagerly questioned about the games ; who were going to enter for the different events, and who were looked upon as likely victors. Agias listened eagerly, and when the heralds were gone he began to make preparations for the journey.

At last the day of departure dawned, and waking early, Agias slipped from the house and climbed the

hill-side above the sleeping town. The dew lay heavy
on the short turf, and the scent of the wild thyme rose
freshly on the cool morning air. In the distance above
the plain towered Mount Olympus. Agias thought that
the gods and goddesses dwelt on its heights and he
turned towards them, and prayed to Zeus that he would
lend him his aid and help him to win in the coming
contest. The sun rose in a cloudless blue sky, and the
plain below shimmered in the heat. The town was
astir, and a little goatherd climbed the hill-side, driving
his flock before him and piping a little wild and
melancholy air to the morning skies. Agias leapt
lightly to his feet and ran down the slope to the town,
revelling in his youth and strength and longing for the
contest before him. His breakfast was simple—figs,
cheese and porridge—and he was soon ready, and set off
with his family and some chosen friends, who were also
going to the festival.

2. The Festival. (a) The Arrival—All the world
was flocking to Olympia : rich men and peasants, philosophers and statesmen, soldiers and artists of every
description. The sculptors and the painters knew that
they would get abundant inspiration for their work, for
they would see the most splendid youth of Greece,
strong and graceful and lithe, and from the victors they
would get commissions for statues and paintings. The
roads were black with people. Clouds of dust rose
into the heat and the sunshine, as the chariots flashed
past, drawn by splendid horses. Many tongues were
heard, for strangers were arriving from distant lands ;
not to compete, as this was a privilege for Greeks only,
but to watch and share in the excitement. Fathers
brought their sons, so that the games might be an
inspiration to them, but women, strange to say, were

absent ; they were forbidden to attend the festival, owing
to some religious law.

There were few buildings at Olympia besides those
connected with the festival, and although some visitors
had put up tents, the mass of the people slept in the
open air, under the shade of the olive and poplar trees,
or by the banks of the river. Agias and his friends
chose a place for their camp, and then went up to the
great temple of Zeus, where all the competitors were
assembling. Here they underwent a solemn scrutiny,
and standing before the great altar which was built in
the open air in the sacred enclosure, they offered up a
sacrifice of a wild boar and swore that they had trained
for ten months in a manner worthy of the festival; that
they would use no unfair means to win a victory, and
that they were innocent of all impiety or irreverence to
the gods. Agias looked around him at his fellow
competitors, as strong and bronzed and eager as he.
What would his fate be, he wondered ! The ceremony
over, he was free for the rest of the day. He made a
round of the race-courses, talked with other athletes,
hunted up old friends, and then went off early to rest,
to be ready for what lay before him.

(b) The Contests—The next day the contests began.
Before the sun was up every good point of view was
occupied. There were no seats so the people lined the
edge of the Stadium and Hippodrome and sat rank
above rank on the steep slopes that rose above them.
The sun blazed down on the vast audience and the dust
rose in clouds. The people had no hats to give them
shade, but nothing could damp their enthusiasm. The
contests lasted three days. Each morning a blast of
trumpets announced the entry of the judges, distinguished
visitors, and competitors, who entered the Stadium in

procession and took their appointed places. The judges
wore long purple robes, and garlands on their heads.
They solemnly swore that they would judge all events
fairly. Each athlete's name was proclaimed in turn by
the heralds, who asked the assembled company if there
were any charge to be brought against him. Then the
games began. Agias watched the events with keen
interest. First came the chariot races. This was the
sport of the wealthy and those of noble birth. Princes
and rulers stood in groups by the side of the course,
and watched their four splendid horses harnessed and
brought to the starting-point. The charioteers stood
firm and erect, dressed in long white chitons or tunics
which fell to their feet. They grasped the reins, knowing
that danger lay before them. The race was twelve times
round the course, and at any one of the twenty-three
turns involved, the chariots might dash one against the
other, and the drivers be thrown to the ground and killed.
But they were sons of princely houses, used to danger and
adventure, and their eyes were steady and their hands firm.

" They took their stations where the appointed umpires
placed them by lot and ranged the cars; then at the
sound of the brazen trump they started. All shouted
to their horses, and shook the reins in their hands; the
whole course was filled with the noise of rattling chariots;
the dust flew upward; and all in a confused throng plied
their goads unsparingly, each of them striving to pass
the wheels and the snorting steeds of his rivals; for alike
at their backs and at their rolling wheels the breath of
the horses foamed and smote. Mishaps followed—shock
on shock and crash on crash, till the whole race-ground
was strewn with the wreck of chariots." [1]

[1] From the description of a chariot race at Delphi, in *The Electra*,
Sophocles. Jebb's translation. Cambridge University Press.

The excitement was intense. People held their breath, and then leapt to their feet, shouting wildly to encourage their favourites. A great roar of applause went up as the winner rounded the post for the last time, and pulled his steaming horses up beyond the goal. He stood dignified and proud, his head thrown back, his hands slightly trembling from the strain, while the owner of the team hastened with his congratulations, and received the prize that his horses had won. There were artists too whose eyes had followed the charioteer, and who had so realized the fineness of his poise and bearing that already they saw in imagination the splendid statues and paintings that he would inspire, and which would bring them fame and render him immortal.

Then came competitions of all sorts: disk-throwing, jumping, boxing and throwing the javelin. These were followed by the foot-races for boys and youths. They were always popular events, and the crowd gathered thickly to cheer on its friends. It was the custom in Greece for all athletes to compete without clothes, in order that their limbs shall have perfect freedom, and there were hundreds of artists among the spectators, who studied the well-knit figures and their graceful movements in order that they might afterwards carve and paint beautiful statues, frescoes, and vases. Agias watched with keen interest as the lithe and lightly built forms flew past like the wind. He singled out a handsome youth with a band bound round his curling hair, and shouted with delight when he won the race, an easy first, and received his crown of wild olive amidst enthusiastic applause.

The moment came at last when Agias must strive for the honour of his town and country. He heard his name called as if in a dream. It seemed to him as if the

words " Agias of Pharsalos in the state of Thessaly "
were echoing back at him from every hill. A long-
robed official was holding the silver urn, and uttering
a prayer to Zeus, Agias plunged his hand in and drew
his lot. He was drawn for the first heat, and at the
blast of the trumpet he closed with his opponent. They
wrestled together, and to his delight Agias found that
he could easily throw him the three times that were
required. He was successful in each of the ensuing
rounds, and panting with excitement, he realized that
he had now reached the final. His opponent was big
and muscular, and the spectators shouted encouragingly,
knowing that there would be a close competition. The
trumpet sounded and the final trial began. It seemed
at first as though the chances were equal. Sometimes
Agias fell and sometimes it was his opponent who lost
a round. The strong bronzed figures swayed and bent,
their muscles standing out like cords. The great crowd
was tense with excitement. Somewhere in that dense
mass of people Agias knew that his friends were watching,
and straining their eyes so that no movement of his
should escape them. He nerved himself for a final effort,
and using every atom of skill and strength he possessed,
he succeeded in throwing his opponent for the third
time.

As he rose and stood in the centre of the vast crowds,
the light of valour in his eyes, his breath coming and
going quickly and unevenly, the wild applause seemed
to sound in his ears like the roaring of a great sea.
Thousands of faces swam before him, and he was dimly
conscious of men standing up, stamping and hurrahing
madly, and above all the echoing words, " Agias, Agias,
Thessaly ! " ringing out into the blazing summer noon.
Flowers and garlands fell thickly round him ; someone

was advancing towards him, and joy surged through him as he realizes that in him Thessaly was victorious for the first time.   He bowed his head, and with a blast of trumpets, the victor's crown of wild olive was placed upon his brow.

(c) The Feast—It was evening.   The last of the games was over, and the victors were making ready to attend the public banquet given by the authorities in their honour.   Agias, rested and refreshed after his labours, threaded his way through the olive trees, which looked silvery and dim in the moonlight.   From every side came sounds of revelry, music, and dancing.   Down on the plain, hundreds of torches lit up the booths and sheds, where a busy trade in cakes, fruit, flowers, and wares of every kind was going on.   The great feast was crowded.   Princes and nobles, sculptors and poets, victors crowned with olive, and officials of the festival reclined on couches, and hundreds of slaves passed to and fro, supplying the small tables with food of every kind.   It was a brilliant scene, and the table was furnished with all the delicacies that the Greeks loved—

> " Couches, tables,
> Cushions and coverlets for mattresses,—
> Plum cake and plain, comfits and caraways,
> Confectionery, fruits preserved and fresh,
> Relishes of all sorts, hot things and bitter,
> Savouries and sweets, boiled biscuits and what-not,
> Flowers and perfumes and garlands, everything."

During the feast music was played, and when the banquet drew to a close, a poet rose from his couch, and recited a poem in honour of the victors.   "O King Zeus, the accomplisher, grant them with light feet to move through life, give them all honour, and sweet hap of goodly things." [1]

---

[1] *Extant Odes of Pindar*, translated E. Myers.   Macmillan.

The guests passed out into the moonlight, and on to the sacred enclosure.   There, in the shadow of the great temple, a sacrifice was offered to Zeus, and representatives of the different states presented costly vessels of gold and silver as offerings to the temple.   The flames leapt on the altar, casting a flickering light on the statues of athletes, that stood like dim ghosts on every side.   Agias looked around him well content, while high above in the summer night " the lovely shining of the fair-faced moon beamed forth, and all the precinct sounded with the songs of festal glee." [1]

3. The Home-coming—All good things come to an end.   The Olympic games were over and Agias was on his way home.   The news of his victory had gone on before him, and as he left the plain of Thessaly and began to climb the spur of the mountain on which his town was built, his reception was being prepared.   As he drew near the town, the great gates were flung open, and a procession of men and girls advanced to meet him. They were singing a chorus in honour of his victory, and in their steps followed a crowd of the townspeople, eager to do honour to the hero of the day.   Garlands were thrown over him, and flowers fell like rain in his path. He might not enter the town by the public gates.   A way had to be made for him that no foot had yet trod, and scores of men attacked the wall with picks and crowbars, until a breach was made through which he could pass.   His family and friends crowded round him, but he would not go home until he had been to the temple, and solemnly and reverently offered his victor's crown as a thanksgiving to the god.   There was nothing else in the world that Agias valued as much as that chaplet of faded leaves.   It was more precious than gold

[1] *Extant Odes of Pindar*, translated E. Myers.   Macmillan.

and silver to him, for he had laboured for honour, not for
material gain. There was another great honour that also
fell to him. In due course his statue would be erected
by the town, and placed near the temple of the gods.
No one in Greece that night was happier than Agias.

"He that has lately won glory in the time of his
sweet youth, is lifted on the wings of his strong hope
and soaring valour, for his thoughts are above riches."

"For if a man rejoice to suffer cost and toil, and
achieve god-builded excellence, and therewith fate plant
for him fair renown already at the farthest bounds of
bliss, has such an one cast anchor, for the glory that he
hath thereby from god." [1]

SECOND STORY—ATHENS AND PHIDIAS

Introduction—Last story. This is a story about a boy who
became a sculptor, one of the greatest artists who ever lived.

1. The Panathenaic Procession—In the town of
Athens, which was built near the blue Ægean sea, lived
a little boy called Phidias. His hair was long, and fell
in curls over his shoulders, and he wore a short white
tunic and sandals. One morning he woke in great
excitement. For the first time he was to be allowed to
watch the great procession in honour of the goddess
Athena, whom the Athenians thought of as the protectress of their town and country. They asked her help
and advice in all their enterprises, and they loved to
honour her in every way. That day a beautiful mantle
of violet and pale gold was to be carried in the procession
and draped on her statue. Every four years a new
mantle was presented to her in this way, and a great
festival with games and music was held in honour of the

[1] *Extant Odes of Pindar*, translated E. Myers. Macmillan.

event. Phidias knew what the mantle was like. It had
been embroidered by some noble Athenian maidens, and
several times he had been allowed to watch, when their
clever fingers traced out the figures of gods and giants
that covered it. He loved all beautiful things, and even
though he was only a child, he would model little figures
out of clay, and draw and paint men and women with
their white tunics and robes.

The day dawned clear and fine. Phidias could hardly
wait to eat his breakfast of barley cakes and honey and
figs, and gave his parents no peace until they were ready
to start. The town was full of visitors from every part
of Greece, and even distant lands from beyond the sea.
Everywhere was bustle and excitement. There were
booths set up in the open places, with wares of every kind
exposed for sale, but to-day the people were thinking
only of the great procession, and the road that it would
travel was already lined with hundreds of men, women,
and children. Phidias and his father and mother secured
a good position, and the boy waited with impatience,
watching the crowds, and wishing that he could see the
mustering of the procession outside the gate of the town
by the Sacred Way. The time slowly passed; the crowd
got denser. In the distance was heard the fishmonger's
bell, which showed that the morning's catch had arrived,
and a slave, who has no leisure of his own, hurried away
from the roadside to attend to the needs of his master's
table.

At last a low murmur showed that the procession had
started. Phidias strained his eyes, and saw in the
distance a cloud of dust. Sounds of music and slow
chanting were heard, and round the bend of the road the
first detachment of cavalry came into sight. The men
wore short tunics and crested helmets on their heads.

They rode proudly, curbing the impatience of their fine
and spirited horses, which tossed their heads, their manes
flowing in the breeze. Soldiers on foot followed, gallant
in bearing, bronzed and strong of limb. Then the
chariots passed, their drivers standing silent, firm, erect.
Next came aged Athenian citizens with long beards and
flowing robes, bearing olive branches ; men carrying trays
on which were heaped cakes and other offerings, and
others leading oxen, cows and sheep, wreathed with
garlands, as offerings to the gods. Then came lines of
men and maidens, singing as they went, and bearing
sacrificial urns, followed by representatives of the whole
body of Athenian citizens. In the centre of the
procession, surrounded by maidens of the utmost grace
and beauty, the sacred mantle was displayed, stretched
on the mast and yard of a wooden ship, which was drawn
along on rollers. Phidias held his breath as it passed.
Never before had he seen anything so solemn and so
beautiful as this procession. He stood spellbound as it
passed along the winding road, up the steep Acropolis
hill. The trampling of the horses and the sound of the
singing grew fainter. Above him the temple of Athena
stood tawny and golden against the deep blue of the sky.
The sunlight glanced from the armour and the spears of
the soldiers. The sound of the music floated down on
the summer air, fainter and still fainter, until it died away.
Now the embroidered mantle was being draped on the
old statue of the goddess Athena, the statue that once a
year was carried down to the sea and washed in the cool
blue water. Phidias was taken home, tired out with the
waiting and excitement. He little dreamt how the time
should come when the Acropolis, newly covered with
great buildings and statues, should owe its immortal
glory to him.

2. The Persian Wars—Time passed. Troubles fell thick and fast upon Greece. The Persians, the people who had conquered Assyria, thought that they would conquer Greece also, and their king sent his army to invade the country. They were a strong and powerful nation, and they thought that they could soon overcome the Greeks. They marched in thousands into the fair Greek country, but the people joined together and fought with the greatest bravery and courage, and defeated them at a place called Marathon. The Persians retired discomfited, but later came again in greater strength than before. Then every Greek that could fight polished his spear and shield, and prepared to drive away the hated foe from the land. They determined to defend the pass of Thermopylæ against the advance of the invaders, but they were outnumbered. The Persian host was so enormous that their arrows came in clouds, until it seemed as though the sun would be hidden. "So much the better, we can fight in the shade," a Greek observed. But bravery and heroism alone could not win the day; thousands fell in the battle, and the three hundred men who defended the pass to the last died a splendid death, fighting until the end.

The Persians then prepared to march upon Athens. The Athenians, knowing that they could not hold the town against the enemy, sent their women and children away to places of safety, and themselves embarked in their ships, which numbered nearly four hundred. The Persians sacked the town, burnt the temples, destroyed the statues, and, marshalling their fleet, prepared for battle. Sitting on a golden throne, Xerxes, King of the Persians, waited to see the Greek ships overwhelmed by his enormous fleet. He did not realize that the Greeks had taken up their position in a narrow part of the bay, where his ships, said to number twelve hundred in all, would only get in the way of each other.

" When, however, day, with its white steeds, radiant to behold, had occupied all the earth, first of all a cheer from the Greeks rang loudly like a chant of triumph, and shrill and clear from the island crags echo returned the cry. And fear was in the hearts of all the barbarians, finding themselves mistaken ; for the Greeks were then chanting a solemn pæan, not as seeking to escape, but as advancing to battle with daring courage.   Next a bugle with its call fired all their line into action, and at once with foaming oars in unison they smote to the word of command the brine.   And rapidly the whole of them came plain into view . . . and the same time a mighty shout would be heard : ' Sons of the Greeks, advance !   Deliver your country, deliver your children and your wives, the temples of your fathers' gods, the tombs of your ancestors !   Now is the contest which decides all ! ' " [1]

The Greeks drove the sharp metal prows of their ships into the broad sides of the Persians, and sheared off their protruding oars.   The enemy's ships, driven one against the other in the narrow waters, were broken up and damaged in the confusion of the fight.   The sea was strewn with floating wreckage, and by nightfall the Greeks were victorious, and the battle of Salamis was won.   Further fighting took place, until at last the day came when the hated foe was driven out of the land.

3. Phidias and the Parthenon—With joy and thanksgiving the Athenians returned to their beloved city, but what a sight met their eyes !   The houses were levelled to the ground, the temple and gateway on the

---

[1] Æschylus, *The Persians*, translated Headlam.   Bell.   (The poet was an eye-witness of the scene.)

Acropolis were burnt, and the statues were broken and
scattered; nothing but desolation could be seen. The
rebuilding was at once begun. Simple houses were
erected for the people to live in, and great walls were
built to the sea and round the harbour in case of further
invasion.

At last an Athenian called Pericles rose to power and
became the greatest ruler Athens had known. He loved
his country more than anything else, and determined to
make Athens a monument to her greatness. The wars
were over; she had conquered magnificently; what could
be done to immortalize her glory and to give praise to
the gods and to Athena? The State had untold wealth
at her disposal, chiefly money contributed by other Greek
states, but also spoil from the Persian wars—gold and
silver armour, jewelled daggers, chariots and treasure of
every kind. Pericles was determined that it should not
be spent by the people in luxurious living, but in some
other and nobler way. He had a friend who could help
him, a famous sculptor, the greatest in all Greece. Who
was he? None other than Phidias, the boy who had
watched the procession, now grown to be a grey-haired
man. Pericles and Phidias had long talks together.
Sometimes the sculptor came to the ruler's house with a
big roll of parchment under his arm on which were
drawn plans of great temples and statues. Poets and
philosophers joined in the discussion, and all made
suggestions as to how the Acropolis could be beautified.
Sometimes Pericles visited Phidias in his workshop.
Roughly-hewn blocks of marble were piled in the corners,
and at one side stood a big furnace for melting bronze
and precious metals. Pupils came and went. The sound
of hammers and chisels never ceased, and beautiful
sculptures by the master's hand stood about the big shed.

Day and night Phidias thought about the work that had
been entrusted to him.

One evening he left his plans and drawings and went
out into the town. Dusk was falling, and the air was
soft and scented with the fragrance of the spring. He
turned his steps towards the Acropolis, which loomed
above him, a dark mass against the fading light in the
sky. Slowly he climbed the steep pathway, and leaving
the noise of the town behind him, threaded his way
among the fallen pillars and blocks of broken marble,
until he stood in the shadow of a bronze figure of
immense height towering up into the night sky. It was
a statue of Athena which he had made and cast some
years before. He stood in silence before the goddess,
praying for her help in his great undertaking. The
moon came out from behind a cloud and lit up an
ethereal world, where the sea and shore and distant hills
showed dimly and mysteriously. Exaltation filled the
heart and mind of the great sculptor, and visions of
immortal beauty haunted him until he saw, as if in a
dream, the new Athens that should arise in answer to his
inspiration. A cool night wind crept up from the sea,
and a bird called. Phidias, roused from his reveries,
turned his steps homeward, and retracing his way through
the sleeping city, reached his house.

The work on the Acropolis was begun at last. News
of the rebuilding of the city was carried far and wide by
the Greek soldiers and traders, and hundreds of artisans
from far and near crowded into the town. The Athenians
were filled with enthusiasm, and the workmen vied with
each other as to the quality of their work. A long train
of hundreds of mules wound to and fro from the quarries
of Pentelicus, some ten miles distant, bringing from them
numberless blocks of marble. Thousands of slaves were

PLATE XIII

ATHENS. THE ACROPOLIS AND PARTHENON SEEN FROM THE TEMPLE OF JUPITER

set to work on the great walls which banked up the sides of the Acropolis hill, while in his workshop Phidias designed sacred buildings and their decorations, and issued orders to the architects and sculptors who carried out his designs. He remembered the Panathenaic procession which he first saw and loved as a child, and with this as his subject he drew out a magnificent frieze, to be carved in stone on the walls of the Parthenon. He also designed figures of the gods and goddesses for the same building, which other artists helped him to carry out, but the great statue of Athena, which was to stand in the *cella* or hall of the Parthenon, was entirely the work of his own hands. To no one else could so great a trust be given.

The building progressed with extraordinary rapidity. The whole city was stirred with enthusiasm. No one cared that his own house was small and plain. It was the glory of Athens alone that mattered. Day by day and year by year the buildings of the Acropolis rose, stately in conception and unsurpassed in harmony and grace. At last the longed-for day arrived, when the last barricade was taken away and the people were free to see the sanctuary of their gods. They crowded up the steep path and the long flight of steps that led to the *Propylæa* or gateway : men, women, and children, poets and philosophers, sculptors and painters, all of them filled with joy and pride in their beautiful city. They were proud to be Athenians, and wanted to give thanks to Athena and the gods, and to take part in the general rejoicings. Beautiful buildings greeted their eyes on every side. Before them the Parthenon, the new temple of Athena, lifted its golden-tinted marbles into the clear air, and glowed with beauty against the blue skies. The outside walls were decorated with beautiful sculptures; figures of the gods and goddesses, and warriors and centaurs. Inside the columns, high on the outer walls of the central chamber, ran the frieze of the Panathenaic procession. The people threw back heads and craned their necks to see all its beauties. Beside a pillar stood a grey-haired man, silently watching the crowds. Someone asked him why he had placed the frieze so high, that the people could scarcely realize its beauty. " The gods can see it," replied Phidias. Inside the temple the crowds stood in awe and reverence. Before them in the half-light towered the great statue of Athena Parthenos. Her face was of softly gleaming ivory : golden draperies flowed from her shoulders in richly glowing curves and folds. On her head was a golden helmet, and one hand rested on a great shield. The statue was so wonderful and awe-inspiring that the people stood spellbound before it. Then they turned, and with soft footfall and in silence passed out again into the dazzling sunshine and left their places for others.

The crowds came and went. The fame of Athens passed from lip to lip. " Come to the splendid land of Athens and see a country rich in loveliness, rich in men. Here is the majesty of inviolate shrines, here are statues and soaring temples, here are processions, sacred, blessed, and through every season of the year flower-crowned feasts and festivals of gods. Here as spring advances, comes the . . . musical delight of dancing, and the deep-toned melody of the flute."[1]

NOTES ON THE STORIES

First Story—*Aim.*—To show the effect of the athletic ideal upon Greek art.

Agias was born at Pharsalos in Thessaly, and lived about the

---

[1] Aristophanes. *The Clouds.*

middle of the fifth century B.C. He was a famous athlete, having won five times at Nemea, five times at the Isthmian games, and three times at Delphi without suffering defeat. His statue by Lysippus was commissioned by a descendant of the family, and was cast in bronze, and probably erected in his native town. The marble replica, recently found at Delphi, was made about the year 338-334 B.C., and formed part of a votive offering. Although it is probably not by the hand of the master, there is no doubt that it was a contemporary work and may very likely have been executed under his supervision. The descriptions of the charioteer, and the youth who won the foot-race, are suggested by the original bronzes at Delphi and Munich. The sculptor, date and original of both of these works are unknown. The bust of the boy dates from about the middle of the fifth century B.C., while the charioteer is a somewhat earlier masterpiece. Different critics have suggested that the whole-length figure represents the charioteer of (a) Hieron of Syracuse ; (b) Arkesilas of Cyrene ; (c) Anaxilas of Rhegium.

The story is imaginary. The details are chiefly taken from *Greek Athletic Sports and Festivals*, by E. Norman Gardiner. The exact order of the events of the Olympic games is not known, and although it is probable that the victors were crowned after each event, it has not been definitely proved. The famous statue of Zeus at Olympia was probably erected by Phidias at a later date than 450 B.C. As this was the time when the festival reached its height, it has been chosen as the moment of the story.

Second Story—Paragraph 1 imaginary. The description of the procession is drawn from contemporary accounts and from the sculptures of the Parthenon. It is not known when the wooden ship was first used to display the peplos, but the custom had probably been instituted by the beginning of the fifth century B.C.

Paragraph 3 imaginary. The saying of Phidias that the gods could see his frieze is traditional. The Parthenon was probably built during the years 447-438 B.C. A detailed description of its sculptures can be found in the explanatory guide, published by the British Museum Trustees (price 1s.).

PART. II.—MATERIAL FOR ADVANCED LESSONS ONLY

History and Civilization—The early civilization of the Ægean was destroyed by northern invaders who came, not only to conquer, but to settle down in the new lands that they had won. These northern people were a vigorous, sturdy, and self-controlled race of soldiers, and their intermarriage with the quick-witted, sensitive, and beauty-loving seafarers of the Ægean may have something to do with the genius of the Greek race, which was in this way the heir of varied and powerful characteristics. It is interesting to note that the Spartans, who had most of the northern blood in their veins, remained to the end a warlike and inartistic people, while the Athenians and Ionians, who were the most artistic of all the Greeks, claimed to be of the purest native descent.

Another cause that helped to foster the genius of the people was the geographical position of the country, which is a land of mountains and hills, with a coast-line so broken that there is no inland spot more than forty miles distant from the sea. Owing to its centre position in the ancient world, its natural harbours, and the extent of Greek enterprise in war, colonization, and trade, the country became the home of all foreign thought and ideas, and mental or physical stagnation was unknown.

The early monarchies of the Homeric times had been superseded by the rise of small independent states, which were ruled over by the heads of noble families, or popular leaders or "tyrants." These states were continually at war with each other, and this engendered a hardy, active, and resourceful people, ever ready to devote themselves to the service of their state. It was, however, the temporary union of these states that resulted in the great age of the Greek genius. The Persian invasions, under Darius and Xerxes, threatened the safety of all, and sinking their differences by force of necessity, the people fought with magnificent courage, and in the battles of Marathon (490 B.C.), Salamis (480 B.C.), Platea (479 B.C.), and Mycale (479 B.C.) completely defeated the enemy.

Then followed a period of unsurpassed intellectual and æsthetic power. The victories kindled in the people a passionate exaltation of civic and religious energy, and the white flame of their genius burnt fiercely, and still lives in some of the greatest masterpieces of literature and art that the world has ever known.

Among the Greeks, there were none more intellectually and artistically endowed than the Athenians, who reached the summit of their power under Pericles (died 429 B.C.). We get a vivid description of the people in the following account by Thucydides, written during the first half of the fifth century B.C. :—

"You have never considered what manner of men are these Athenians. . . . They are revolutionary, equally quick in the conception and the execution of every new plan—they are bold beyond their strength ; they run risks which prudent people would condemn ; and in the midst of misfortune they are full of hope. . . . They are always abroad—for they hope to gain something by leaving their homes. . . . Their bodies they devote to their country as though they belonged to other men ; their true self is their mind, which is most truly their own when employed in her service. When they do not carry out an intention which they have formed, they seem to have sustained a personal bereavement; when an enterprise succeeds, they have gained a mere instalment of what is to come ; but if they fail they at once conceive new hopes and so fill up the void. With them alone to hope is to have, for they lose not a moment in the execution of an

idea. . . . To do their duty is their only holiday, and
they deem the quiet of inaction to be as disagreeable as
the most tiresome business." [1]

The fourth century saw the growing power of
Macedonia, a half Hellenic province to the north of
Greece. By the end of that century Greece had come
under its rule, and, as a Macedonian province, became part
of the immense Hellenic empire of Alexander the Great
(356-323 B.C.). This famous general conquered Persia,
extended his dominions as far as Parthia, Bactria, and
Northern India, and conquered Egypt. After his death
his dominions were divided among various lesser rulers,
none of whom were strong enough to hold the vast empire
together. Eventually three kingdoms were established :
Macedonia and the two Macedonian kingdoms of Ptolemy
in Egypt, and Seleucus in Syria, the latter including Mesopotamia and Seleucia, the capital of the kingdom ; Persia,
Media, Bactria, and other "upper provinces," together
with most of Asia Minor. During the third and second
centuries B.C. the growing power of Rome made itself felt,
and in the year 146 B.C. Greece became a Roman
province.

Religion—The early Greeks, who like other primitive
people deified unseen agencies controlling natural phenomena, expressed their worship of them as their Ægean
ancestors had done, in a veneration for stones, trees and
pillars. We cannot tell if the deities were supposed to
be connected with these objects in some occult way, or
if the stones and trees were only regarded as their symbols,
and we do not know also at what time the people first
began to imagine their gods in human form. There is
little or no evidence of their sculptured representation in
the Homeric poems, but their conception was to a great

[1] Jowett's translation. Clarendon Press.

extent furthered and developed by the early Greek epics, and not long afterwards the first human representations must have been attempted.

The pillar was gradually developed into some sort of stiff human semblance by sculptors who in this way exercised no little control over the popular thought concerning the national deities. By the sixth century B.C., although the old rigid figures were still preserved and worshipped in the temples, the gods were represented by human figures in archaic form, and the Greeks conceived their deities as men and women fashioned like themselves, dwelling on Mount Olympus in Thessaly, and sharing, to a certain extent, their own thoughts and emotions. By the fifth century the sculptors had gained enough power over their material to emphasize the individual characteristics of each god and goddess. It must be remembered, however, that the Greek people were of mixed race, and that many varying beliefs were held in different parts of the country where different gods were held in veneration. Besides their cult of the Olympic deities the Greeks believed also in a very ancient form of religion, which consisted in the worship of mysterious nature goddesses. The most important of the gods of Olympus are as follows :

Zeus, the son of Cronos and Rhea, the father of most of the gods and the supreme ruler over them. He was the giver of victory in battle and the god of all manly force and excellence. He was said to have been born in a cave on Mount Ida, Crete. Attributes : a thunder bolt ægis (skin-covered shield), or eagle.

THE BROTHERS AND SISTERS OF ZEUS

Hera, his consort, representing the female principle in nature and the goddess of marriage. Generally represented with a crown, ægis or pomegranate, or a peacock, her sacred bird.

Demeter, the earth mother and goddess of corn and harvest, and mother of Persephone, who with Pluto (Hades) ruled in the realm below of the dead.

Poseidon, god of the sea when represented with a trident or fish, and of springs and rivers, when he is often given the form of a bull. He was also the god of horses.

Hestia, the virgin goddess of the hearth, who received the first offering at every feast. Represented as a draped and often veiled figure.

THE CHILDREN OF ZEUS

Athena, the goddess of wisdom and of the arts and sciences. The special protectress of Athens. Generally represented in armour, with an owl or an ægis in which is set the head of a gorgon (which she slew, either by herself or with the help of Perseus).

Apollo, the sun god (Phœbus), and the god of music and youth. He was also the lord of oracles, and was said to have been born on the island of Delos. He was represented in early days as a bearded man, but in later times as a very effeminate and degraded type. Attributes: a bow and lyre, or a branch of bay.

Artemis, the goddess of wild nature, the virgin huntress, and also the goddess of the moon ; especially associated with Apollo. Attributes : a stag, lion, or other wild animal, and a bow and arrow, and sometimes a torch.

Hermes, the messenger of the gods, and the giver of increase, especially of flocks and herds. Also the god of wayfarers, commerce, cunning, and theft, and of luck and treasure trove. Attributes : a caduceus (snake-wreathed

wand), winged feet or sandals, a staff, a winged cap, and
sometimes a purse. In early art he was represented as
bearded, later as a beardless youth. His son was the
god Pan, the protector of flocks and god of the country.
Pan is generally represented with goats' legs and horns,
holding pipes.

Dionysus, or **Bacchus,** taken as an infant by Hermes
to the nymphs of Nysa, who, with the help of Satyrs and
Silenus, guarded his youth. The god of wine, the leader
of the rout, and the patron of drama. Represented in art
as a bearded man in rich drapery ; later as a youth, often
effeminate in type.

Ares, the god of war. Generally represented as an
armed soldier, with torch and spear.

Hephæstus, the god of fire, lame through being hurled
into the sea by one of his parents. Represented with
hammer, pincers, and smith's cap.

Aphrodite, according to some myths the daughter of
Zeus, and by others described as born of the sea foam.
She is the goddess of love and of all feminine grace and
beauty. In some of her forms she has a tortoise for a
symbol, in others a goat. Until the fourth century she
was represented as a draped figure, afterwards either
draped or undraped.

The Greeks held no fixed creed and dogma. They
were lovers of proportion and harmony, and their conception of the soul was, to a large extent, æsthetic.
" Virtue will be a kind of health and beauty and good
habit of the soul, and vice will be a disease and deformity
and sickness of it." They troubled themselves little with
any definite beliefs as to a life after death, for Greek
thought was controlled by intellect and reason, and halted
on the threshold of a region where the spirit of man alone
could penetrate. So the Greek was content with a vague

and undefined belief that the spirits of the dead descended to Hades, the nether world, and, after purification, passed to the happy place where the souls of heroes dwelt.

The dead were cremated or buried, and, in order that necessities should not be wanting during the journey to the other world, food, jewellery, and other articles were placed in the tombs. Armour was buried with the men, and mirrors with women, while a coin was placed between the lips as a fee to Charon, who would ferry the ghost over the river Styx.

Athletic Festivals—Together with Greek religion, the national athletic festivals, or games, served to shape and mould Greek art. They were conceived, however, in a very different spirit from our modern athletics. To the Greek, with his worship of harmony and proportion, training of body went hand in hand with training of soul : a good soul must dwell in a beautiful body, and athletic power was of the highest educational importance.

The festivals were primarily religious in character, and were held in honour of the various gods to whom the athletes dedicated their strength. The temple, the prayer, the sacrifice, and the choral hymn were the background against which they were set. To compete in the games was a sign of special distinction, and the victor of any event brought great honour to his town and state. There was no mercenary motive involved, for the prize consisted of a wreath of olive or bay. Poetic recitations and musical competitions also formed part of the programme, and in this way æsthetic influences were added. The barriers between different states were broken down, a sacred truce was proclaimed, and a sense of unity prevailed. People had common interests and prayers, and a feeling of good-will and charity to each other. New friendships were made, and a renewal of old ones took place. The games fostered the ideals of fairness and honour, and excellence in athletics was only won, "God helping, by cost and toil."

The Greeks lifted these festivals into a high imaginative atmosphere, to which literature and art added their lustre. Style and grace in the contests were imperative. In order to have absolute freedom, the Greeks wore no clothes in the competitions, and it is easy to see how this fact influenced Greek art. The sculptors and painters had unlimited opportunities for studying the male form in its most perfect development, and they soon became past masters in its portrayal. The most famous festivals were the Olympic games, held in honour of Zeus, at Olympia, every fourth year; the Pythian games at Delphi, in honour of Apollo, held every third year; the Nemean games, held every second year in the vale of Nemea; and the Isthmian games, held every fourth year under the presidency of Corinth. In later days the rise of professionalism robbed Greek games of much of their value, and they never again reached the high level that they held in the fifth century B.C. The traditional date of the founding of the Olympic games is the year 776 B.C.

ART. HISTORIC OUTLINE

Greek art can be divided broadly into the following periods :—

1. **Beginnings of Greek Art, 900-600 B.C.**—Period of Oriental influence. Greece enters into relations with Egypt, 664-610 B.C. Trade with Phœnicians brings Assyrian influence. Rude wooden and stone images of the gods.

2. **The Sixth Century or Archaic Period, 600-500 B.C.**—Rise of plastic art in marble and bronze.

Schools of athletic sculpture at Argos and Sicyon.
Doric style of architecture introduced into Greece,
Sicily, and Magna Græcia ; Ionic style into Asia
Minor.

3. **The Fifth Century, or great age of Literature
and Art. (a) Period of Transition, 500-450
B.C.**—Persian wars. Rapid development of
sculpture ; many masterpieces produced. Introduction of Ionic style of architecture into Greece.
Sack of Acropolis, 480 B.C. Calamis, Pythagoras
of Rhegium, and Myron. Perfection of architecture and vase painting.

    (b) Period of Maturity, 450-400 B.C.—
Great age of sculpture. Phidias, Polyclitus, Poly-
gnotus, and Apollodorus. Dedication of Parthenon,
438 B.C. Supremacy of Athens under Pericles.

4. **The Period of Late Fine Art, 400-320 B.C.**—
Scopas, Praxiteles, Lysippus, Zeuxis, and Apelles.
Production of Attic tomb-stones and Sidon
sarcophagi. Great age of painting and terra-
cottas. Introduction of Corinthian style of architecture, c. 350 B.C.

5. **The Hellenistic Age, 320-100 B.C.**—Death
of Alexander the Great, 323 B.C. Spread of
Hellenistic culture throughout the East. Schools
of Rhodes and Pergamum.

Architecture—The earliest form of Greek temple
consisted of an open-air altar ; the second of a building
in the form of cell roofed with overhanging stones ; the
third was made of unbaked brick, with wooden columns
and a wooden roof ; while as a final development, influenced
by the Egyptian temple, came the famous stone buildings
of the Doric and Ionic orders.

A Doric temple consisted of three main parts: the interior chamber or *cella,* the vestibule or porch, and, at a later date, an outer colonnade. The pillars were ornamented with sharply edged flutings ; they rose straight from the ground, and had plain capitals or top blocks. The Ionic temple was built on the same plan, but usually had no colonnade, and instead was ornamented by a portico of pillars at one or both ends. Its columns were slender, and their flutings were blunted ; they rose from bases and had capitals ornamented with *volutes,* or curved shapes like rams' horns. There was also a third form of building, the Corinthian temple, the columns of which had capitals decorated with acanthus leaves, but this was a later form chiefly used by the Romans.

Greek temples emphasized the national love of lucidity and purity of style. Everything superfluous was removed from them, and only the essentials of noble architecture were left. But this harmony and apparent simplicity was the result of delicate and subtle calculation. Fergusson has remarked that the sensitiveness of a Greek's vision was equivalent to a new sense. This opinion was evoked by the results of some measurements of the Parthenon, which showed that any possibility of monotony or false effect in the building was avoided by a series of irregularities, unnoticeable in themselves, but of the most subtle architectural importance. For example, corner stones were slightly enlarged, pillars were made to swell a little, midway between top and bottom ; platforms and flights of steps were imperceptibly curved ; and columns were of not quite equal height, and were separated by unequal distances.

Greek temples, like those of Egypt and Assyria, were not used as places of assembly for worshippers, but were intended as special shrines for the gods, and sometimes as

treasuries. They were generally surrounded by sacred
enclosures, containing lesser buildings, altars, and dedicatory statues. Inside they were dim and mysterious, as
the only light that could penetrate came through the main
entrance, or by faint infiltration through thin slabs of
marble in the roof.

The Greek built fine gymnasia for their athletic contests, open-air theatres, *agoræ*, or open places of public
assembly surrounded by colonnades, entrance gateways, or
propylæa, and many lesser forms of buildings, but it is the
temple that is the supreme triumph of Greek architecture.
When building a temple, the Greek architect put on one
side all transient thoughts and all reflections of everyday
life, and concentrated his art on the expression of an
eternal principle of life, the worship of an unseen god. His
architecture is severe, intellectual, full of repose, and of an
austere and serene beauty, and has been the ruling force
in architectural design until the present day.

Sculpture—Greek sculpture, as has already been
stated, was the outcome of Greek religion, and owed much
of its excellence to the importance the people attached to
bodily perfection and the subsequent popularity of the
national games. The country was rich in possession of
beautiful marbles, of fine quality, particularly those from
the islands of Paros and Naxos, and from the quarry of
Pentelicus. The latter marble, which was used almost
exclusively by the Attic sculptors, contained a certain
amount of iron in its composition, which gave to temples
and statues that had been exposed to the weather an
exquisite golden tint.

Sculpture was frequently painted, although no attempt
was made to create the illusion of living form. A conventionalized scheme of colour was preferred, and marble
statues were seldom completely painted, the colour being

reserved instead for the details of the statue and applied within strictly artistic limits. Bronze statues were often gilded. Decorative temple sculpture, which was more frequently painted, falls into four principal groups : (1) The Doric frieze, consisting of alternate grooved blocks (triglyphs), and plain slabs (metopes), decorated with sculptured reliefs, the whole forming a frieze above the outer colonnade ; (2) the Ionic frieze, which decorated the top of the inner plain wall, and which consisted of an uninterrupted band of sculpture ; (3) the decorations of the pediments, or triangular gables, at each end of the temple ; (4) the *acroteria*, which were ornaments, or statues, placed on the roof of the temple, above the pediments. The Parthenon is an example of a temple containing both the Doric and Ionic frieze. Primitive Greek statues were usually made of wood, but in later centuries bronze and marble were the chief materials used by Greek sculptors. There were also famous statues made with a wooden core, which was overlaid with gold and ivory, and had sometimes the addition of marble for the nude portions. The great statues of Zeus and Athena, by Phidias, were made in this way.

In forming an estimate of Greek sculpture it must be borne in mind that original works are rare in comparison with copies. The Hermes of Praxiteles is the only known example of an original statue by one of the eight greatest of the Greek masters, and for the rest we are forced to be content with copies, either the few which are early or contemporary, or the vast majority which are inferior works of the Hellenistic or Græco-Roman period.[1] We have, however, a number of fine originals,

---

[1] As we have no knowledge of the exact part taken by Phidias in the execution of the Parthenon sculptures, we cannot attribute any individual work to him.

the authors of which are unknown, and also early statues which were evidently produced under the influence of a great master's style. There is also much fine architectural sculpture still remaining.

Even the fine originals and copies that have escaped destruction have often been half ruined by a process of so-called restoration, when treatment with acids has completely defaced the beauty of their surfaces. There are also a great number of statues produced in the Græco-Roman age which did not profess to copy any one original, but instead to reproduce an earlier type of sculpture. These are often very cleverly executed and may easily deceive the amateur. The best comment on originals and copies, and one to be recommended to all who advance the opinion that Greek art is dull and insipid and lacking in individuality, is the reproductions on the opposite page, which speak for themselves.

The following is a short sketch of the chief periods of Greek art and of the work of the most famous sculptors :—

FIRST AND SECOND PERIODS

The rapid development of Greek sculpture has no parallel in the history of art. Up to the beginning of the year 600 B.C. votive figures showed only small resemblance to the human form, but after that period a change soon made itself felt. The Oriental influence of Egypt and Assyria was gradually absorbed, and sculptures reminiscent of Eastern work, but original in character, were produced. The growing popularity of athletic contests led sculptors to a fresh observation of the human form and greatly influenced the schools of Argos and Sicyon. As a result of increased technical skill the figures of the gods and goddesses soon were

PLATE XIV

GRÆCO-ROMAN COPY OF MELEAGER. VATICAN, ROME

HEAD OF MELEAGER. VILLA MEDICI, ROME
BY, OR AFTER, SCOPAS. (FOURTH CENTURY, B.C.)

made more attractive and life-like in appearance, to the delight of a people who believed that unless a statue were beautiful, the deity might not care to inhabit it.

These early statues have not any very pronounced individualities, and it is often impossible to tell whether a certain type of male figure, which is frequently met with in early art, represents an athlete or the god Apollo. A smile that is often a grin is also characteristic of the figure sculpture of the sixth century, and probably represents the effort to give life or benignity to the face. Another characteristic is the way in which the eyes are often treated, for in the effort to give to them their true effect their lines were exaggerated, and were rendered in a staring and prominent manner. Towards the end of the sixth century some fine and dignified work was produced, somewhat rigid and severe in treatment, but holding the promise of beauty as yet unborn. An example of the sculpture of this time is found in the "Harpy Tomb" from Xanthus, in Lycia, which may be considered an early work by a Greek artist. It dates from about the year 520. B.C.

THIRD PERIOD

With the fifth century we come to the great period of Greek art and literature. The wars with the Persians had called out all the self-sacrifice, courage and endurance of the people and had united them in a tremendous effort to secure, not each his own personal triumph, but the triumph of Greece. It was an age when the people had a profound faith in their gods who had succoured and preserved them. Intellects were keen as swords and minds were filled with a vision of a life of perfect harmony, free from all exaggeration, when body and soul should

be developed for a common end. National aspiration
was voiced by Plato in his prayer, "Give me beauty in
the inward soul, and may the outer and inward man be
at one."[1]

The art of the fifth century was the expression of these
ideals. It was calculated to illumine human thought and
not merely to reflect the passing life that gave it birth.
It contained an appeal, not for the moment, but for all
time. All that was intrinsically worthy it sought to
express with simplicity and truth. It was an impersonal
art and followed the highest conception of a type rather
than an actual human representation. Pliny tells us that
until an athlete had been a victor three times his features
were not represented in his votive statue, and those of
the traditional type of athlete took their place, while in
the same way the bust of Pericles, by Cresilas, shows
rather the head of an ideal ruler than the actual portrait
of the man. The so-called ideal types were of the
greatest power and force, and were both minutely observed
and highly differentiated, but they did not stoop to immortalize the transitory likeness of a single individual.
Cicero tells us that Phidias "when he was making the
statue of Zeus or of Athena did not derive his image from
some individual, but within his own mind there was a
perfect ideal of beauty, and gazing on this, and in contemplation of it, he guided the craft of his hand after its
likeness."

The spirit in which Greek art of this period was conceived is best illustrated by two quotations from Plato :—
"Must it then be only with our poets that we insist they
shall create for us the image of a noble morality, or
among us create none? Or shall we not keep guard over
all the workers for the people and forbid them to make

[1] *Phædrus*. Jowett's translation. Clarendon Press.

what is ill-customed, and unrestrained and ungentle—
either in likeness of living things, or in buildings, or in
any other thing whatsoever that is made for the people?
And shall we not rather seek for workers who can trace
the inner nature of all that may be sweetly schemed; so
that the young men, as living in a wholesome place, may be
profited by everything, in work fairly wrought, may teach
them through hearing and sight—as it were a breeze
bringing health to them from places strong with life."[1]

The second quotation is taken from a glorification of
inspiration or the divine madness of the spirit. "The
third kind is the madness of those who are possessed with
the Muses; which taking hold of a delicate and virgin
soul, and there inspiring frenzy, awakens lyrical and all
other numbers; with these adorning the myriad actions
of ancient heroes for the instruction of posterity. But
he who, having no touch of the Muses' madness in
his soul, comes to the door and thinks he will get into
the temple by the help of art . . . he, I say . . . is not
admitted; the sane man disappears and is nowhere when
he enters into rivalry with the madman. The soul which
has seen most of truth shall come to birth as a philosopher,
or artist, or some musical and loving nature. Thus far I
have been speaking of the beauty of the fourth and last
kind of madness, which is imputed to him who, when he
sees the beauty of the earth, is transported with the
recollection of the true beauty: he would like to fly
away, but he cannot; he is like a bird fluttering and
looking upward, and careless of the world below; and he
is therefore thought to be mad. And I have shown this
of all inspirations to be the noblest and the highest."[2]

The first half of the century constitutes a transitional

[1] *Republic.* Jowett's translation. Clarendon Press.
[2] *Phædrus.* Jowett's translation. Clarendon Press.

period in sculpture, which links up the early sculpture of
archaic form with the more realistic sculpture.   One of
the earliest artistic centres at this time was the school of
sculpture at Ægina.   It produced such work as the
pediment sculptures of the principal temple on the island,
which are now in Munich (casts, British Museum).
Recent excavations on the Acropolis have proved that
an equally important early school must have existed at
Athens, for the sculptures of the first temples have been
found, either as they were thrown to the ground, or else
walled up in the buildings erected during the rebuilding
of the Acropolis.   A great deal of the original colouring
is still to be seen on many of these figures, and they show
how the grin of the archaic heads has been modified and
tempered to a smile of subtle sweetness.   During this
period the Greek sculptors gradually mastered the art of
representing the human figure in a life-like manner, and
we notice that for the first time in the history of art
sculptured figures are no longer bound by the law of
" frontality " (see page 44).

This transitional style is represented by sculptures of
exquisite grace and freshness and by certain masterpieces
of such grave and unforgettable beauty that they stand
high in the history of art.   Perhaps the most famous of
these is the bronze figure of a charioteer, now at Delphi,[1]
while some of the figures from the pediments of the
temple at Olympia show the same noble dignity.   The
so-called Ludovisi Throne, in the National Museum,
Rome, also dates from this period, and many of the most
beautiful of the Greek vase paintings.

The most famous sculptors of this time were **Pythagoras of Rhegium, Calamis,** and **Myron** of Athens,
who were at the height of their powers between the years

[1] See frontispiece.

480-440 B.C., that is, between the sack of the Acropolis
and the eve of the dedication of the Parthenon. Unfortunately all work of the two former sculptors has been
lost, and we have not even a copy to echo, however
faintly, the beauty of the lost originals. Pythagoras was
a sculptor of Olympic victors, and suggestion has been
made that the so-called Choiseul-Gouffier athlete in the
British Museum is an old copy after one of his lost
originals. Of the masterpieces of Calamis we read most
of the statue of Sosandra, which stood on the side of the
path that led up to the Acropolis and was famous for
" the noble, unconscious smile " of the goddess.

The work of Myron, who came from Eleutheræ in
Bœotia to work in Athens, is better known to us than
that of his two contemporaries, for several marble versions
of his famous statue of the Discobolus (Disk-thrower)
have come down to us. The best copy perhaps is that
in the Palazzo Lancelotti in Rome, and shows the athlete
at the instant when he pauses with hand outstretched
before the throw. The statue is a wonderful study of
violent action, checked for an instant, and immortalized,
and is a great technical achievement for so early a date.
A second statue, which probably is a copy after another
original, is the statue of Marsyas, a satyr, in the Lateran
in Rome, representing him as he draws back suddenly at
the sight of the goddess Athena. The great sculptors
who followed Myron were Phidias and Polyclitus.

Phidias, considered the greatest of the Greek
sculptors, was born in Athens about the year 500 B.C.
He is said to have studied painting, and to have learnt
his sculptor's art at the school of Ageladas of Argos,
famous for its bronze work and mastery over form. His
youth was spent during the stirring times of the Persian
wars. As a small boy he would hear of the great Greek

victory at Marathon, and later it is very probable that he
fought for his country at Salamis and Platea. Of this,
however, there is no record. His first work for the
Athenians was probably executed during the political
supremacy of Cimon, which began about the year 470 B.C.
It was at this time that he made the colossal bronze
figure of Athena which stood on the Acropolis. So great
was its height—some 70 feet including the pedestal—that
from far out at sea the golden point of the goddess's spear
could be seen by the sailors as it glittered in the sunshine.

When the last of the Persians had been driven out of
Greece the time was ripe for a pæan of praise and thanksgiving, and to Phidias and Pericles we owe the immortal
form in which it crystallized. Nothing was wanting,
neither the inspiration, the organization, the money, nor
the master hand and mind. The Athenians yielded to
Pericles the entire direction of his scheme ; the spending
of the vast wealth of the Delian league, and the treasure
that formed the spoil of the wars. The Acropolis hill,
devastated by the Persians, was levelled and banked up,
and in less than twenty years had become not only the
splendid sanctuary of the gods, but also a national
museum of Greek art at its greatest.

There is no record of the exact part taken by Phidias
in the work of the Acropolis. We know that the general
conception and artistic scheme of the buildings were his
and that he supervised and directed all the work for
Pericles, but except for the great statue of Athena which
the master made for the Parthenon, we do not know if
any of the sculptures are by his hand. This is the
account given by Plutarch. " As the buildings rose, stately
in size and unsurpassed in form and grace, the workmen
vied with each other that the quality of the work might
be enhanced by its artistic beauty. Most wonderful of

PLATE XV

HORSEMEN FROM THE PARTHENON FRIEZE

all was the rapidity of construction. Pheidias managed everything and was his (Pericles') overseer in all the work."[1]

Ictinus was the architect of the Parthenon, and the skill of many hands is displayed in its sculptures, which consisted of a frieze of over 520 feet in length, fifty colossal figures belonging to the pediments, and about ninety sculptured metopes. Needless to remark, no one man could have designed the whole of these works in detail, and their execution must have been entrusted to a number of workmen, but we know that the spirit of the work belongs to Phidias alone and that he may himself have undertaken the execution of some of the most important figures.

The most famous works of Phidias were the statues of Athena Parthenos at Athens, already mentioned, and the statue of Zeus at Olympia. The former statue repre-sented the goddess as a majestic standing figure, fully armed, her hand resting upon a shield. It embodied the worship of the Athenians for the great goddess who symbolized the Attic genius, and to whose protection they attributed their victory.

The statue of Zeus, the supreme god of all the Hellenes, was probably commissioned at a slightly later date, and represented the son of Cronos as seated on his throne, crowned with a wreath of olive. The story runs that on being asked what conception of the god was to be followed, the sculptor answered by repeating the lines of Homer : "So spake the son of Cronos and nodded his dark brow, and the ambrosial locks waved from the King's undying head, and he made great Olympus to quake." No work of art has received such supreme and reverent praise as was awarded to this statue. Quintilian spoke of it as one " whose beauty seems . . . to have added something to the received religion, so adequate to the

[1] *Select Passages from Ancient Writers.* Stewart Jones. Macmillan.

divine nature is the grandeur of his work."[1]   This is the account of Dion Chrysostom. " If there be any mortal whatsoever that is heavy-laden in spirit, having suffered sorely many sorrows and calamities in his life, nor yet winning for himself sweet sleep ; even such a one, methinks, standing before the image of the god, would forget all things whatsoever in his mortal life were dire, and hard to be endured, so wonderfully hast thou, Phidias, conceived and wrought it, and such light and such grace shines upon it from thine art."

These statues were of great height and were made of gold and ivory laid upon a wooden core. This may seem to us a curious method of sculpture, but we may be sure that no work of Phidias could be other than of great beauty. It must also be remembered that statues made in this manner were designed for the *cellæ* of the temples, where their richness would gain in effect by the subdued light.

Both these masterpieces of Phidias' have perished, and also his early bronze statue of Athena and a third version of the goddess, known as the Lemnian Athena, which was also executed for the Acropolis, and was said by many to be the most beautiful of all. The general design of the Athena Parthenos is preserved for us in some small and very inferior versions in Athens and Madrid, and a copy of her shield known as the " Strangford shield " is in the British Museum. (The figure of a middle-aged, bald-headed man raising his sword above his head is said to represent the sculptor himself, and the whole design of the relief may be reminiscent of his share of the Persian wars.) A copy in Dresden and a fine marble head in Bologna are said to represent the Lemnian Athena, but there are no statues that preserve to us with

[1] *Select Passages from Ancient Writers.*   Stewart Jones.   Macmillan.

any exactitude the design of the Zeus or the early bronze Athena. On the other hand, all representations of Zeus that date from the second half of the fifth century are to a great extent inspired by the version of Phidias.

Clouds rest upon the last years of the master. Tradition says that political enemies of Pericles, and others jealous of the great sculptor's fame, charged him with embezzling some of the gold that was entrusted to him for the making of the Athena Parthenos. This charge he was able to confute by weighing the gold armour of the goddess, which he had had the foresight to make detachable. He was also accused of profanation, having introduced portraits of himself and Pericles on the shield of the goddess. Other accounts state respectively that he was exiled from Athens, was poisoned, and was put to death in prison. It is impossible to test the truth of these statements, but we can only conclude that his life ended in trouble. Although all original works by his hand have been lost, his fame is immortalized in the Parthenon and its sculptures. From them we can learn the perfect harmony that existed between the inspiration and realization of his ideals, and his unrivalled genius in grouping and design. His art, like all the great art of Greece, can bear the test of mutilation, and even fragments are in themselves beautiful. Phidias would stand a dim, uncertain figure among the ranks of the past, were it not for the living spirit that quickens in his marbles. In the words of Cicero and of Plutarch—"There blooms upon them a certain freshness untouched by time, as if there dwelt in them an ever-animating spirit, a life that never grows old." "There dwelt in his mind a certain idea of surpassing beauty, the sight and intense contemplation of which directed his art and hand to produce a similitude of it."

Polyclitus, who grew to be the head of the famous Argive school of sculpture, was ranked with Phidias as one of the two greatest sculptors of the age. He excelled in making statues of athletes, and in his statue of the Doryphorus (or Spear Bearer), which became known as the "Canon," he embodied his ideal of male proportions, an ideal which set the standard until the time of Lysippus. A heavy and mechanical marble copy of this statue is preserved in the Naples Museum, while in the British Museum we have a copy of the Diadumenus, a youth binding a sacred fillet round his brow before receiving the victor's wreath. A third statue by Polyclitus is represented by various figures of Amazons, the most famous of which is in the Vatican Rome.

FOURTH PERIOD

The fourth century witnessed a change in art. It has been called the psychological period of Greek Art, as opposed to the ethical period of the fifth century. The Greeks were no longer united against a common enemy, but were engaged in incessant wars with each other. A feeling for individuality had grown up as opposed to the former devotion to the State, and a greater luxury had taken the place of the former simplicity of living. Work was undertaken for individuals rather than for the State, and although the people still worshipped their gods it was not with the old passion of faith. Whereas the deities were formerly represented as seated or standing, omnipotent and majestic, they were now for the first time depicted rather as human beings than as immortals, engaged in some action or conscious of the spectator. Models were used for their production, and the art of portraiture began

to be practised. It must not be thought that these
changes resulted in an art other than great. It is true
that the splendid austerity of fifth century art had gone,
never to be recaptured, but very fine work was still
produced, work full of a mellow loveliness, and charged
with an emotional force and a dramatic intensity of
expression that illuminated, but never transgressed, the
inherent Greek love of harmony and control.

The most famous sculptors of the fourth century were
Scopas, Praxiteles, and Lysippus. **Scopas**, who was
perhaps the greatest of them, excelled in his power of
depicting a passionate and fiery spirit. His work was
dramatic and full of intensity, but was never contorted
or theatrical. We do not know if any originals by his
hand still exist. There is an antique Greek head placed
on a statue of Meleager in the Medici Gardens, Rome,
which may be by him, but is more probably a close
study in his style, and there are also some heads from
Tegea which, though much mutilated, bear the impress
of his genius. We know that he was working on the
tomb of Mausolus, Prince of Caria, in the year 351 B.C.,
but this work was shared by three other sculptors, and
we cannot tell if any of the broken sculptures in the
British Museum, which represent all that is left of this
famous mausoleum, are the work of the master. One, a
small relief of a charioteer, is so beautiful that we may
well imagine this to be the case. The drum of a column
from the temple of Ephesus, also in the British Museum,
is either by him or shows his influence, and the beautiful
statue of Demeter, in a small ante-room near by, could
not have been produced had he not lived.

The work of **Praxiteles** was more admired by the
Greeks and Romans than that of any other sculptor.
The result of this was that an enormous number of

copies of his statues were made, and were it not for the
discovery of the Hermes at Olympia, we should find it
very difficult to make an exact estimate of his work.
The Hermes was found buried under the earth on the
spot where it fell nearly two thousand years ago. It is
the only instance of a Greek original straight from the
hand of an identified master, and although it was considered an inferior work of Praxiteles, it reveals all his
power of transmitting to marble a sensuous beauty and
grace. The most famous copies of lost originals by
Praxiteles are the Aphrodite of Cnidus, the " Apollo
with the lizard," at the Vatican, and the Satyr or Faun
in the Capitoline Museum. All these works, however,
betray an over-sweetness which would not have been
found in the originals.

Lysippus was the most prolific of the Greek sculptors. He is said to have produced over a thousand works,
but as they were almost all of bronze, we have a
reason for the disappearance of so large a number. He
began life as a bronze founder, but soon rose to be the
chief genius of the Sicyonian school. His work was the
result of a close study of nature, combined with a great
reverence for the work of the masters that had gone
before him. In his own words, he was said to have
reproduced men "not as they are, but as they appear to
the eye," which represents an extraordinarily modern
point of view. His work was characterized by a strength
and severity of type which is in strong contrast to the
more sensuous charms of the sculpture of Praxiteles.
Lysippus was the favourite sculptor of Alexander the
Great, whom he served in the latter part of his life, and
in this way he stands between the older art of Greece
and the newer art of the Hellenistic period. He made
many portraits of the emperor, whose head became a type

for contemporary sculpture. We are able to form an estimate of the work of Lysippus by the recent discovery of the fine statue of Agias at Delphi. The original was no doubt cast in bronze, but this version appears to be a marble replica, which, if not by the master's hand, was probably executed in his workshop under his direct supervision. A copy of his statue of the Apoxyomenus, or man with a scraper, which constituted the sculptor's canon of art, is one of the treasures of the Vatican. It shows an athlete in the act of scraping off the sand and oil after an athletic contest. Lysippus executed statues that varied in height from sixty feet to several inches. A small and very beautiful bronze statuette in the British Museum, representing a seated figure, may be from his hand.

Among fine fourth century work, two different branches of the sculptor's art may be mentioned. One is represented by a series of marble sarcophagi found at Sidon, which are probably the work of a pupil of Lysippus, and which show, in one instance, the hunting scenes of Alexander; the other by some gravestones dug up in the old cemetery at Athens, and decorated with dignified and beautiful figures that point to their being the work of craftsmen who had been trained in the school of the Acropolis.

FIFTH PERIOD

With the conquests of Alexander, Greek art acquired new characteristics. Wherever the great general conquered an ancient city or established a new one, there he left Greek sculptors and craftsmen behind him. In this way the art of Greece, which had already begun to be known in other countries, was spread still further to far

distant quarters of the globe, where it grew to be a
powerful influence on the local schools of art. As
examples of work influenced in this way, we have the
Buddhist sculptures of North India and China, and the
Græco-Egyptian heads from Alexandria.

These new and foreign influences also reacted upon
Greek art itself. It became more cosmopolitan. Statues
full of charm and sweetness were produced, but the
old characteristics of repose, strength, and dignity had
vanished. Sometimes we find them partially recaptured, as, for example, in such fine statues as the
Aphrodite of Melos, known as Venus of Milo (probably
a work of the second century B.C.), and the Victory of
Samothrace, which was set up to commemorate a victory
at sea in the year 306 B.C., and which is also preserved
in the Louvre. But these works are only echoes of
former ideals, and the most important centres of art
during the Hellenistic age were the schools of Pergamum
in Asia Minor and the island of Rhodes. These schools
produced works which, though full of strength and vigour,
were theatrical and sensational in type, and lacked all
feeling of repose, as is shown in the famous altar of
Pergamum, now in Berlin, and in such figures as the
Laocoon in Rome and the Farnese Bull at Naples. A
number of religious sculptures were produced by these
schools, but we find in them no assurance of faith, but
rather an interested attempt to reconstruct old myths.

During the Hellenistic age many fine portrait busts
were produced. Up to this time portrait sculptures were
largely idealistic in character, and were generally represented by whole-length figures or else by *herms*, which
were plain, squarely-shaped pillars with the tops carved
into the forms of heads. The Hellenistic portraits, on
the other hand, generally took the form of busts, and

PLATE XVI

BUST OF EUTHYDEMOS I OF BACTRIA
REALISTIC WORK OF THE HELLENISTIC AGE. (C. 200 B.C.)

HEAD OF AGIAS
IDEALISTIC WORK OF THE FOURTH CENTURY B.C.
(PROBABLY A CONTEMPORARY COPY AFTER AN ORIGINAL BY LYSIPPUS)

TYPES OF GREEK PORTRAITS

were works of great vigour and realism, dominated by
the individuality of the subject (see Plate XVI.).

The Greek colony of Alexandria, founded in 332 B.C.,
also possessed a flourishing school of art.   The sculptured
reliefs that were characteristic of this school reflected
the pastoral poetry that was then popular, and were
something in the nature of *genre* pictures in stone, while
a second form of art that became popular there was
the naturalistic sculpture of children, until then seldom
attempted.

Mention must also be made of the Hellenic kingdom
of the Seleucids, the Macedonian dynasty which ruled
in Syria, Mesopotamia, and the surrounding countries after
the death of Alexander.   Their capital of Seleukia, built
where the Tigris and Euphrates converged, has been
called "the descendant of ancient Babylon and the
precursor of Baghdad."   Here the Seleucids ruled from
the year 312 B.C. until after the year 130 B.C., and here
Greek art and the art of the East met.   In the words of
Miss Gertrude Bell : " In the flux and reflux of civilization,
Seleukia has been fixed upon as the crucible into which
East and West alike threw their gold—the fertile mint
from which a coinage of artistic forms and conceptions
flowed to the furthest limits of Asia and Europe."   A
second great centre of Græco-Oriental culture was Antioch,
the later capital of the Seleucid kingdom of Syria, and
one of the most famous cities of the Near East.   As an
example of the art produced during this period, we have
the fine bust of Antiochus III., the greatest of the Seleucids,
which is now in the Louvre.

The account of the influence of Greek sculpture upon
the art of the Romans will be found in the next lesson.
It was this Græco-Roman art which produced most of the
copies and imitations of ancient statues, including such

affected and theatrical works as the Medici Venus of the Uffizi and the Apollo Belvedere of the Vatican.

Painting—The ancient classic writers have much to say on the beauty of Greek painting, but all traces of the great work that was produced have disappeared. Beyond a few scattered specimens of minor work, we have to rely for our knowledge on what information we can get from three sources. These are the painted Greek vases and stelai (tombstones), the Græco-Roman and Etruscan wall paintings, and the portraits on Egyptian mummy cases, which chiefly date from Roman times. From these sources we have to form an estimate of what must have been a very great art.

We know that a school of painting was in full vigour in Ionia towards the end of the eighth century B.C., and that some fine painted sarcophagi were produced there between the years 600-500 B.C. (a fine example is in the British Museum); but it was not until the fifth century that we hear of the first great Greek painter, Polygnotos. He executed large wall paintings of a monumental character, such as the "Painted Porch" at Athens and the loggia at Delphi, and we are told that he freed art from its ancient rigidity and in this way gave the lead to the sculptors. His work probably consisted in line drawings, washed in with colour, and there is no doubt that it had the splendid qualities that marked the art of this age. A second great painter, who followed Polygnotos, was Apollodorus, who introduced effects of light and shade, and aimed at painting men "as they seemed to be."

During the fourth century a great advance in technique and *chiaroscuro* was shown, and easel painting became popular. Famous painters of this period were Zeuxis (420-380 B.C.), who came from Heraclea, a Greek colony in South Italy, and settled in Ephesus; and Apelles, probably an Ionian-Greek from Asia Minor, who became the favourite painter of Alexander. They painted both historical and mythological subjects, and their work no doubt reflected the ideals of the day, showing the same characteristics that were evident in contemporary sculpture. There were many other famous Greek painters, but very little is known of them.

Vase Painting—The great majority of painted Greek vases have been found in the tombs, although a certain number have been discovered, in a more or less broken condition, on temple sites. The latter were no doubt used as votive offerings for the gods, but there is more uncertainty as to the purpose for which the tomb vases were made. Some were evidently designed for funeral purposes only, and having been filled with fragrant perfume and sweet oil and placed near the corpse, were then buried in the tomb for use in a future existence. Others again were objects of household use, or were given as presents or as prizes in the Pan-Athenaic games.

Among the most familiar types of Greek vases are the *amphora*, or double-handed vase, for water or for storing food or wine ; the *krater*, or mixing bowl ; the *kylix*, or shallow two-handled goblet ; and the *lekythos*, or tall vase with a narrow neck, used for holding oil.

The early vases, dating from the end of the seventh and a greater part of the sixth century B.C., were painted with black figures on a red or cream-coloured ground. The subjects were generally drawn from mythology and the epic poets. Towards the end of the sixth century new methods were introduced, and during the fifth century the figures were left to stand out in the natural red colour of the clay, against a black glazed background, or were painted in polychrome, against a white background. The subjects were varied, and reflected every phase of Attic life ; the decoration showed a highly developed sense of composition and linear design, and the art reached the height of its perfection. The decay of the Athenian potteries took place at the close of the fifth century, and the production of red-figure vases passed to other places, especially to the Greek colonies in Southern Italy and Sicily. The art never again reached its former high standard of beauty.

Terra-cottas—The making of terra-cotta statuettes was an art of very early origin in Greece, and during the fourth and third centuries B.C. attained great popularity. Numberless small statuettes were produced and were buried in the tombs for the use of the dead, in place of more elaborate offerings, or else perhaps were put there as votive offerings for the gods. This habit became so popular that it seems probable that the statuettes came to be regarded as a usual form of grave furniture, without any particular religious significance. The cemeteries of Tanagra in Bœotia, as well as many others in different parts of Greece, have yielded an immense number of these statuettes. They are delicately coloured, full of charm and grace, and are strongly reminiscent of the style of Praxiteles. It is possible that they were sometimes used as household ornaments before their burial in the tombs, or else as votive offerings to be placed in shrines. They are very varied in subject, and scenes and figures from everyday life and figures of deities are frequently met with.

Coins and engraved gems must also be mentioned, as under the skilful hands of the Greeks their production was raised to a fine art, testified to by the many beautiful specimens preserved in the national museums.

Extracts

" The faithful, immortal, anointed, adored,
Dear city of men, without master or lord,
Fair fortress and fostress of sons born free,
Who stand in her sight and in thine, O Sun,
Slaves of no man, subjects of none.
A wonder enthroned on the hills to the sea,
A maiden crowned with a fourfold glory,
That none from the pride of her head may rend ;
Violet and olive-leaf, purple and hoary,
Song-wreath and story, the fairest of fame,
Flowers that winter can blast not nor bend,
A light upon earth as the sun's own flame,
A name as his name—
Athens, a praise without end."

SWINBURNE, *Erechtheus*.

LESSON IX

ROMAN ART

PART I.—ELEMENTARY LESSON IN STORY FORM

INTRODUCTION—Last Lesson—A time came when the Greeks were no longer the greatest nation in the world. Their country was conquered by the Romans, a people who lived in Italy and who became as powerful as the Greeks had been, and established a great empire that stretched from Great Britain to Mesopotamia. This is a story about a Roman boy.

1. **The Portrait Bust**—One morning there was much bustle and confusion in a sculptor's workshop in Rome. The sculptor himself was heated and busy, giving orders to his assistant, and superintending the work of his son, who was occupied in putting the room into something like order. On every side there were blocks of stone and marble; chisels and hammers lay in confusion among chippings of stone and marble dust, while various statues, some only roughly hewn, and others nearing completion, stood about the shed. The sunshine streamed in at the open door and windows, and the dust that rose in clouds with the boy's vigorous brushing seemed to quiver and dance in the rays of sunlight that fell in broad strips across the threshold.

"By Jupiter, but it is hot!" exclaimed the sculptor, mopping his brow, and turning to the young Greek who helped him in his work. "You get on with your copy of my old Greek statue in case it may take the fancy of our visitor when he arrives; leave me and the boy to finish

the rest." The father and son dragged the sculptures
about, and had hardly got several cleverly executed
portrait busts into a good position before a clatter of
wheels was heard outside and a carriage was pulled up by
its driver so suddenly that the horses were nearly pulled
back on their haunches. Throwing the reins to a servant,
a young man leapt to the ground and entered the shop.
He was Titus, the son of a famous Roman general called
Vespasian, and a favourite of the Emperor himself, in whose
palace he lived.

The sculptor and his son and the young Greek bowed
low before Titus while he began to examine the sculptures.
" I have heard of your skill," he said to the sculptor,
" and I have come to see for myself what you can do.
If your work pleases me you shall make my portrait ;
now tell me which is your work, and which is the work
of your young Greek here, for in these days the work
of Greek and Roman is so alike that it is hard to tell
one from the other." The sculptor pointed out the
copies of famous Greek statues made by his assistant ;
" but here you have my own work," he added proudly,
pointing to the row of portrait busts. " Ah, the portraits,"
answered the young soldier, examining them carefully.
" Yes, this is the art in which we Romans excel. I see
that you have great talent. You shall start work upon
my portrait to-morrow."

The sculptor beamed with pleasure and again bowed
low. With a commission from Titus his way was indeed
made. In the meantime the sculptor's son had been
making himself useful, moving the sculptures into a good
light and placing a chair for Titus when necessary, while
his eyes rested with undisguised admiration upon the
fine visitor, who was a popular and well-known member
of the Emperor's household. The boy himself was an

attractive figure, with his open, honest face, bright eyes and sturdy limbs, and the young soldier glanced keenly at him several times. What are you going to do with yourself?" he asked him suddenly; "are you going to be a sculptor like your father?" The boy shook his head. "I want to travel and see the world," he said eagerly. "Then you will just do for me," answered Titus, looking at him kindly. "I am off directly to fight in our distant provinces, and I need a new boy among my personal servants. I like the look of you; will you come?" The boy flushed crimson with surprise and delight, and the father bowed his thanks at the honour afforded to his son, although in his heart he was filled with sorrow at the thought of losing him.

Soon after the visitor took his leave, and the next day a block of marble, and clay for a first model, were sent up to the palace and the sculptor began to make the portrait of Titus. Each day the work was continued, until the head was finished, and a second Titus lived in the marble, a Titus with the same low and prematurely lined brow, the same full curved lips, and the same short, thick, curly hair.

2. Britain—The day came when Titus set off with his legion to serve in the provinces, and with him went the sculptor's son, sad at parting with his parents, yet wild with excitement at the thought of the adventures that lay before him. Then followed months of journeyings, long marches and nights under the stars, and intervals of service in different countries, until at last a time came when the legion was ordered to Britain, a wild and remote island of which the boy had sometimes heard soldiers speak.

It was a cold and windy day when the soldiers set sail for the island. Their boats were tossed by the wind, and the boy was drenched to the skin with the flying spray, but though he sat numb and cold, huddled up in a corner, he knew that as a Roman he must be hardy and brave and not complain. At last the shores of Britain came in sight. All that the boy could see through the driving rain was a line of white cliffs, while the waves tossed and broke upon the shores, retreating with a long low rattle of pebbles in their wake. As soon as the boats were near enough to shore, the Roman soldiers leapt into the sea and waded to land. There were strange men on the shore, at whom the boy gazed with interest. Instead of wearing bright shining armour, helmets with plumes, and gleaming breast-plates, and carrying shining shields and sharply-pointed spears, as the Romans did, these strange Britons, who were strong and hardy-looking men with long hair and beards, wore short woven tunics and carried roughly made spears, shields, and bows. The Britons looked with distrust at the newcomers, but did not molest them, for they knew that the Romans were the masters of the southern part of the country and they dare not rebel or they would have been killed.

Then followed long months on the island. Wherever the master went the boy had to follow. Sometimes they passed months in one Roman town, sometimes in another. Sometimes they had to march north, where the country was wild and rugged, and where they went in deadly fear of their lives, for the north of Britain had not been won as the south had been, and there were not only enemies, but wild beasts on every hand. The Romans sheltered in small military camps, and in the long evenings the boy would sit by the fire hugging his knees, listening to the howling of the wolves outside and the moaning of the wind round the walls and towers, and he would wonder if he would ever see again the sunny skies of his beloved Italy, and the shrines and temples of

Rome. Sometimes, when the time hung heavily, he would get pieces of stone, and chip and carve them into figures of men and animals, in the way his father had shown to him, and he would try also to teach a British youth, a slave and camp servant, to do the same. The things that they made were very rough and rude, but they served to pass the time and kept the boys amused.

3. The Conquest of Judea—The years passed, and the boy grew tall and strong. He still served his master, Titus, who was very fond of him and liked to have him near. Titus himself had won fame by his prowess as a soldier, and one day the order came that he was to travel with his legion to other parts of the Empire. So they left the cold northern shores of Britain behind them, and following the great Roman roads they came to other countries, where they served until Titus was ordered to Judea, to join his father Vespasian, the famous Roman general, and help him to quell the insurrection of the Jews. But they had not been long in Judea before the Roman Emperor died, and Vespasian was chosen to be emperor in his place. This meant that he had to leave Judea and fulfil his duties as Emperor elsewhere. So Titus was left as the head of the army, to finish the conquest of the Jews by himself. He decided to march upon Jerusalem, the capital of the country, and soon the Roman army was encamped under the walls of the town, which stood high on a hill above them, defended on three sides by impregnable rocks.

The night before the assault Titus strode up and down before his camp fire, deep in thought, and busy planning the next day's assault. His generals came and went, consulting with him as to the best plan of attack, while by the door of his master's tent the boy polished the shining armour of Titus and his bright spear and shield. He

felt sorry for the Jews. He wished that Titus would
spare them, but he knew that the Romans' ideal was to
have a great empire and that they would never allow
their subjects to rebel.

Night fell, and the clamour of the camp died away.
The glow of the fires lit up the inanimate figures of the
soldiers, stretched on the ground, sleeping heavily. The
watchmen passed to and fro, their steady tread breaking
the stillness. Here and there in the town above a light
burnt. The boy slept.

The camp was astir with the dawn, and in the
early morning the siege began. But the Jews fought
stubbornly, and the task of Titus was no easy one.
Week after week passed, and first one and then another
of the city's defences were taken. The poor Jews suffered
terribly, for they had hardly any food, and each day the
great stones, hurled from Roman catapults, battered down
a fresh part of their walls. At last the day came when
the greater number of the Jews felt they could hold out
no longer. They sent a message to Titus asking him if
he would allow them to leave the city in safety, and this
he did, as he did not wish to hurt them. But inside the
walls of the Temple of Solomon there were other Jews
who refused to surrender, so the Roman soldiers threw
burning brands over the walls, and soon a great flame
shot up, and some of the Jews escaped, and some died
fighting, and the capture of the city was complete.

The Roman soldiers rushed into the burning temple
and dragged from the flames the golden candlestick with
its seven branches, which had been carried by the children
of Israel through the wilderness. The victorious army
bore their treasure back with them to Italy, and the
soldiers raised it high on their shoulders when they
entered Rome. The citizens carried it to a resting-place

in one of the great Roman temples, while the air rang
with the blasts of trumpets and the shouts of the people
as they welcomed Titus, the darling of the army, and his
victorious soldiers.

The Colosseum—You can imagine how glad the boy
was to see his parents again. When they first saw him
they could hardly recognize him, for he had grown so big
and strong and was so bronzed and handsome. What
stories he had to tell them! They were never tired
of hearing of his adventures in Britain and Judea,
although they too felt sorry for the poor Jews, who had
lost their beautiful city and their temple and golden
candlestick.

A great number of the Jews who had been taken
prisoner and brought back to Rome were now set to
work upon building a huge amphitheatre or oval building
lined with seats, open to the air above, and with a big
space in the middle where fights were to take place.
The Emperor Vespasian had commanded the building to
be erected, and he and his son Titus, who now shared
with his father the task of governing the great Roman
Empire, used often to drive there in their carriages and
watch how the work was progressing. It was such an
immense and massive building that it took many years to
erect. Before it was finished the Emperor Vespasian had
died, and when it was opened Titus was the Emperor who
took his place on the marble throne under the silken
canopy. When he sat down, and the shouting that
greeted his entrance had died away, what a sight met his
eyes! All around him, tier upon tier, were tens of
thousands of Roman citizens, dressed in their best for the
great occasion. Up above, on the roof of the gallery,
numbers of sailors swayed to and fro the great striped
silk awning that sheltered the people from the burning

PLATE XVII

ROME

a. COLOSSEUM. *b, c.* ARCHES OF CONSTANTINE AND TITUS. *d.* PALATINE HILL (SITE OF PALACE OF THE CÆSARS). *e, f.* FORUM

sun, while the air was full of the perfume of scented water, which was sprayed from the walls. But what was to happen in the arena, the open space in the centre of the building? What had all these people come to see? They had come to see fights, fights of animals and fights of men, and although most of the Romans loved to see such cruel sport, there were some among them who hated it, and the boy, the servant of the Emperor, was one of the first to slip away, vowing that no one, not even his royal master, would make him witness such sights again.

So the boy wandered about the deserted streets outside, while from within the roar of the lions, and the shouts of the great crowd, half mad with excitement, rose and fell continually, now echoing like thunder and then suddenly checked for a tense and sickening moment of silence. When the show was finished for the day, the crowd burst from the huge building like a tide, the people fighting and scrambling as they went for the food that was being distributed on every hand by order of the Emperor Titus, who wished to please the people, and provide a fitting ending to the great day.

5. The Arch of Titus—There was another building in which the Emperor took a great interest, and this was a big triumphal arch which was being erected by the Romans in his honour, and in memory of the capture of Jerusalem. But when he stood before it, watching the men as they set stone on stone, he knew that he would never live to see it finished. He was not yet forty, but he felt a fatal illness creeping upon him, and it was not he but his servant who saw the completion and the solemn dedication of the arch. It was the boy, now a strong and vigorous man, who looked on the carved reliefs that decorated it, and saw the figures of the triumphant citizens bearing the golden candlestick, and of

Titus, seated in his triumphal car, and crowned with laurel by the goddess of Victory.

Notes on the Story—The boy and his actions are imaginary throughout. Busts of Titus are in the British Museum and the Vatican. Paragraph 2.—Imaginary. Titus served both in Britain and Gaul. Paragraph 3.—Capture of Jerusalem by Titus, 71 A.D. Camp scene imaginary. A full description of the siege and of the triumph held on the return of the army to Rome can be found in Josephus' *Antiquities of the Jews.* The writer was an eye-witness of the scenes. The Colosseum was opened in the year 80 A.D. Death of Titus, 81 A.D.

The destruction of Pompeii took place in the year 79 A.D. It could be introduced into the story, and would serve excellently as an introduction to photographs of the excavations, but there is no space in which to include it here.

Titus, who was born in the year 40 A.D., was of a kindly disposition, but was impulsive and luxurious in his habits. He showed unusual clemency for a Roman during the siege and capture of Jerusalem, and was greatly beloved by the army and also by the Roman people after his accession. His reign was one of great extravagance, and at his death he left the Imperial exchequer in a greatly reduced condition.

PART II.—ADDITIONAL MATERIAL FOR ADVANCED LESSONS ONLY

History, Civilization, Empire, etc.

Period of Kings	B.C. 753-509.
Period of Republic	B.C. 509-27.
Period of Empire	B.C. 27-A.D. 305.

The small city-state of Rome was founded by the Latins, a people who occupied the whole region south of the Tiber, and by the Sabines, who lived among the hills near by. These differing tribes of the same race built a common market-place or forum, and became one people. They steadily grew in power, and

not only conquered the entire Italian peninsula, but
founded the vast Roman empire which reached its
furthest limits under the Emperor Trajan (98-117 A.D.),
when Roman rule was extended to such distant outposts
as Britain, North Germany, Gibraltar and North Africa
in the West, and Asia Minor, Mesopotamia, Armenia,
Syria and Egypt in the East. The heart of this great
system was Rome itself, and from it the great Roman
roads spread out, leading to the farthest limits of the
Empire and carrying with them the civilization and
dominion of the great Roman people.

These Romans were a hardy, self-confident race, whose
strenuous and practical character was produced by
continual warfare. It is recorded that the Temple of
Janus in Rome, which was only closed in times of peace,
stood open for a period of six hundred and fifty years
(from Numa to Augustus), except during a short interval
between the first and second Punic wars.

The difference between the Greeks and Romans has
been well described by Mommsen. "That Hellenic
character which sacrificed the whole to its individual
elements, the nation to the single state, and the single
state to the citizen ; whose ideal of life was the beautiful
and the good, and only too often the pleasure of idleness ;
whose political development consisted in intensifying
the original individualism of the several centres, and
subsequently led to the internal dissolution of the
authority of the State ; whose view of religion first
invested the gods with human attributes and then denied
their existence ; which gave full play to the limbs in the
sports of the naked youth, and gave free scope to thought
in all its grandeur and in all its awfulness ; and that
Roman character, which solemnly bound the son to
reverence the father, the citizen to reverence the rules,

and all to reverence the gods; which required nothing and honoured nothing but the useful act, and compelled every citizen to fill up every moment of his life with unceasing work; which made it a duty even in a boy to modestly cover the body, which deemed every citizen a bad citizen who wished to be different from his fellows; which viewed the State as all in all, and a desire for the State's extension as the only aspiration not liable to censure."[1]

During the third century A.D. the power of Rome began to wane, although, during the reign of Diocletian, the glories of the Empire were for a time revived. In the fourth century the Empire was divided by Theodosius into the empires of the East and West. The history of the Eastern or Byzantine Empire will be described in the next lesson. In the West, Ravenna became the Imperial residence in 404 A.D., while a series of disasters ensued in the fifth century. The invasions by northern Germanic tribes, who were sweeping like a tide over the Western Empire, culminated in Italy in 410 A.D., when Rome was sacked by Alaric the Goth. In 455 A.D. the city was sacked once more, this time by Gaiseric, King of the Vandals, after which it stood empty for forty days. Theodoric the Ostrogoth reigned in Italy from the years 493-526 A.D., and after his death, from the year 536-552, a continual warfare raged between the Goths and the Byzantine armies of Justinian. In the year 552 Rome was recaptured by Narses for Justinian, and shortly afterwards the entire peninsula became part of the East Roman or Byzantine empire.

[1] *The History of Rome.* Bentley.

MAIN FACTORS IN ROMAN CIVILIZATION AND ART

A. **Etruscan**—The Etruscans were a branch of the ancient Ægean race. They settled in Italy about the year 1000 B.C., over-ran the region of modern Tuscany, which became known by the name of Etruria, and also conquered Umbria, the districts bordering on Latium, and certain tracts of country in the south of the Peninsula. Little is known of the Etruscans, either of their origin or history. They seem to have had no literature, and numerous inscriptions, chiefly found in the tombs, are all that is known of their language. Their religion seems to have contained a strong Ægean element, and to have been modified by the varying beliefs of the people with whom they came in contact, for although the Etruscans were probably a rich and rather stupid land-owning race, there were also many traders among their number, who introduced foreign ideas to Etruria. The chief Etruscan god was probably Tinia or Tina, the wielder of the thunderbolt, who was worshipped, in association with two goddesses, in all Etruscan cities.

Etruscan art was composed of several different elements. In the work of the earliest period, dating from about 900-800 B.C., the influence of the art of the local indigenous peoples inhabiting the Peninsula is apparent. During the years 800-600 B.C. Etruscan metal work showed a marked improvement, while the presence of early Greek vases in the tombs testifies to the beginning of Etruscan and Greek intercourse. This intercourse had a very great effect upon Etruscan art. Ionian Greeks came to settle in the south of Italy at an early date, and their Etruscan neighbours learnt much from them, largely through the commercial relations established between the two nations.

Etruscan art reached its height during the years 600-300 B.C. It was still markedly Greek in character, although the scarabs, carved ostrich eggs, and objects from the Egyptian delta which have been found in the tombs of this period show that an infiltration of Eastern, as well as Greek influences, must have taken place. The Etruscans had a strong love of realism in art. This showed itself in the portrait work, which is the most noteworthy feature of Etruscan art, a feature which gained a full expression owing to the funeral customs of the people. One of these customs, which was probably derived from the East, consisted at first in shaping the jar for the ashes into a rough semblance of the deceased. Gradually the idea of a vase or urn was lost, and instead a small receptacle was used for the ashes, and was crowned with either a bust of the deceased or his seated figure. A still more popular form was that of a sarcophagus, either small or large, upon which a figure or figures were placed in a reclining position. A characteristic example of Etruscan art is the large sarcophagus from Cervetri, dating from about the year 500 B.C., and now preserved in the British Museum. There are also some beautiful wall paintings in the tombs which date from this period, and are strongly Greek in character, while dating from the fifth century we have some very fine examples of gold jewellery and many good bronzes.

Architectural remains consist almost entirely of walls and gates to cities and tombs, and the foundations and terra-cotta sculptures and enrichments of several temples. In the year 294 B.C. the chief Etruscan towns surrendered to Rome, and towards the end of the third century B.C. Etruscan civilization was merged into that of the all-conquering Roman people, and the Etruscans ceased to be an independent race.

B. **Greek**—Greek influence, already an important factor in Etruscan art, exerted an independent and powerful influence also upon the art of the Romans. From very early times the dwellers on the Tiber had been familiar with the arts of Greece, for Greek colonies bordered Latium on the south, and Greek wares had been dispersed by the Carthaginians. Pliny tells us that in the year 496 B.C. two Greek artists, Damophilus and Gorgasus, helped in the decoration of a temple near the Circus Maximus, while Livy, writing of 186 B.C., speaks of Greek artists fetched from their native lands to prepare the festivals and games decreed by Roman generals.

The story of the conquest of Greece by Rome is illustrated by a series of pictures, tragic to all lovers of art, in which victorious Roman generals tore down the statues from the shrines and the decorations from the temples and public buildings, and bore them back to Rome, not as objects of special beauty, but as symbols of victory and the loot of war. In the life of Paulus Æmilius, Plutarch describes the return of the victorious general from Greece in the year 168 B.C. and the festivities that took place in Rome in his honour. "The triumph took up three days. On the first, which was scarcely sufficient for the Show, were exhibited the images, paintings, and colossal statues taken from the enemy, and now carried in two hundred and fifty waggons." Before this date hundreds, if not thousands, of statues had been brought from Syracuse, Macedonia, and Ætolia, the result of conquests in the years 212, 197 and 187 B.C., and later, in the year 146 B.C., the fall of Corinth served as a signal for a fresh series of lootings, when the most sacred shrines of the gods were not spared, and Athens, Delphi, Epidaurus, and Olympia were stripped of a great number of their treasures, in order that the palaces and gardens of the Roman aristocracy might be ornamented in the current fashion. In the early years of the Empire, Nero is recorded to have carried off five hundred bronze statues from Delphi alone, the greater number of which must have perished in the disastrous fire of his reign. This growing taste for Greek art was deplored by many of the sterner Romans, who felt that the strength of the people lay in conquest and administration. This belief was summed up by Virgil in his well-known lines in the *Æneid* :

> " Others belike, with happier grace
> From bronze or stone shall call the face,
> Plead doubtful causes, map the skies,
> And tell where planets set or rise.
> But Roman, thou, do thou control
> The nations far and wide ;
> Be this thy genius, to impose,
> The rule of peace on vanquished foes,
> Show pity to the humble soul
> And crush the sons of pride." [1]

But Greek art had come to stay, and from being at first a fashion of the moment and a sign of national supremacy, it became the dominating influence in the art of the people. As a result of this popularity a number of Greek artists came to settle in Rome. There was little request for their skill in their own country, which lay wasted and dismantled, while in Italy they found both a ready market for their work and pupils eager to learn the art that was in such great request. There is no doubt that the production of work for a rich and ignorant public had a bad effect upon Greek artists, some of whom turned their art into a mere commercial business, and chiefly occupied themselves with the copying of antique statues and types which soon became property comm on to all.

[1] Conington's translation. Longmans.

Religion—Roman religion was composed of many differing elements, for to the first early beliefs of the city-state were added a multitude of Greek and Oriental ideas, accumulated through years of conquest and intercourse with other nations. The early Romans believed in certain supernatural beings or powers, who were not visualized or defined as creatures of definite sex or appearance, but were supposed to dwell in certain places, persons or objects, and were reverenced as objects of worship. The activities of these deities were eminently practical, and the people were only interested in them in so far as they served them.

These deities were essentially local in character, and were held to inhabit definite places, cities, villages or houses. The Roman farmer believed in Vesta, the spirit of the hearth fire ; in Penates, who guarded his store closet ; in Janus, who guarded his doorway and who was invoked and worshipped daily ; and in the Lar, who watched the boundary of his land. The *paterfamilias* was looked upon as a natural priest and ruler of the family, who had in control the domestic worship.

The State religion was an expansion of this family cult. The King was held to be the father of the State, and held certain sacrificial functions, while the Vestal Virgins guarded the hearth of the State, and kept the sacred fire alight in the temple and near the palace. In later years the King was not only supreme ruler of the State while he lived, but was deified and worshipped after his death, a custom derived in part, no doubt, from Egypt.

In later art, when the gods were represented in human form, the Lar was generally depicted as a youthful male figure, clothed in a tunic, and often with a laurel or jar or bowl of wine in his hand, and with his feet lightly resting on the ground, as if in an attitude for dancing. The

genius, or spiritual embodiment of the father of the family
was usually represented as a male figure in a toga, often
standing between two Lares, and frequently in the act of
pouring a libation from a horn. This genius was also
supposed to take the form of a snake, representations
of which are frequently met with in Etruscan tombs.
Romans also believed that the spirits of the dead, on a
certain day of the year, were allowed to revisit the earth,
after the removal of a large stone, which was supposed to
keep them underground.

During the Republic a number of deities were worshipped,
both Greek and Roman in character. The chief gods
were Jupiter, the god of lightning, the " best and greatest,"
who had been known as Tinia, or Tina, by the Etruscans,
and Mars, the god of war, who was connected also
with the harvesting of crops and with growth. With
Jupiter was associated the goddess Juno, the special protectress of women. The goddess Minerva was also
Etruscan in origin, and was connected with the art of
wind instruments. Hercules and Apollo were among the
most famous of Latin deities, and also Ceres, Venus, and
Mercurius, identified later with the Greek goddesses
and god, Demeter, Aphrodite, and Hermes. Among the
principal Oriental deities who became popular during the
Empire were Serapis, Isis and Mithras. Serapis was
generally represented like the Greek god, but was marked
by a cylindrical head-dress, or *polus*, while Isis, beloved
by women because of her grief for her son, was represented, not in classical dress, but in Egyptian costume,
with a head-dress of a solar disk and cow's horns. The
worship of Mithras was essentially a cult of the army,
and for this reason altars and reliefs of the god have been
found on far distant boundaries of the Empire. Mithras
was originally a Persian sun deity, and his cult spread

westwards, and became so popular that at one time it constituted a serious rival to Christianity. The god is generally represented sacrificing a bull, and it is believed that the group is symbolic of the sun's victory over the earth and moon, the latter being represented by the curved horns of the animal. The dagger in the god's hand symbolizes the rays of the sun opening the fertile veins of the earth. The cult was introduced into Rome before the end of the Republic, but it was not until the third century A.D. that it attained its great popularity.

Art. General Characteristics—Just as the Romans were a strenuous, practical, and unimaginative race, so is their art realistic, full of force, and stamped with practical intelligence rather than with spiritual and imaginative qualities. Roman art is, to a great extent, a further development of Hellenistic art on Italian soil, but it is not this alone, for the people, although they were largely borrowers, not originators in art, moulded the æsthetic ideals of the Greeks into a Roman imperial art of their own, an art into which their own strength and forceful personality passed. Material power and might, and the glory of dominion, are felt in every line and curve of Roman architecture, from the splendour of the forum, baths, and amphitheatre to the personal pride expressed by triumphal arch and column. Every Roman aqueduct, wall, and road speaks of the engineering ability and unswerving purpose of the empire builder, and no one who has followed the line of Hadrian's wall in Northumbria, through driving mists and over crag and heather, can read unmoved the sermon of its stones.

In sculpture, as well as in architecture, Roman art was the servant of the State. Emperor and aristocrat, empress and citizen were alike eager to have their memory kept green by means of portrait bust, or historic relief, and the State was equally anxious that great names and great deeds should be held in remembrance as a spur to further effort. In this way the characteristic and essentially Roman art of the portrait bust and historic relief, which are realistic and narrative in character, is in marked contrast to the impersonal and idealistic art of the great age in Greece.

With the rise of Byzantium the glory of Rome began to fade, and Eastern ideals made themselves felt, but to the end Roman art preserved the human form as the dominating idea of art, and, although weak and enfeebled, yet had enough strength to impose it upon the forms of the Christian Church, which was in spirit entirely hostile to it.

Architecture—The Roman architects won their chief right to fame by the splendour of the domes which they built and by their discovery of the possibilities of the arch as an architectural form. It was a form known to the Egyptians and other early races but it had been employed by them in underground tombs ; the Greeks also used it occasionally, both for construction and decoration, but the Romans made the form their own, and using it in many and beautiful ways, opened up fresh possibilities of design, and laid the foundation of the medieval architecture that was to come. One of the most effective uses to which they subjected the arch was in the building of colonnades, while the form was also used as a purely decorative feature in the ornamentation of blank walls.

Another feature of Roman building, which was essentially native in character, was the use of cement for architectural purposes. Large quantities of lime and *pozzolana*, a species of volcanic earth, were found in the ineghbourhood of the city, and were used by Roman builders, at first timidly, and then with increasing effect, as they realized the great strength and potentialities of the material.   The boldness of design of the later Roman buildings, and the immense domes and vaults that often crowned them, owed their existence in a large measure to the employment of this material.   There has been much controversy as to the origin of these Roman domes. They may have been copied from the smaller structures of a similar type common in the Near East, or it is possible that large domes had been erected in the eastern Hellenistic cities, and that these had been the inspiration of the Roman designs.   In any case the dome became a favourite feature of the Roman architect, who preferred it to the flat roof that had been universal in the buildings of the Egyptians.

The immense solidity of Roman building may have been partly due to the influence of the Etruscans, some of whose great walls are still to be seen in old Italian towns, such as Volterra and Perugia.   It is difficult to estimate to what extent the Romans borrowed from the Etruscans in architectural matters, as Etruscan architecture in Rome was buried under the reconstructions of Augustus, who boasted that he found Rome of brick and left it of marble, while in other parts of the country there are scant Etruscan architectural remains.

It is a much simpler matter to decide what Roman architecture owes to Greece.   The Romans used all three Greek orders, the Doric, Ionic, and Corinthian, but owing to their lack of imagination, they were frequently guilty of abusing these forms and employing them in a way which betrayed an utter lack of refinement and appreciation.   The Roman forum was copied from the Greek *Agora* or market-place ; the amphitheatre was a develop-

ment of the Greek theatre ; the circus was modelled on
the Greek hippodrome, while the baths were to a certain
extent an offspring of the Greek gymnasia.

The early Roman buildings of the Republic were made
of tufa, which was covered with stucco for decorative
purposes, and was frequently ornamented with decorations
in terra-cotta. With the advent of Augustus a fresh
development of architecture took place. This great
Emperor is said to have restored eighty-two temples, and
the buildings that he erected must have been numberless.
Their marble elegance, however, was not appreciated by
all, for Juvenal wrote that in the Rome of the Republic
"nowhere did marble spoil the native tufa." Nero was
also a great builder, but the disastrous fire of the year
64 A.D. destroyed not only the larger number of his
buildings, but reduced a great part of Rome and its
treasures to ashes. The power and luxury of the
Flavian period is reflected in some of the most splendid
and typically Roman buildings, such as the Colosseum
and the triumphal arch of Titus, and fine buildings
continued to be erected during the second and third
centuries, as, for example, the great baths of Diocletian
and the Temple of the Sun at Baalbec.

The Romans regarded their secular buildings as equal
in importance to their temples. Among the most important of them were the amphitheatre, basilica, and the
thermæ or baths. The Colosseum of the Flavian
emperors is the most famous example of its kind. This
vast oval building measures a third of a mile in circumference, and it is estimated that it held at least 50,000
spectators. The columned decoration of the exterior
shows this architectural scheme in all its beauty, and
also illustrates how a different style has been used for
each story, first the Doric on the lowest, next the Ionic,

and lastly the Corinthian order on the third story. The plain wall that crowns them is probably of later date. The Colosseum is perhaps the most typical of all Roman buildings, and shows, in the words of Blomfield, "the masculine intelligence of Roman architecture in its highest level." The amphitheatre, erected before the Colosseum, had been made of wood, but after this date all the chief Roman towns, both at home and in far distant provinces, erected amphitheatres after the new model. A number of them are still standing and are terrible witnesses of the ghastly and brutal scenes that were enacted within their walls.

Roman basilicæ were large halls, oblong in plan, and frequently divided into aisles by rows of columns and arches to support galleries for spectators, while an apse containing a tribunal was placed at one or both ends. These halls were used as courts of justice or exchanges, and the earliest of them was erected by Cato in the year 184 B.C. The great baths, which date for the most part from the rich and luxurious days of the later empire, were enormous buildings with vaulted roofs, and contained, besides the baths themselves, a series of lecture rooms, libraries, lounges, and halls for gymnastic exercises. Another favourite architectural form was the triumphal arch, which was erected in commemoration of civil, or more frequently military, services. The earliest of these was put up in San Rémy in memory of victories of Julius Cæsar, while the latest, which is at Rheims, is assigned to the year 360 A.D. The three most famous examples in Rome are the arches of the Emperors Titus, Septimius Severus, and Constantine, while a beautiful and severely simple example is the arch of Augustus at Aosta. Arches, which were frequently single or triple in form, were surmounted by a sculptured group, generally representing an emperor on a chariot drawn by four horses. They were often decorated by fine reliefs also. Another favourite form of historic memorial was a column upon which were set forth, in sculptured relief, the histories of campaigns. The most famous examples are the columns of Trajan (a hundred and twenty-four feet in height), and the column of Marcus Aurelius, both in Rome.

The Roman aqueducts and bridges, which were considered as purely building and engineering works by their makers, are nevertheless fine and dignified monuments, often admirable in proportion and form. The remains of the earliest aqueducts, which date from the fourth century B.C., and which lie like "the gigantic vertebræ of antediluvian monsters," upon the flowery stretches of the Campagna, are familiar to all visitors to Rome, while the Pont du Gard, near Nîmes, is the most famous of the provincial examples.

Roman temples are for the greater part adaptations of Etruscan and Greek models. Many of the circular temples are very beautiful, as, for example, the little temple of Mater Matuta in the Forum Boarium, which dates from the time of Augustus. The Pantheon, the finest and most impressive of the Roman temples, built in the year 27 B.C. and re-erected later by Hadrian, is also to a large extent circular in character, as its main feature is a vast and massive rotunda, to which a portico is attached. The non-circular temple generally had a triple *cella*, which was an Etruscan characteristic, and was also built upon a raised *podium* or platform, which is probably also Etruscan in origin. The portico of the temple was frequently enlarged and was given special prominence, while a columned ambulatory often flanked the building on either side, until its course was arrested

by the fourth wall, which was brought out to meet it.
Among the Greek styles, that of the Corinthian order
became the most popular among the Romans, and was
universally employed in their buildings. In summing
up the characteristics of Roman architecture, Professor
Lethaby says : " Rome was lacking in the things of the
Spirit. There is little wonder—the first early wonder at
mysteries—left in Roman art ; the dew of the morning is
dried up ; it is the greatest Philistine style. The architecture, as ever, mirrors the soul of the nation." [1]

Sculpture. General Characteristics—The greater
number of surviving Roman sculptures are in marble,
and works in bronze are rare. The favourite and typical
forms of sculpture, as has already been mentioned, were
portrait busts and historic reliefs, and although decorative
temple sculptures in marble were produced, they were, for
the most part, mechanical and monotonous groups following Greek models. A great number of the historic reliefs
are chiefly interesting for their narrative, rather than for
their artistic qualities. There are, of course, many fine
examples, such as the beautiful *Ara Pacis* of Augustus
and the reliefs on the arch of Titus, but, generally speaking, they have not the true decorative instinct or a
realization of the limitations of material and technique.

The growth of the art of sculptured portraits can be
traced to the ancient Roman custom of modelling wax
masks of the dead. This was done in all aristocratic
households, and the masks, when coloured, were preserved
in small shrines and produced at subsequent funeral
celebrations, when they were worn by men who in this
way personified the ancestors of the deceased. The
uncompromising realism of the Roman portrait busts

[1] *Architecture* (Home University Library). Lethaby. Williams &
Norgate.

was a natural result of this practice. At the end of the second century B.C. wax masks were first superseded by busts in marble, but the influence of wax technique is apparent in these early works of the Republic, and also a lack of life and animation. Gradually the sculptor gained command over his material, and the later busts of the Republic are full of life and excellent characterization. Certain lines of Vernon Lee's, often quoted, may perhaps be quoted again here, as they express so well what is to be said of Roman portrait busts.

"But when Greek art had run its course, when beauty of form had well-nigh been exhausted or begun to pall, certain artists . . . began to produce portrait work of quite a new and wonderful sort, the beautiful portraits of ugly old men, of snub little boys, work which was clearly before its right time. . , . Of this Roman portrait art, of certain heads of half-idiotic little Cæsar brats, of sly and wrinkled old men, things which ought to be so ugly and yet are so beautiful, we say—at least, perhaps unformulated, we think, 'How Renaissance!' and the secret of the beauty of these few Græco-Roman busts, which is also that of Renaissance portrait sculpture, is that the beauty is quite different in kind from the beauty of Greek ideal sculpture and obtained by quite different means." There are other lines too which come into our minds when we think of this fine art by which Rome has perpetuated the memory of her sons,

"Toute passe . . . L'art robuste.
  Seul a l'éternité,
    Le buste
  Survit à la cité.

  Et la médaille austere
    Que trouve un laboureur
      Sous terre
  Révèle un empereur."

The production of Roman sculpture can be divided into the following seven periods :—

1. The Republic, B.C. 509-B.C. 27—By the beginning of the first century A.D. native art was nearly forgotten in Rome, and but for a few sentences, such as the remark by Pliny the Elder as to the "ancient art of statuary native to Italy," we have little or nothing to tell us of what it was like. There are very few traces of it still surviving, and the famous wolf of the Capitol, formerly thought to have been Roman work, is now attributed by many authorities to Ionian Greeks. There is no doubt that the chief influence in early Roman art was that of the Etruscans. Livy tells us that after the fall of Veii, in B.C. 396, the ancient Etruscan images of the gods were carried with reverence to Rome, and according to Pliny as many as two thousand statues of bronze were transferred to the capital after the sack of Volsinii, in 265 B.C.

With the decay of Etruria and the new vigour that made itself felt in Rome after the Punic wars, a national art began to grow up, similar in many respects to Etruscan art, but stamped with a rough force and realism and a strong fidelity to life that was essentially Roman in character. The famous *Arringatore* or orator, now in Florence, may be an example of later Republican art, in spite of its Etruscan inscription, for although it betrays Greek influence, this is not yet strongly marked. The busts of the husband and wife in the Vatican, known as Cato and Portia, are other well-known examples of the art of this period.

It was not until the first century B.C. that Greek ideals first began to be felt with any certainty, but from this time onwards their influence was paramount in Roman art. The sculpture of the Republic was confined almost exclusively to portraiture. The law of the growth of portrait busts has been determined by Bienkowski, who points out that busts of the Republic are only carried down to the part immediately below the collar-bone.

2. The Julio-Claudian Dynasty. *A.* **Augustus (28 B.C.-14 A.D.)**—With the establishment of the Empire, and the age of peace and prosperity that marked the reign of Augustus, Roman art took on new characteristics. The Emperor, who was a great admirer of Hellenic culture, did all that he could to foster the artistic traditions of Greece in his own dominions, with the result that numberless Greek artists flocked to Rome and an important school of Græco-Roman sculpture was developed. In the words of Horace, " Captive Greece o'ercame her savage conqueror and introduced the arts to rustic Latium," while the fine and " rustic " native art of realistic portraiture was for the moment checked. Hellenic art was transformed into a Roman Imperial art and a large number of sculptures were produced, many being cold and lifeless copies of the types and statues of ancient Greece, while others were fine specimens of Hellenic art, reinforced by Roman power and individuality. It is very difficult to tell whether the works of this period are by Greeks or Romans, as the sculptors of each nationality caught certain characteristics from the other, and we must be content to label it " Græco-Roman " work.

Besides the Hellenic school and the school of imitators and copyists, there was a second body of Augustan sculptors who established a realistic school of relief, based upon a careful observation of nature. This school developed the idealistic tendencies of the Alexandrian school and produced some delicate and carefully observed work, full of tenderness and playful fancy, and strongly Hellenic in character. The most famous reliefs of the

Augustan age, however, are those from the *Ara Pacis*, or
Altar of Peace, which was erected by the Senate between
the years B.C. 13-9 in celebration of the victories of the
Emperor in Spain and Gaul. It was the first of the great
Roman monuments to be decorated with historic reliefs,
and consisted of the altar and high enclosing walls. The
decorations of these walls were partly in the shape of
renderings of natural forms, such as leaves, birds and
flowers, and partly consisted of a procession of priests,
nobles and people, on their way to sacrifice after the
victories ; in fact, it formed a Roman equivalent to the
frieze of the Parthenon. These beautiful reliefs are Greek
in form and, to a great extent, Greek in spirit, but a
number of the figures are portraits and the procession is
Roman in character. Although the monument has long
been destroyed, a number of the reliefs have been preserved, and perhaps the fact that they have been scattered
is not to be regretted, for according to Mrs Strong, the
decoration of the great altar was controlled by no
dominating idea, and the reliefs gain in beauty when
studied separately and not as a complete decorative
scheme.

The realism of the Roman portrait busts was to a great
extent changed during this period to the more idealized
and typical representations of the Greeks. The heroic
heads of Augustus are many of them very fine, while at this
time also certain female heads were first produced which
represented living Imperial personages in semi-mythical
guise. The busts of this period, like those of the Republic, include little more than the neck. There are also
some fine whole-length statues dating from the Augustan
age, the most famous of which is the statue of the
Emperor from Prima Porta. A noticeable feature of the
heads of the Augustan reliefs is that for the first time the

full importance of the eye seems to be realized, and in the words of a recent critic, " The sculptor allowed the direction of the gaze to diverge from that of the head."

B. **Other Principals of the Julio-Claudian Dynasty. Tiberius (14-37 A.D.), Caius Cæsar (Caligula) (37-41 A.D.), Claudius, (41-54 A.D.) and Nero (54-68 A.D.)** —The remaining members of the Julio-Claudian House had little time to spare from the cares of war and government for the cause of art.   They were collectors, and loved to amass treasure in their palaces, but they did little to encourage native art, which, left to itself, first declined into a cold and mechanical echo of Hellenism, and then slowly began to return again to native tradition.   The busts of the middle of the century show an actual facial likeness to the model, but have not yet gained power enough to express once more the informing spirit.   Owing to the great fire of Nero's reign very few of the Julio-Claudian monuments have been preserved.

Reigns of Galba, Otho and Vitellius

3. **The Flavian Dynasty.   Vespasian (69-79 A.D.), Titus (79-81 A.D.), Domitian (81-96 A.D.)**—The series of foreign victories of the first of the Flavian emperors was followed by a succession of brilliant, if often terrible, triumphs and celebrations in Rome.   The enthusiasm of the people was stirred, and a great age of Roman art set in, perhaps the greatest and certainly the most truly Roman of the periods of artistic output.   Vespasian forwarded the cause of the arts in every way that he could; protected and favoured the men of letters, and formed a magnificent collection of works of art which he placed in the Forum and Temple of Peace.

The artificiality of later Hellenic culture had died out, and native tradition had again to a certain extent asserted itself, having gained in the meantime both in execution and conception by contact with Greek ideals. It was an age of genuine artistic effort. The number of native artists was greatly increased, and a large amount of work was produced by sculptors of Greek descent who were now naturalized as Roman citizens. Certain Græco-Syrian influences from the East made themselves felt and were apparent in the richer decoration of architectural forms, while the art of portraiture reached a high level, heads being rendered with force, subtlety, and distinction, and showing a strong feeling for characterization. The busts were carried down to the line of the shoulders, and those of the women are generally marked by the high *toupets* of curls which were fashionable at the time in court circles.

With the exception of portrait busts very little Flavian sculpture remains. The most famous reliefs of the period still existing are those on the arch of Titus, which is the next great monument of its kind that has been preserved after the *Ara Pacis* of Augustus. The arch was erected in commemoration of the capture of Jerusalem by Titus in 71 A.D., but although it was probably commenced during the reign of Titus, it was finished and dedicated after his death by his brother Domitian. The reliefs on the arch, illustrating incidents in the campaign, are examples of what has been described as the illusionistic methods of certain of the Flavian sculptors, who became absorbed in expressing not an actual imitation of an object or scene, but rather the impression which it produced. Wickhoff has described the relief showing the return with the candlestick to Rome (see Plate XVIII.) in the following words:—" A frame is simply thrown

open and through it we look at the march past of the
triumphal procession.   We are to believe that the people
are moving there before our eyes ; . . . the plastic art
tries to attain by its own methods the same effect as
would a highly developed art of painting—the impression
of complete illusion.   Beauty of line, symmetry of parts,
such as a conventional art demands, are no longer sought
for.   Everything is concentrated on the one aim of
producing an impression of continuous motion." [1]

Reign of Nerva, 96-98

4. Trajan (98-117 A.D.)—The reign of Trajan,
which was a military and strenuous one, showed a decline
in the artistic qualities of the Flavian dynasty.   The
brilliance of execution was preserved and many fine
works were still produced, but on the whole a certain
lack of spirit and decline in vitality set in, and sculptures
were apt to be wooden and insensitive on handling.   The
portrait busts show the whole shoulder and upper part of
the chest ; *toupets* were still worn, and the pupils of the
eye were for the first time represented.

The most famous monument of the reign is the
Column of Trajan, which is ornamented by a long winding
spiral of continuous decorative reliefs, composed of about
four hundred slabs and illustrating the campaigns against
the Dacians.   There are no less than 2500 figures in
these reliefs, and the Emperor appears among them
nearly a hundred times in connection with the various
scenes of the war.   These reliefs, besides being of great
historic interest, are also interesting from the artistic
standpoint, although they cannot take high rank as works
of art.

[1] *Roman Art.*   Wickhoff, translated Sellers.   Heinemann.

PLATE XVIII

ROMAN PORTRAIT BUST.   TIME OF TRAJAN (?)

THE RETURN TO ROME WITH THE CANDLESTICK FROM JERUSALEM
RELIEF ON THE ARCH OF TITUS.   FLAVIAN DYNASTY

5. Hadrian (117-138 A.D.)—Hadrian, spoken of by
his contemporaries as "the Greekling," was a man of
Hellenic and philosophic sympathies. He revived the study
of Greek and even Egyptian artistic models, with the result
that the sculpture of his reign was eclectic in tendency
but often dull and academic in manner owing to the lack
of internal response to the ideals thrust upon it. Art
attained a widespread popularity during this reign, and
many buildings were erected by the Emperor, both at
home and in the colonies, while ancient monuments were
enlarged and restored. A great number of the Roman
sarcophagi also date from this period. Although many
of them were interesting works, they were apt to be over-
decorated with crowded figures, and they do not take
high rank among Roman works of art.

The portrait busts of Hadrian's reign show part of the
upper arm, and the representation of the pupils of the
eye becomes more common. The Emperor was also the
first ruler to be represented with a beard, a fashion which
rapidly became popular. The idealistic tendencies in art,
occasioned by the renewed study of Greek sculpture, are
well expressed by the numerous busts of Antinous, a
Bithynian youth and great favourite of the Emperor's,
who was drowned in the Nile, possibly by his own desire,
as some mystic sacrifice required on behalf of his patron.
This voluntary death aroused a fresh passion of devotion
in Hadrian, who deified his favourite and caused endless
idealized portraits of him to be executed. These portraits
exerted an important influence on contemporary sculpture,
and established a type, the popularity of which lasted during
the whole of the reign.

**6. The Antonine Dynasty. Antoninus Pius (138-
161 A.D.), Marcus Aurelius (161-180 A.D.), Com-
modus (180-192 A.D.)**—With the Antonine dynasty, the

first signs of decadence in Roman art became apparent.
The influence of the Greek revival, now dying out, was felt
but weakly, and sculptors became occupied with new
technical problems, such as the differentiating between the
texture of hair and skin, by highly polishing certain surfaces,
and a free use of the drill for the rough surfaces of hair and
beard. The eye was also again carefully studied. Although
the age was one of gradual decline, many fine works were
still produced, such as the bronze equestrian statue of
Marcus Aurelius, which, if uninteresting in detail, is
splendid in general effect ; and the portraits of the elder
and younger Faustina. The busts of this time generally
include the upper arm and the whole of the chest.

Reigns of Pertinax and Didius Julianus

7. The Third and Early Fourth Centuries—The
third and early fourth centuries witnessed the steady
decay of the Empire and also of Roman art. During the
second quarter of the third century the Roman dominions
were torn by eternal strife, and few works of art were
produced except sarcophagi and portrait busts. The
latter art continued to hold its own, in spite of artistic
decay, and although as an art it had fallen to a lower
level than that to which it had previously attained, and
over-elaborate treatment was afforded to the representation
of detail and colouristic effect, occasional masterpieces,
such as the portrait of Philippus Arabus in the Vatican,
and the bust of Caracalla, were still produced, During
the first half of the third century, busts had grown to be
almost half-length figures, while the pictorial effect of
hair and beard was rendered by numberless small pick-
marks of the chisel.

During the third century a steady growth of Oriental

influence took place. Fresh Oriental religious cults were adopted, many of which were derived from the Hellenic centres of Asia Minor, and the Oriental love of pattern began for the first time to be felt. After the fall of Gallienus, in 268 A.D., very little sculpture was produced in Rome, while in the fourth century few portrait busts were executed.

The reign of Constantine shows Roman art in its last phase. In the execution of reliefs the sculptors were chiefly occupied with the new colour effects, and work was largely executed in two planes, so that effects of light and dark, not softly graduated effects of light and shade, might be obtained. This was no doubt the result of the Oriental love of pattern, as opposed to Western representative relief, and to this cause also, as well as to the growth of Christianity, the growing lack of interest in the human figure may be attributed. Riegl states that the arch of Constantine, erected after his victory over Maxentius, is spiritual as well as æsthetic in interest, and "stands where the antique passes over into the medieval world." The figures in Constantinian reliefs show marked formal characteristics and are the precursors of Romanesque sculpture.

Painting and Mosaic Work—Roman painting never reached a high level. The frescoes found in Pompeii, and in the excavation of Roman palaces and villas, show that the art was based on that of the Greeks, and in particular on the art of the Hellenistic city of Alexandria.

At the time of Augustus, subjects from the epic poets and from mythology were frequently used, while somewhat later idyllic scenes in the manner of the Alexandrian School became popular. The early paintings also show a love and observation of nature, but this seems to have

died out to a large extent during the first century A.D.
Among other examples of paintings are the portraits
on Egyptian mummy cases, mentioned on p. 182, but
these, although executed under Roman rule, are Græco-
Egyptian in origin.

The mosaic art was introduced into Rome from Egypt
about the middle of the second century B.C., and became
so popular that by the time of the Antonines it had
spread to the remotest provinces. The small cubes or
tesseræ were chiefly made of marble, and the decoration
of floors and walls by this process became a common
practice in every Roman house. The art developed on
somewhat similar lines to that of painting, and employed
the same subjects as well as purely decorative and
geometrical designs. It was, however, in Byzantine
art that it reached its most splendid expression.

Metal Work, Gem Engraving and Pottery—The
Roman craftsmen produced some fine metal work. Vases
in precious metals were more frequently executed than
bronze reliefs, and the art was influenced to a certain
extent by the Hellenic school of metal chasers established
since early days in Asia Minor. Gem engraving, with
which should be classed cameo cutting, reached a high
level during the age of Augustus, when such famous
specimens as the cameo in Paris representing the deified
Emperor and his family, and the cameo portraits of
Augustus and Livia in the British Museum, were produced. Roman pottery never reached the level of that of
the Greeks. The native potters, however, produced an
original ware of their own, which was first manufactured at
Arretium (Arezzo) in the second century B.C. Its chief
characteristic was a brilliant red glaze, which was frequently
decorated with moulded figures in the same medium.
This ware, which is incorrectly known as Samian ware,

was afterwards produced in Gaul and certain centres in Germany, but it was never made in Britain, although it has been frequently found there.

Roman Art in Britain—Although Julius Cæsar had visited British shores in the year 55 B.C., the Roman occupation of the country did not begin until the conquest of Claudius in A.D. 43, when Aulus Plautius was left as governor until the year 47. The southern part of the country was first occupied, and the advance towards Scotland did not begin until the time of the great Roman General, Agricola, who governed the country during the years 78-85. There are many scattered camps between Northumberland and Aberdeen which may be attributed to Agricola, and although the great wall of Hadrian was not built until the year 124, the inception of both this and the Antonine wall, built some years later between the Forth and the Clyde, are probably due to the military genius of the great General.

Very little is known about Roman Britain except what has been learnt through archeological research. The country was a remote and outlying province and was only to a certain extent civilized by her conquerors. The northern districts were always more or less unsettled, although it has been estimated that a hundred thousand souls dwelt on the seventy-mile line of Hadrian's wall Among the chief Roman towns were Lindum (Lincoln) Eboracum (York), Camulodunum (Colchester), Glevum (Gloucester), Deva (Chester), Aquæ Sulis (Bath), Verulamium (St Albans), Calleva (Silchester), and Viroconium (Wroxeter). The last two of these towns have been excavated, and much light has been thrown in consequence upon the history of the period.

There were many forts in the region of the wall, and also one or two small fortified towns, such as Luguvallium

(Carlisle) and Corstopitum (Corbridge).   Although these towns were largely military in character, the historian Josephus speaks of "the place for handicraft trade" that they contained, and the excavations that have recently taken place prove that works of art, even if rude in character, were produced there.   Among the most interesting specimens found is the "Corbridge lion," which shows a certain rough vigour and strength which is obviously local in character.   In the south, one of the best examples of local art is the bearded Gorgon found at Bath, a typical specimen of Romano-British work.

The Roman era in Britain lasted, broadly speaking, for 350 years, and came to an end about the year 400 A.D.

LESSON X

BYZANTINE ART

PART I.—ELEMENTARY LESSON IN STORY FORM

INTRODUCTION—Last Lesson.—About three hundred years after the time of the Emperor Titus, the Roman Empire was divided into two parts, the Western Roman Empire with Rome as its capital, and the Byzantine or Eastern Roman Empire, with the town of New Rome, or Byzantium (now called Constantinople), as its chief town. A different Emperor ruled in each capital, but the subjects of the Emperor in Byzantium were chiefly Greeks, not Romans. This is a story about something that happened during the reign of a Byzantine Emperor called Justinian.

1. **Anthemius of Tralles**—In a town called Tralles, near Ephesus, in Asia Minor, there lived a Greek family consisting of a father and mother and their five sons. The parents thought that no one could ever have had such clever boys as they had, for there was hardly anything that they could not do. They not only loved their games and got into scrapes and mischief like any other boys, but they loved their books too, and seemed to learn their lessons with no trouble at all. They delighted to talk and argue and write, and in the winter evenings they would get their father or mother to tell them stories about the ancient Greeks who had lived hundreds of years before. "Ah," the father would say, "those were great days. Now the Romans are the powerful people, but then it was our race which ruled the world and kept the Persians at bay. The Greeks of those days were the

223

most brilliant people the world has ever known. Think of Pericles, the wise ruler of Athens, and Phidias, who planned the wonderful statues and friezes of the Parthenon. Where are our great men now ? " The old man would sigh and the mother would say, " Now, my sons, you, when you grow up, must do great things and show that the Greeks have not lost their ancient power and skill."

There was one of the brothers who perhaps more than all the others loved to hear the old stories. His name was Anthemius, and there was nothing he could not do with his clever hands and quick brain. He would sit hugging his knees, his eyes wide, like one in a dream, as the soft voice of his mother went on and on, telling of kings and heroes. Then the falling logs of the fire with their sudden shower of sparks would bring him to himself with a start, and the boys would be packed off to their beds, and Anthemius would dream of all the wonderful things that he would make, churches and bridges and machines of every kind.

As the boy grew up he spent more and more time with his models and plans. He was for ever experimenting with buildings and machines, until the people around became interested and asked him to build things for them. Whatever he built was well made and solid, and when he planned a church or a house it was beautiful also. No wonder his fame began to spread and he was sent for to build in far-distant towns.

Then one day a most wonderful thing happened ; a messenger arrived on horseback, dusty with long journeying and wearing the Imperial livery. What did he want ? He had come bearing an order to Anthemius from the great Emperor Justinian, who bade him to come and settle in Byzantium and work for the Imperial family.

No greater honour could fall to Anthemius, and in company with the messenger he set off joyfully for the famous capital of New Rome. After several days' travelling they came to the coast, where they took passage in a trading ship, and soon the breeze had filled its big sails and they were slipping through the warm blue waters, past the sun-burnt islands of the Ægean Sea towards Byzantium.

2. Byzantium—At last one morning a call from the watch told Anthemius that Byzantium was in sight. He hurried on deck in great excitement to see the wonderful city where the glories of the East and West met. He had often heard how the Emperors had ransacked their wide dominions for splendid statues and marbles to decorate their capital, and now he was to see the splendour and the treasures himself. The walls and towers grew nearer, bright in the clear morning light, and soon the ship was in the busy harbour, and Anthemius had passed the walls and was on the way to the Emperor's palace.

The streets were full of people of every nationality : Roman soldiers with the sunlight glancing from their shining spears and helmets ; dusky traders from the East, busy in bartering their richly coloured rugs and embroideries ; numberless bearded monks, deep in argument as they passed ; Syrians and Arabs from the East, in their white and coloured robes, and everywhere Greeks, going about their morning's business. Great buildings lined the streets, bright with coloured marbles, and ornamented with splendid Greek statues. In the vast hippodrome or circus some of the finest of the statues were placed, among them four splendid gilded bronze horses, which Anthemius thought were some of the most beautiful things he had ever seen. There was little time, however, to examine all the beautiful works of art, and he

was hurried on by his guide to the palace, with only time
for a glance at the big Forum and the Church of Sancta
Sophia, which stood near by.

If Anthemius had been dazzled by the brilliant scene
outside he found himself still more amazed at the richness
of the palace within. He was taken through a series of
ante-rooms and great halls until he found himself in the
presence of the Emperor and prostrated himself upon the
ground before him. Justinian, who was a spare man of
middle age, slightly bald and clean shaven, and plainly
dressed, received him kindly, and at once questioned him
about his work, asking him what he had already done,
and discussing plans for future buildings in the city.
They were soon joined in their talk by the Empress
Theodora, whose magnificent robes and amazing beauty
astonished Anthemius, although he thought her face somewhat hard. The architect was not sorry when the exciting interview was over and he was free to go to the
lodgings that had been provided for him and rest after his
travels.

3. The Nika Rebellion—Then began happy and
busy years for Anthemius. His genius was the delight
of the Emperor, who kept him continually employed in
the further building and decorating of the city. Often,
after a hard day's work, Anthemius would go to the great
hippodrome and watch the chariot races and the athletic
contests. The roughest of the people would go wild with
excitement over a closely-contested race, and afterwards,
at night, would sometimes march through the city streets
singing and shouting, before their excitement had died
down, and they were driven home by the soldiers on
guard. One winter's night some of the crowd behaved so
badly that Justinian ordered the leaders to be put to
death, so that order might be restored in the city. At

this the mob became more angry than ever, and serious riots began. The people chose the word *Nika* or "conquer" for their watchword, and began to fight in the streets, shouting out that the Emperor must die, and a new one be elected in his stead. Almost all Justinian's soldiers were away fighting the Persians, and very few were left to guard the palace or to check the riots in the streets. The crowd, getting more and more out of hand, set fire to some of the public buildings, and soon the flames began to spread. In a few days a great part of the city lay in ashes; the church of Sancta Sophia was burnt to the ground, and the palace itself was threatened.

Justinian ordered the chief treasures of his palace to be placed on a ship, and himself prepared to fly, but he had not counted on the Empress Theodora. Facing the Emperor and his trembling councillors she said, "No time is this to ask whether a woman should be bold before men, or valiant when men are afraid. They who are in extremest peril must think of nothing but how best to meet what lies before them; to fly, if ever it be expedient, would now not be so, I declare, even if it preserved us. For a man born into this life not to die is impossible; but for one who has been Emperor to become an exile is not to be endured. Let us never come to be without this purple robe, nor live to see that day when men shall cease to call me their sovereign lady. If you, Emperor, wish to escape, it is no hard matter. Here is the sea, and there lie the ships. But consider that you may not one day wish that you had not exchanged your mean safety for a glorious death. For me, I love the ancient saying, 'How brave a sepulchre a kingdom is!'"

These words of Theodora's fired the Emperor and his advisers with fresh courage. The Byzantine general Belisarius collected all the available troops, and sallied

out, and, after sharp fighting, the mob was routed, order
was restored, and the day was won for Justinian.

4. The Building of Sancta Sophia—But what a
sight met the Emperor's eyes when he first went out to
see what harm had been done to his splendid city ! Many
of the magnificent buildings were now piles of charred
ruins.   Curious crowds of people were hurrying to and
fro, commenting and bewailing, and coughing and rubbing
their eyes as drifts of smoke were blown past on the wind
from the smouldering piles of masonry.   Every now and
then a block of stone or piece of timber would fall with a
crash, sending up a fire of sparks, while blackened marbles
stood gaunt and solitary against the grey winter sky.   As
the Emperor, followed by attendants and soldiers, passed
to and fro among the ruins, the people whispered and
pointed covertly, and Justinian, throwing his head back,
vowed to himself passionately that he would live to rule
over a city more magnificent than the city that had just
been so scarred and blackened.   He would build up a new
Byzantium, greater than any that had gone before it, and
the first building that should arise should be a great new
church dedicated to Sancta Sophia, or Holy Wisdom,
which should stand where the ruins of the old Sancta
Sophia now smouldered.   No time should be lost.   The
new church should be begun at once.   Who should be its
architect ?

A familiar figure, now grey-haired, was seen approaching, and recognizing Anthemius of Tralles, Justinian sent
a command that he should speak with him, and before the
interview was finished the planning of the new church had
been entrusted to the great architect.   Anthemius returned
home full of joy at the thought of the task that lay before
him, and Justinian busied himself in dictating an edict
to be sent by messengers to the heads of the different

Byzantine provinces, ordering them to search at once for any old marbles or relics of ancient classical temples in their dominions, and despatch what they might find with all possible speed to Byzantium.

Before a month was over the new church was begun. Anthemius had worked day and night at the plans, with the help of Isidorus, another Greek architect, and had designed a splendid new building, to be surmounted by an immense dome. Every day ships, laden with marbles, carvings, and foreign woods, arrived at the quays, and cartloads of bricks were unloaded at the site of the new church. The sound of hammering and sawing never ceased ; hundreds of workmen came and went, and scarcely a day passed when the Emperor was not to be seen encouraging the workmen and talking to Anthemius, who was never far away from his beloved building. As the years passed the great shell of the church reached up far above the houses, and dominated the town. Then the dome was added, its immense weight supported by the great walls, and borne up by many marble columns and springing arches. Lastly, an army of decorators filled the building. They lined the church with coloured marbles, and covered the vaults and domes with mosaics, which were made of tiny cubes of glass, all gold and silver and richly coloured, cemented together in the form of patterns, and of figures of saints and angels. After five years of work the great church was finished, and a dedicatory service was prepared.

5. The Opening Ceremony—On the day of the opening of the new church the whole town buzzed with excitement. There was to be a great procession of the clergy and the court, and every one was eager to take part in the service of dedication. The town was gaily decorated and at an early hour the line of route was crowded with men, women, and children, eager to see the Emperor and to follow him into the new building. After many hours of waiting the patience of the crowd by the church was rewarded and a quick whisper of excitement passed from lip to lip, " They are coming, the procession has started ! " A sound of solemn chanting was borne on the wind and then the procession came in sight, passing with slow tread under the shadow of the great walls. The armour of the soldiers shone in the sunlight ; the heavy scent of the incense rose into the fresh wintry air, and the boys' voices rose and fell above the deeper tones of the priests' chanting. In the centre of the procession the Patriarch, or High Priest, sat in state in the Emperor's chariot, which was drawn by splendid horses in jewelled harness, while walking on foot by its side was Justinian.

As the great doors were reached, and swung open before the Patriarch and the Emperor, the choir broke into a glad chant. " Lift up your heads, oh ye gates, and be ye lifted up, O ye everlasting doors," the boys sang joyfully. The Emperor stepped forward and entered the church, followed by all the people. He advanced to the pulpit and gazing around him at the great vault above and the richly glowing walls, he threw his arms wide and exclaimed, " Glory be to God for thinking me worthy to finish such a work : Solomon, I have excelled you." But there was another present whose heart was full of a deeper joy than Justinian's. Anthemius, in his place of honour, stood silent and still. The sound of the singing surged past him ; the blaze and glory of the sunlight beating back from the gold and richness of the mosaics dazzled him, but he seemed neither to see nor hear. His heart was full to overflowing to think that he, Anthemius, had been allowed to raise this majestic church to the honour of God, and his eyes were wide, even, as when

PLATE XIX

INTERIOR OF THE CHURCH OF SANCTA SOPHIA, CONSTANTINOPLE
(From a water-colour by Arthur E. Henderson, F.S.A.)

a child, he had listened to his mother's stories, and had seen visions and dreamed dreams.

Notes on the Story—**Paragraph 1**—Imaginary ; founded on the account of Agathias. **Paragraph 2**—Imaginary. Details of architecture and statues taken from contemporary chronicles. **Paragraph 3**—The Nika rebellion lasted from the 15th to the 28th of January, 532 A.D. The circus parties of the " Blues " and the " Greens " had developed into political parties at this time. For full details see any Byzantine History. **Paragraph 4**—Imaginary. Justinian actually sent the edict demanding the old marbles, and he also watched the building of the church. **Paragraph 5**—Minor details of procession imaginary. The chant " Lift up your heads " was sung at the re-dedication of the church, after its restoration due to the earthquake, but we do not know if it was sung at the first dedication. Details concerning Anthemius imaginary. The words of Theodora, and of Justinian on entering the church, are traditional.

PART II.—MATERIAL FOR ADVANCED LESSONS ONLY

Byzantium—In the year 330 A.D. the Emperor Constantine transferred the seat of empire from Rome to Byzantium, now known as Constantinople, and christened by him " New Rome." Byzantium had been founded by Greek settlers about the year 657 B.C., and had for long been under Roman rule, but it was not until the reign of Constantine that the city first became important. The Emperor saw that Byzantium was in nearer relation to the East and commanded a finer military position than that of old Rome, and would make a better trade centre, and he also realized that the new religion would gain greater freedom than would be possible for it in the ancient pagan capital. Although Constantine brought many of the Roman nobles with him to his new capital and numbers of Roman merchants, craftsmen, and troops, the city was largely populated by Greeks, and Greek remained the common tongue although the Court spoke Latin.   The city also, although avowedly Christian, still contained pagan shrines.

In the year 395 A.D. the Emperor Theodosius divided the Empire into the two Empires of the East and West and apportioned one to each of his two sons.   The Western Empire fell shortly afterwards before the attacks of the Goths and Vandals.   The Eastern or Byzantine Empire, on the other hand, steadily grew in power and dominion. Among its most important cities were the great Hellenistic centres of Alexandria, and Antioch in Syria, but these gradually assumed a second place as Byzantium itself became the centre of the Empire.

Among the people who came to settle at the new capital were Greeks from Asia Minor and Alexandria, Copts, Jews, Armenians, Syrians, Persians, and wandering craftsmen from the Roman guilds.   As time passed a welding together of these varying elements took place and Byzantium became not only the centre of the Christian East, but one of the most important cities of the Middle Ages.   Splendid buildings were erected there by the emperors, and the treasures of Rome, Greece, Sicily, and Asia Minor were used in its decoration.   Among the hundreds of statues that ornamented the city were the four Greek bronze horses, which were probably brought to Byzantium by the Emperor Theodosius II. (408-450 A.D.) and which were taken to Venice in the thirteenth century by the Doge Enrico Dandolo.   There was also a great bronze statue of Athena from the Acropolis at Athens which stood on a column in the forum, until in later years it was melted down for purposes of war.   It is quite possible that this statue was none other than the famous early work of Phidias.

Byzantium reached the height of its glory under the Emperor Justinian (482-3-565 A.D.), who was a man of humble origin and hard in character, but of great force and determination. His famous generals Narses and Belisarius extended the Eastern Empire on every hand; they destroyed the rule of the Vandals in Africa, captured Southern Spain from the Goths, reconquered Italy from the Gothic kings, and concluded a peace with the Persians, who threatened the Byzantine provinces in Asia Minor. Justinian had a passion for building. He repaired the fortifications of his capital and erected numberless buildings within their shelter. It is said that during his reign Byzantium boasted eight aqueducts, eleven forums, twenty-four thermæ or great baths, and numerous palaces, churches, theatres, and other public buildings. To the glories of ancient Greece and Rome were added the splendour and colour of the East, and it was to this blending of East and West that the city owed its magnificence.

During the seventh century many of the Byzantine provinces were captured by the Arabs; in the eighth and early ninth centuries a great iconoclastic controversy raged ; and from the end of the ninth to the middle of the eleventh century the splendour of the Empire was revived under the rule of the Macedonian dynasty. The beginning of the end came in the year 1204 A.D., when a coalition of Venetian merchants and Crusaders sacked Byzantium and elected a Frankish emperor in place of a Greek. In the year 1261 the Greeks recaptured their capital and ruled over a kingdom that had become weakened by inroads of Bulgarians and Turks.

In the year 1453 A.D. the capital itself fell into the hands of the Turks and the Byzantine Empire came to an end. The crescent or new moon which had been the symbol used by the Greeks for their capital was also appropriated by the conquerors, and from this time onward it became symbolic of the Turk.

Early Christian Art—In the year 313 A.D. the Emperor Constantine issued from Milan the famous edict which gave the official sanction to Christianity. It granted to Christians the permission to build churches, restored to them their confiscated property, and gave them the right of holding public offices. Up to this time the Christians had worshipped for the most part in secret, in catacombs which they hollowed in the earth, in deserted temples, or in caves and private rooms, and they had erected but few buildings of their own. With the publication of the edict they could hold their services without fear of danger, and at once numbers of new churches were erected.

The most important of these early buildings were erected in Rome and in Syria, and in consequence the so-called " Early Christian " style was composed of elements from Rome and from the Hellenized East. The greater number of these churches took the form of oblong halls divided by rows of pillars into long aisles, and were terminated by an apse and sanctuary. There has been endless discussion as to derivation of these Constantinian basilicæ which were probably modelled on one or other of several types of Roman buildings. A second early Christian architectural form was the circular baptistery or tomb, which probably followed the design of the Roman circular temple.

Among the early Christian buildings erected by Constantine in the Near East were the basilicæ that marked the seven sites that he had newly dedicated in the Holy Land. The Christians in Syria soon followed the Emperor's example, and a number of churches were built in different parts of the country. The architects of these buildings were probably for the most part Asiatic Greeks, but they were aided no doubt by Syrians and Persians. In the Hellenistic cities of Ctesiphon and Seleucia, Persians and Greeks had for many years lived side by side, and as a result, an interchange of artistic ideas and methods of construction had taken place. These early Christian buildings in Syria had in consequence markedly oriental features, and in some instances consisted of a simple rectangle with a dome from which the Greek cross type of building was afterwards evolved.

Early Christian art gave birth to two important architectural styles. One was the Romanesque style, which grew up slowly in the West and out of which Gothic art was finally evolved. The second was the Byzantine style.

The growth of Christianity gave fresh impulse, not only to architecture, but to the lesser arts also. The fathers of the Church turned to artists for aid, in order that their buildings, by means of carvings, paintings, and mosaics, should be a preaching of the Word. In a sermon of St Basil's (A.D. 379) we find the following exhortation, " Rise up now, I pray you, ye celebrated painters of the good deeds of this army. Make glorious by your art the mutilated images of their leader. With colours laid on by your cunning, make illustrious the crowned martyr, by me too feebly pictured. I retire vanquished before you in your painting of the excellences of the martyr. . . ."

Among the most frequent early Christian symbols, the majority of which are preserved to this day, are the following :—A lamb alone, with a nimbus and sometimes a cross, or else a throne alone—Jesus. A dove—the Holy Spirit. Two hands holding a crown—the Eternal

Father.   A peacock or an eagle—the triumph of the
Church, or of Christ.   The phœnix of Arabia—eternal
life.   The stag—baptism.   The eagle, ox, angel, and
lion—the four Evangelists SS. John, Luke, Matthew, and
Mark.   Lambs issuing from two huts and walking in a
meadow by a river towards Jesus, who stands or sits by
the river's source—The Pilgrim Church : the faithful
coming from Jerusalem or Bethlehem to meet at the
spring of eternal life.

**Byzantine Art.   Historic Outline and General
Characteristics**—Byzantine art has been divided into
the following four periods :—

**1. From the Foundation of Constantinople
(330 A.D.) until the Beginning of the Iconoclastic
Period**—This represents the experimental period and
the golden age of its achievement.   Figure sculpture had
not yet become dominated by Eastern ideals, and was
largely realistic in treatment, but by the sixth century
mosaics were splendidly conventionalized and attained
great beauty.   The Byzantine style of architecture became distinctive about the year 450 A.D.   Great development of trade.   The great buildings of this period were
S. Sophia, the early basilicæ in Rome and the early
churches at Ravenna, etc.   The artistic centres of the Near
East, at first Alexandria and Antioch, then Byzantium
itself.

2. The Iconoclastic Period—The Emperor Leo III.
(717-740 A.D.) was an adventurer from the mountainous
regions of Isauria.   We are told by Gibbon that he was
" ignorant of sacred and profane letters ; but his education,
his reason, perhaps his intercourse with the Jews and
Arabs had inspired the martial peasant with a hatred of
all images."   One reason for this hatred can be found in
the fact that many of the people were beginning to

endow the images with mysterious power, believing that they could work miracles and were in some occult way the medium of the saints. In spite of the opposition of the people, whose sympathies were monastic, and who were led by the priests themselves, Leo joined himself to the iconoclastic party, which thought the growing power of the monks a danger to the State. He began to wage war against all sacred imagery, causing numberless works of art to be destroyed, and prohibited the further production of religious art of a monumental kind. He further determined to enforce his beliefs by an edict of the General Council of the Church, but in this he was defeated by Pope Gregory II., who pronounced his ideas as heretical.

The iconoclastic controversy brought monumental art only to a standstill. Hundreds of artists and craftsmen, prohibited from following their callings, turned from religious to Hellenistic motives, and devoted themselves to ivory and goldsmith's work, miniature painting, and conventional decorative design, Eastern in inspiration. By about the middle of the ninth century, mosaic and painted figures began to be used once more in decoration, and a general artistic revival set in, furthered by the growing prosperity of the empire under the Macedonian dynasty.

3. From the Beginning of the Macedonian Dynasty (Basil I., 867 A.D.) to the Sack of Constantinople (1204 A.D.)—The second great age of Byzantine art. It was two-fold in character, being imperial and secular, and inspired by classic tradition, while at the same time the monastic art of the times continued and preserved its strict and severe traditions. Masterpieces of each type were frequent, both historic and ecclesiastical. The greatest existing building of this style and period was S. Marco, Venice (eleventh century).

4. From the Restoration until the Turkish Conquest (1453 A.D.)—Although many fine works of art were produced during this period, it was, on the whole, an age of artistic decline and slow decadence. As the Empire was impoverished, fewer works were executed in precious metal and ivory.

Byzantine art had no period of struggle and slow development, and passed through no archaic stage. It represented the union of the mature styles of the nearer East and West, and showed small desire to draw fresh truth from nature, being content instead to blend the stored fruits of its knowledge for the production of its masterpieces. Its chief element was not so much the art of Rome, but of Sassanid Persia, and the Hellenized East. It was from the East that it acquired its dislike of realistic representation, its love of domed and vaulted buildings, and its delight in oriental decorative pattern and sumptuous richness of colour. It was above all a great decorative art—formal, splendid, ceremonial, and reflecting the set ritual of the Court and the Church. We find the key to it, not in nature and the spontaneous joy and beauty of life, but in some such scene as Gibbon has described, when telling of the visit of Luitprand, Bishop of Cremona, to the Emperor Constantine VII. in the year 948 A.D., "When he (Luitprand) approached the throne the birds of the golden tree began to warble their notes, which were accompanied by the roaring of two lions of gold. With his companions, Luitprand was compelled to bow and to fall prostrate, and thrice to touch the ground with his forehead. He arose, but in the short time the throne had been hoisted from the floor to the ceiling, the Imperial figure appeared in new and more gorgeous apparel, and the interview was concluded in haughty and majestic silence." Here we have all the set pageantry and convention of Byzantine decoration, which was magnificent for its purpose, but which, in the end, was destined to lose its power and force owing to its lack of fresh stimulus and inspiration, and its divorce from life.

Byzantine art was sternly controlled by the Eastern Church which turned in perhaps not unnatural reaction from the pagan love of form, as shown in the sculptures of Greece and Rome, and employed art instead in a decorative manner only, as an expounder of dogma, and an expression of East Christian ideas. In this way it forms an interesting contrast to Gothic art, the product of the Western Church some centuries later, which mirrored faithfully every joy and sorrow of the human heart.

Mosaics and Painting—In the second Council of Nicea, held in the year 787 A.D. the following statement, found in the Acts, shows the attitude of the medieval Church towards painting. " It is not the invention of the painter which creates pictures but an inviolable law, a tradition of the Church. It is not the painters but the Holy Fathers who have to invent and dictate. To them manifestly belongs the composition, to the painter only the execution." This paragraph is interesting in connexion with both Byzantine mosaics and painting. It shows us once more how tradition took the place of nature, and led to both the greatness and weakness of Byzantine art.

The fine qualities have been well described by Mr Dalton. " If the art of the Christian East is lacking in freshness and enthusiasm, it is spared solecisms and ' uncertainties of inspiration.' The restraint of an ever-present law may impoverish imagination, but it forbids rhetoric, and lends to the artistic language the stately

grandeur of a liturgy.   The mean and trivial accidents of
life do not intrude into the sphere of these high abstrac-
tions ; the vulgar and the foolish thing does not come
nigh them. . . . This art avoids false pathos, false unction,
feeble sentiment.   It is neither over-violent nor over-sweet.
. . . Perhaps it was after all a happy destiny which held
the East-Christian art of the Middle Ages in a servitude
so august and transcendental. . . . It is greatest, it is
most itself, when it frankly renounces nature ; its highest
level is perhaps attained where, as in the best mosaic, a
grave schematic treatment is imposed, where no illusion
of receding distance, no preoccupation with anatomy, is
suffered to distract the eye from the central mystery of
the symbol.   The figures that ennoble these walls often
seem independent of earth ; they owe much of their
grandeur to their detachment.   They exert a compelling
and almost a magical power just because they stand upon
the very line between that which lives and that which is
abstracted." [1] The weakness of Byzantine drawing and
painting   became   apparent   after   the   Restoration.
Byzantine art had never been dramatic, and had never
been filled with the warmth of human joys and sorrows,
and when the artistic creeds became outworn and lifeless,
the artists had lost their imaginative power, and were
content to copy drawings which were often in themselves
copies, and to accept such guidance as has been preserved
to us in the " Guide to Painting," a collection of artistic
precepts collected by the monk Dionysius, in the sixteenth
or early seventeenth century from the works of an earlier
and famous Byzantine painter, Manuel Panselinos of
Thessalonica, who may have lived as early as the thirteenth
century.   In this guide, exact directions are laid down
for the execution of all well-known scenes from Bible

[1] *Byzantine Art and Archeology.*   O. M. Dalton.   Clarendon Press.

PLATE XX

CHRIST CROWNING ROMANUS III AND EODOCIA
IVORY. LATE XITH CENTURY

THE EMPEROR JUSTINIAN WITH THE BISHOP MAXIMIANUS, SUITE, AND GUARDS
MOSAIC IN THE CHURCH OF SAN VITALE, RAVENNA. C. 547 A.D.

history. As an example of the tyranny imposed, the following extract may be quoted :—

Adoration of Magi

" A house. The holy Virgin seated, holding the infant Christ who blesses. Before her, the Magi present their gifts in golden shrines. One of the kings, an old man with a great beard and head uncovered, kneels and gazes on the Christ ; with one hand he proffers Him his gift, and with the other holds his crown. The second king has very little beard, the third none at all. Joseph stands in wonder behind the holy Virgin. Outside the grotto a youth holds the three horses by the bridle. In the background, the three Magi are again seen returning to their country ; an angel goes before to show the way." [1] We also read of the saint who was to be portrayed with " complexion the colour of wheat; hair, eyes, brown ; grand eyebrows and beautiful eyes ; clad in beautiful clothing ; humble, beautiful, faultless," a type that was final and changeless to the Byzantine mind.

Byzantine painting was generally executed in tempera upon plaster or a wooden panel, the outlines of the design being often drawn in with gold. Some of the frescoes are still existing, and the paintings, which were exported by the merchants, have been spread far and wide. Numberless miniatures were also produced in the monasteries, and these and the panel pictures exercised an immense influence upon the art of other countries, particularly upon Italian art which was brought into so close a touch with that of Byzantium. Even until the present day the Byzantine tradition is the chief force in the painting of many parts of Greece, Russia, and Asia Minor.

[1] Didron's *Christian Iconography.* Trans. Margaret Stokes. Bohn.

Mosaics were the most splendid expression of Byzantine decorative art. The art, which was an ancient one, had probably been derived from the East, and was raised to a position of importance in Egypt in Ptolemaic times. From there it spread both to the East again and to the West, where in Rome it grew to be very popular. The Romans, however, chiefly employed *tesseræ* (small cubes) of coloured marbles for their mosaics, while the Byzantines preferred glass *tesseræ* of various colours. Gold and silver *tesseræ* were made by laying gold and silver leaf upon the back of the glass and then covering the leaf by a second thin film of glass to protect it. The mosaics were placed in position by means of cement, and the glowing richness of the solemn figures against their golden backgrounds formed a sumptuous and splendid decoration to dome or wall.

From the time when the Roman princess, Galla Placidia, returned from Constantinople in the beginning of the fifth century and took up her residence at Ravenna, until the end of the sixth century, this town, which had become the artistic centre of Italy, was the most famous centre of the mosaic industry, and was renowned for the magnificent mosaic decorations of its churches. In the early days Venice was under artistic allegiance to Constantinople, and among later mosaics those in the churches of S. Marco and the cathedral at Torcello, dating from the eleventh century, may be mentioned. Fine mosaics were also produced in the Sicilian churches in the twelfth century, although in Sicily the Byzantine craftsmen were probably helped by their Western pupils.

Sculpture—One of the immediate effects of Christianity was a distaste on the part of the Christians for monumental figure sculpture, which to their minds was associated with the rites of pagan worship. This dislike was also shared by the all-conquering Arabs, who read in the preachings of Mohammed a prohibition of anything appertaining to idol-worship, a fact which no doubt had its influence on the Byzantines who were in constant touch with the Mohammedans. At this time also, the general trend of opinion as to artistic decoration in the Near East was in favour of elaborate pattern as opposed to a naturalistic treatment of forms, and Byzantine art, being partly Eastern in spirit, shared to a certain extent the common preference.

As the nude was not studied as in classic times such few figures as were carved soon lost their close relation to life. Figure sculpture became a dependent of architecture and was chiefly concerned with the depicting of members of the Imperial family, high officials, or famous characters from sacred story. Delicate gradations of relief were avoided, and carvings were largely confined to two planes so that a strong effect of light and shade, without half tones, should be obtained, and the effect of strong pattern produced. Some of the most beautiful Byzantine sculptures are shown on the capitals of columns and on the pulpits, or ambones, in the churches. Here we find the most delicate patterns of natural forms, plants, birds and animals, and also entwined scroll-work and geometrical designs. Among the most famous of the carvings are those in ivory, the diptyches, *ikons*, caskets, bookcovers, and tablets, many of which were originally coloured and gilded. The goldsmith's work, tapestry weaving, and the art of enamelling also attained great beauty, and served to keep the Eastern tradition alive in Europe.

Architecture—Once or twice in the world's history a people have become suddenly creative as builders. This was the case with the Byzantines, who drawing their inspiration from the massive buildings of the Romans, and those of Sassanid Persia, and the Hellenized Orient, produced a splendid style of their own, one which showed in the words of Choisy, " The Greek spirit working on Asiatic elements." After the time of Justinian the dome became the dominating feature of the Byzantine style which in this way became sharply differentiated from the Early Christian style. The differing artistic elements that were incorporated into the Byzantine system of building were gradually unified and controlled by the ritual of the Catholic faith and grew to be a Hellenic and oriental expression of Christianity. The ancient building which by every line suggested repose and solidity now gave place to one in which a continual striving, stress and thrust, met by counter pressure, produced a completely new and modern constructional style.

This new architecture was continually experimental ; it was " vividly alive and inventive, frank, bright, and full of colour and yet as rational in its choice and application as in the construction." It showed the Greek genius in its final triumph, changed, orientalized, but still splendidly creative. The old Corinthian capital was superseded by new and beautiful forms, one being the so-called impost capital, in which the impost and capital, instead of being two stones, were merged into one. The engineering which made brick walls support enormous domes was unsurpassed. The summing up of the Byzantine style in its complete beauty is found in Justinian's church of Sancta Sophia.

Sancta Sophia—The first church of Sancta Sophia (Holy Wisdom) was built, according to the historian Socrates, by the Emperor Constantine, who joined it to the Church of Irene which had been erected by his father. It was dedicated in the year 360 A.D., thirty-four years after its foundations were laid, and was twice

injured by fire, the second occasion being at the time of
the Nika rebellion, when it was razed to the ground.
The new church of Justinian was built by a Greek,
Anthemius of Tralles, with the help of another Greek
architect, Isidorus of Miletus. It was begun on
23 February, 532 A.D., and was finished and dedicated on 26 December, 537. In the year 558 it was
damaged by an earthquake and restored by Isidorus,
Anthemius being dead. In the chronicle of Procopius,
which was probably finished by the year 558 or 559 A.D.
we read that " Anthemius of Tralles, the most skilled in
the builders' art, not only of his own but of all former
times, carried forward the king's zealous intentions,
organized the labours of the workmen and prepared
models of the building,"[1] while, Paulus, an official and
poet of Justinian's court, wrote that " Anthemius, skilled
in setting out a plan, laid the foundations."[2]

Agathias, a second historian, although he was not a
contemporary of Anthemius, came to Constantinople in
the year 554 A.D., and has left us further particulars of the
great architect. He says that Anthemius " was the man
who devised and worked at every part," and " gave to the
walls strength to resist the pushing arches, which were
like active demons."[3] He then adds some interesting
particulars of the architect and his family.

" Now this Anthemius was born at Tralles, and he was
an inventor of machines ; one of those who apply designs
to material, and make models and imitations of real
things. He was distinguished in this, and had reached
the summit of mathematical knowledge, just as his brother
was distinguished in letters. Besides these, there were
three other brothers. Olympus, famous for his knowledge
of law, and Dioscorus and Alexander, both skilled in

[1] *Sancta Sophia.* Lethaby & Swainson. Macmillan. [2] *Ibid.* [3] *Ibid.*

medicine. Of these Dioscorus lived in his native land, and Alexander in Old Rome. But the fame of the skill of Anthemius and Metrodorus reached the Emperor, and they were invited to Constantinople, where they spent the rest of their lives, each presenting wonderful examples of his skill. One taught letters, the other raised wonderful buildings throughout the city, and in many other places ; these, I think, even if nothing were said about them, as long as they remained unharmed, would be sufficient to win for him perpetual glory."[1]

In planning S. Sophia, which is one of the finest buildings in the world, Anthemius was probably influenced by three types of churches already erected in Constantinople. These were the church of S. Sergius, which was square and domed ; the church of S. John Studius, which was Basilican in form ; and the Church of the Apostles, which was built in cruciform style. S. Sophia seems a synthesis of these three types, and shows, as its most striking characteristics, the introduction of the impost capital, and the merging of all subsidiary spaces in one great central building. The immense dome, which dominates the city, seems " poised rather than supported ; no dome floats like that of S. Sophia." The outside of the church, as is often the case in Byzantine buildings, is somewhat gaunt and bare, but the inside, in spite of the whitewash, which by order of the Mohammedans now covers almost all the mosaics, is magnificent. There is no better description of it than that written by Procopius, who saw it in the first flush of its new glory.

" The church . . . presents a most glorious spectacle, extraordinary to those who behold it, and altogether incredible to those who are told of it. In height it rises to the very heavens, and overtops the neighbouring build-

[1] *Sancta Sophia.* Lethaby and Swainson. Macmillan.

ings like a ship anchored among them, appearing above the rest of the city, which it adorns, and forms a part of it.   One of its beauties is that, being a part of, and growing out of the city, it rises so high that the whole city can be seen as from a watch tower. The length and breadth are so judiciously arranged that it appears to be both long and wide without being disproportionate. . . .

Let us now proceed to describe the remaining parts of the church.   The entire ceiling is covered with pure gold, which adds to its glory, though the reflections of the gold upon the marble surpass it in beauty.   Who could tell the beauty of the columns and marbles with which the church is adorned ?   One would think that one had come across a meadow full of flowers in bloom !   Who would not admire the purple tints of some and the green of others, the glowing red and the glittering white, and those too which Nature, painter-like, has marked with the strongest contrasts of colour ?   Whoever enters there to worship perceives at once that it is not by any human strength or skill, but by favour of God, that the work has been perfected ; the mind rises sublime to commune with God, feeling that He cannot be far off, but must especially love to dwell in the place that He has chosen ; and this is felt, not only when a man sees it for the first time, but it always makes the same impression upon him, as though he had never seen it before." [1]

EXTRACTS

A description of S. Sophia, being part of an opening ode by the Court poet and official Paulus, recited on

[1] *Sancta Sophia*. Lethaby and Swainson. Macmillan.

December 24th, 563 A.D., perhaps in the church itself, or in the hall of the Imperial Palace.

"Whoever raises his eyes to the beauteous firmament of the roof, scarce dares to gaze on its rounded expanse sprinkled with the stars of heaven, but turns to the fresh green marble below, seeming, as it were, to see flower-bordered streams of Thessaly, and budding corn, and woods thick with trees; leaping flocks too, and twining olive-trees and the vine with green tendrils, or the deep blue peace of summer sea, broken by the plashing oars of spray-girt ship. Whoever puts foot within the sacred fane would live there for ever, and his eyes will fill with tears of joy. Thus by divine counsel, while angels watched, was the temple built again.

"At last the holy man had come, and the great door of the new-built temple groaned on its opening hinges, inviting the emperor and people to enter; and when the inner part was seen sorrow fled from the hearts of all, as the sun lit the glories of the temple. 'Twas for the emperor to lead the way for his people and on the morrow to celebrate the birth of Christ. And when the first gleam of light, rosy-armed, driving away the dark shadows, leapt from arch to arch, then all the princes and people with one voice hymned their songs and prayer and praise; and as they came to the sacred courts, it seemed to them as if the mighty arches were set in heaven.

"Yet who, even in the measures of Homer, shall song the marble pastures gathered on the lofty walls and spreading pavement of the mighty church? These the iron with its metal tooth has gnawed, the fresh green from Carystus, and many-coloured marble from the Phrygian range, in which a rosy blush mingles with white, or it shines bright with flowers of deep red and silver. There is a wealth of porphyry too, powdered with bright stars, that has once laden the river-boat on the broad Nile. You would see an emerald green from Spata, and the glittering marble with watery veins, which the tool has worked in the deep bosom of the Jassian hills, showing slanting streaks blood-red and livid white. From the Lydian creek came the bright stone mingled with streaks of red. Stone, too, there is, that the Lybian sun warming with his golden light has nurtured in the deep-bosomed depths of the hills of the Moors, of crocus colour glittering like gold; and the product of the Celtic crags, a wealth of crystal like milk poured here and there on a flesh of glittering black. There is the precious onyx as if gold were shining

through it ; and the marble that the land of Atrax yields, not from
same upland glen, but from the level plains ; in part fresh green as
the sea or emerald stone, or again like blue cornflowers in grass.
With here and there a drift of fallen snow . . . a sweet mingled contrast
on the dark shining surface." [1]

---

[1] *Sancta Sophia.*   Lethaby and Swainson.   Macmillan.

LESSON XI

ARAB ART

PART I.—ELEMENTARY LESSON IN STORY FORM

INTRODUCTION—Last Lesson.—This is a story about a young prince who was born rather more than two hundred years after Sancta Sophia was built by Justinian. This prince was not a Greek or Roman, but an Arab. Many of his fellow-countrymen lived wandering lives in the desert and slept in tents at night. Others dwelt in big cities, for the Arabs had grown to be a very powerful nation, and had conquered a great many countries.

1. The Caliphate of the East. Abderrahman's Escape—Abderrahman was a tall young Arab prince. He had reddish hair, parted in two long curls, ruddy cheeks, and a keen and clever face. He lived far away in Syria in a town called Damascus. Inside in the palace there were beautiful rugs and carpets, and gold and enamelled cups and plates, and rich silk hangings, covered with embroidery. Outside, in the courtyard, palms and orange trees made a welcome shade from the burning sun, and when night fell and the moon rose, the nightingales sang enchantingly, and little fountains, full of gold and silver fish, plashed and murmured and threw their crystal showers into the fragrant dusk.

Abderrahman was as happy as the day is long until a terrible thing happened. A wicked and cruel man of the House of Abbas determined that Abderrahman's family should rule no more in Damascus and that he himself should be the Caliph or governor. He was so powerful

250

that no one could stop him. He had all Abderrahman's family put to death, and would have killed the young prince too, if he had not happened to be away in the country at the time.

Being warned by friends of the danger that he was in, Abderrahman called his young brother and his friends and they fled together secretly, to a little village on the banks of the river Euphrates. Here they pitched their tents and rested, thinking themselves out of danger. They did not know that the enemy, led by the sons of the House of Abbas, was marching after them, their black banners fluttering in the wind.

One evening, when Abderrahman was sitting in his tent, sheltering from a storm of rain and wind that was passing over the land, and watching the great river as it rushed along between its banks, swollen and turbulent, he heard sounds of disturbance from the direction of the village. He was just going to look what was happening when his brother burst into the tent crying, " Away, away with thee, O brother, for yonder black banners are the banners of the house of Abbas ! "

Abderrahman gave one look at the approaching horsemen, and calling to his friends to follow, rushed to the river where there were bushes and trees that would afford some cover from the enemy. Hardly had he left his tent before it was surrounded by the soldiers, who quickly ransacked it, and furious at finding their quarry escaped, turned in the direction of the river.

Abderrahman saw that one chance of safety only was left to him. Calling to the others to follow suit he plunged into the great river just as the soldiers reached its banks. Baulked in their purpose, the soldiers shouted aloud in their anger, but they dared not follow the young prince because of the wild rush of the water. At first

Abderrahman thought that all was over. The current ran so swiftly that time and again he felt himself to be battling against it in vain. Fortune favoured him, however, and at last he reached the other side in safety and sank down exhausted by his faithful servant Bedr, who had kept close to his master's side and had braved the river with him.

2. The Years of Wandering—Then followed years of wandering. Abu Abbas, the enemy, was Caliph in Damascus, and Abderrahman dared not return to his old home. But in spite of this he found many friends. The Arab kingdom was a very large one, and in Egypt and Morocco the young prince found wandering tribes who befriended him, and who sympathized with his family rather than with that of the new Caliph, the usurper. These wandering Arabs and Berbers asked Abderrahman to live with them and share their tents, for they were charmed by his noble bearing and his courage and energy. He was very happy in his new life, for all Arabs have an instinctive love of the desert. Yet sometimes, when he sat before his tent in the evening, and watched the sun as it set, turning the world to a vision of gold and flame, his eyes would search the interminable wastes of sand which lay around him like a great and limitless sea, boundless and forsaken, and he would wonder if beyond them a new kingdom waited for him. The old Caliphate of the East was closed to him. Why should not he, Abderrahman, rule over a new and glorious Arab kingdom in the West?

His thoughts turned to Spain, the country that lay beyond Morocco, across the Straits. There were Arabs living there, and some of them had begged him to settle in the country and govern them. The thought of the beautiful and fertile land never left him, and one day,

when he was by the sea, he felt he could wait no longer.
He called his faithful Bedr, and pointing across the
Straits to where the Spanish shores were faintly visible
through the haze of heat and sunshine, he said, " See,
yonder is Spain ; take a boat, cross over, and see what
welcome will await me if I follow thee as a new ruler and
leader for the people."

Then followed long days, when Abderrahman waited
by the sea-shore, always watching until the boat should
return and Bedr should bring him tidings of Spain. One
morning when the prince was kneeling on the shore in
the sunshine, saying his prayers, a white figure against
the blue sea, he heard a shout. The boat was in sight,
and soon Abderrahman could recognize the figure of
Bedr standing on the bows. By him were some strangers,
Arabs, whom he did not know. What news did they
bring ? At last the boat reached the shore, and Bedr
fell on his knees before his master, kissing his hand. He
told him that he had brought friends, eager to welcome
him to Spain. Abderrahman, full of delight, was soon
ready to start and the boat set sail again for Spain.
How he watched the shores of the new land as they
became clearer and more distinct every hour ! How
soon would he be ruler over them ?

At last the ship slipped into the harbour, where many
Arabs were waiting to welcome their new ruler. But
there were other Arabs too, who were not eager to meet
him, and Abderrahman had many battles to fight before,
with the help of his friends, he captured the town of
Cordova and settled down there to rule the land.

Cordova and the Mosque—Abderrahman determined
that Cordova should be one of the most beautiful towns
in the world. He remembered Damascus where he had
lived as a child, and decided to copy some of its most

famous buildings. First he set to work to beautify the old Cordova palace or alcazar. When the rooms were richly furnished with exquisite rugs, silks, and embroideries, and costly and beautiful objects of every kind, the new Sultan turned his thoughts to the garden. He dearly loved flowers and choice fruits ; so calling a clever botanist and giving him money he said to him, " I want you to go to far-away lands and collect rare and choice plants, trees, and seeds of every kind, and what you find, bring back to me, so that my fair gardens and this beautiful town shall break into bud and blossom from end to end."

There was another plan that Abderrahman had made, and for this he cared more than for all the others. He believed in the teaching of an old Arabian called Mohammed, the Prophet, long since dead, and this was one of the things that he said, " Whosoever builds for God a place of worship, be it only as the nest of a grouse, God buildeth for him a place in Paradise." So Abderrahman determined that he would please God and Mohammed by building a great mosque or church, as like as possible to the mosque at Damascus where he had worshipped as a child. He sent for clever builders, and ordering hundreds of his own Arabs to make ready, the work was soon begun.

Day after day Abderrahman came to watch the progress of the building. How fast it grew ! It stood high above the river, and had great walls which enclosed an open court which Abderrahman planted with orange trees and palms. At one end of the court was a covered-in space, and day by day fresh columns were added to support its roof. Abderrahman thought that even then the mosque was beautiful, but if he had only known, his successors were to make it far more wonderful still. Then, in their day, the mosque would glow with colour and richness. A

PLATE XXI

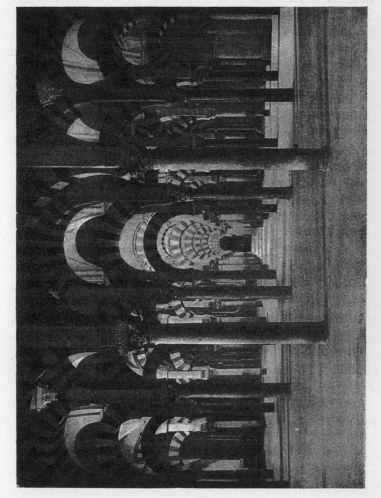

INTERIOR OF THE MOSQUE, CORDOVA

forest of columns, made of porphyry, jasper and coloured marbles of every sort, and bright with inlay of lapis-lazuli would support the roof. The Byzantine Emperor would send from Byzantium a shipload of little glass cubes for the mosaics, and wonderful jewels and ivory and sweet-scented woods would be brought from far distant lands to increase the beauty of the great mosque.

Abderrahman wandered through the building day after day, standing in the dim light among the shadowy aisles, gazing up at the horse-shoe arches above him, and some-times ascending the pulpit and preaching to the people who had already begun to crowd the mosque. The servants of the building strewed flowers up and down among the pillars and arches, and their fragrance mixed with the sweet scent of ambergris and aloe wood which burnt in the swinging censers hanging from the roof.

One evening Abderrahman left the mosque and turned to retrace his steps to the palace. Rich carpets were spread for him to walk on ; servants followed him, and the people bowed as he passed. But he was tired. He was growing old and he walked slowly. The mosque was not finished, and he knew that the task of completing it must be left to his son. On reaching the palace he signed to his servants to leave him, and entering the gardens, he sank down upon a marble seat. The dusk fell ; the water lilies in the fountain basins gleamed palely in the dim light and the dew lay thickly upon the leaves and flowers. A nightingale burst into song in a bush near by, and its mate answered it joyfully from among the fragrance of the orange blossom. Down by the river the frogs croaked in a monotonous chorus. Abderrahman rose and returned slowly to the palace, but he could not sleep. At midnight he heard faintly in the distance the cry of the watcher at the mosque, "God is great, to pray

is better than to sleep." At four o'clock his cry sounded
faintly again, "Day is breaking, let God be praised."
The old man could not sleep, but he was happy, for, when
he had passed away, he knew that his great mosque would
remain, his lasting memorial throughout the centuries.

Notes on the Story—Abderrahman I. was the son of Moawia, and
grandson of the Caliph Hisham Ibn Abdil-Malek. (See under
"Caliphate of the West.") The story is founded on the full account
given by the old Arabian historian Ibn Hayyam in his *Muktabis*, and
quoted at length in Al Makkari's *History of the Mahommedan
Dynasties in Spain*, which was written in the sixteenth century and
translated into English in 1843. It has been chosen rather than any
other story in Arab history because it brings in both the Caliphates,
and also because an Arabian mosque in Spain is more accessible to
Europeans than one in the East, and in consequence is better known
to them. The last scene of the story is imaginary and also the scene
in the desert.

A convent now stands on the site of Abderrahman's palace of Ressafah,
and with the exception of the mosque and bridge and a part of the
walls and towers, very little remains of the buildings of the Omayyad
princes of Cordova.

PART II.—MATERIAL FOR ADVANCED LESSONS ONLY

The Arabs. Civilization, Religion, Wars, Dominion
—The Arabs, or inhabitants of the Arabian peninsula,
were a people composed of various tribes, which differed
from one another in character, customs and religious
belief. Modern Arabians describe the period before the
birth of Mohammed as "the time of ignorance," but it was,
in point of fact, an age of great culture. Before the time
of the Persian Conquest of Arabia in the sixth century
A.D. the Yemenite Arabs had enjoyed centuries of refined
and luxurious civilization. A legendary queen of Yemen,
the Queen of Sheba of the Bible, paid a visit to the court
of King Solomon at Jerusalem about the year 1000 B.C.,

while some of the Arabian inscriptions that have been
found have been attributed by some scholars to the ninth,
and by others to the sixteenth, century B.C. Sana, the
capital of Southern Arabia, was a city of much wealth,
and the accounts of its beauty and luxury, when conquered
by the Persians, read like a fairy tale. At the time of
this conquest many of the Yemenite Arabs were driven
out of their country and took refuge in what they called
"the wilderness of Egypt," and it was here that their
friendship with the Copts began, which was to play so
important a part in connection with Arab Art.

Whereas a large number of the Yemenite Arabs were
Christians of the Monophysite sect, like the Copts, the
mass of the people worshipped jinns and fetiches of
the simplest kinds, and vaguely acknowledged "Allah the
God." Over three hundred tribal idols were kept in the
Ka-ba at Mecca in the sixth century, while the chief object
of worship was a black stone, preserved in the sanctuary.

With the coming of Mohammed, all this came to an end.
The wealth and prosperity of the country, which owing
to the growth of shipping and the subsequent loss of the
caravan trade had been on the decline, were strengthened
and renewed and the great era of Arab civilization began.
This era of supremacy lasted from the death of the
Prophet until the fall of the Caliphate of Baghdad
in 1258 A.D.

The prophet, or Apostle, as he was called, was born at
Mecca in Northern Arabia, in the year 568 or 569 A.D.
He believed himself to be divinely appointed as the
mouthpiece of the Deity, and held that his chief duty
was to abolish the old Arabian pagan beliefs, particularly
all forms of idol worship, and in their place to substitute
and restore the ancient religion of Abraham, or, as he
called him, Ibraham. He preached the unity of God and

the resurrection of the body, but not the doctrine of the Trinity or the beliefs of the New Testament. Certain Arabian customs and beliefs were incorporated into the new doctrine, which was called Islam by Mohammed, but was more generally known as Mohammedanism, and a declaration of all of these beliefs was collected by the prophet in the Koran, which was composed of a series of tracts or pamphlets, written by him at various times.

Religious wars were an essential part of the creed of Mohammed, although the Jews and Christians, the " people of the Book," were often allowed to pursue their religion in peace, and tribute only was exacted from them. The Yemenite Arabs were tolerant and gentle to their enemies, but the Syrian Arabs allowed small quarter to the heathen and followed the doctrines of the Koran—" Fight in the cause of Allah ! . . . The spoils are Allah's and the Prophet's. When you meet those who misbelieve, strike off their heads. . . . Ye shall be called out against a people endowed with vehement valour, and shall fight them or they shall become Moslems. . . . Allah promised you many spoils." And again, " Stir up the faithful to the fight. Twenty of you who stand firm shall vanquish two hundred, and a hundred shall put a thousand to flight . . . and be ye steadfast and fear Allah and if the foe come upon you in haste, Allah will succour you with five thousand angels." The Arabians soon gave way before the Moslem troops, which, led by the prophet, carried all before them and even captured Mecca. The conversion of the people soon followed, and fired with fresh zeal, Mohamed conceived the idea of sending missions to all sovereigns and rulers, promising them safety on the condition that they embraced Islam.

Then followed the extraordinary story of Moslem conquests. Mohamed died in the year 632 A.D., but still

possessed by religious fanaticism, the followers of the
Prophet swept like a tide westward and eastward.
Nothing could stop these Arab hordes. The neighbouring countries fell before them, and before a century had
passed Mesopotamia, Persia, North Africa, Southern
Spain, Syria, Western Turkistan, Sind (North India)
and Egypt formed part of the Arabian Empire, although
in certain instances the countries were only partially
subjugated. The followers of the Prophet have been
known ever since by the name of Saracens, which was
the name given by the Christians of the Middle Ages to
their Mohammedan opponents, in particular to those in
Europe and the Near East.

The Eastern and Western Caliphates—On the
death of Mohammed a ruler was appointed to follow him,
who was known as the Caliph or " Successor " (from the
Arabic *khaleefa*). He was obliged to be of the tribe of
the Prophet, and was chosen by popular election, according
to the old Arab custom in electing their Chief. The
Eastern Caliphate was established in 632 A.D., with the
appointment of Abu-Bekr. Its history falls into three
main divisions :

1. The rule of the first four caliphs, the immediate successors of Mohammed.
2. The rule of the Omayyad caliphs, 661-744 A.D.,
   Damascus the capital.
3. The rule of the Abbasid caliphs, 763-1258 A.D.,
   Baghdad the capital. (Capital transferred to
   Samarra, about eighty miles north of Baghdad,
   during the years 836-861.) During this dynasty
   the power of the Arab Empire reached its height
   under the rule of the Caliph Abu-Jafari, known
   as Mansur (754-775), and that of his grandson,
   the Caliph Harun al-Raschid, the splendour and

luxury of whose court had been immortalized in *The Thousand and One Nights.*

At the time of the Abbasid succession, Abderrahman, a princely refugee of the house of the Omayyads, fled from the East and eventually found shelter in Spain. A large number of the Spanish Moslems were sworn to fealty to the Omayyads, and they gladly welcomed the young prince and invited him to rule the country. After much fighting with hostile Arab tribes he established his rule in Cordova, and it was here that his descendant, the great Abderrahman III., founded in the beginning of the tenth century the independent Caliphate of the West. This Western Caliphate became a brilliant centre of Arab culture, renowned for its learning and art, and famous for its schools, palaces, and great mosque.

In the year 1009 A.D. civil war broke out, the Caliph Hisham II. was deposed, and a succession of Pretenders were set up, and were deposed or killed, until, in the year 1031, the rule of the Omayyads at Cordova came to an end. (The Yemenite tribes, however, acknowledged as their Caliph the deposed grandson of Abderrahman III., Hisham II., until his death in about the year 1060.)

The Moslem Occupation of Spain—The history of the Moslem occupation of Spain is an extremely complicated one owing to the incessant feuds which raged between the various conquering tribes inhabiting the peninsula. All that need be said on the subject here is that the chief among these Moslem tribes were the Yemenite and Mudarite Arabs (two eternally hostile tribes), the Berbers of N. Africa and the Moors. The term Moor is generally used to designate the entire Moslem population of Spain, but this is incorrect. The Moors or Almohades were a North African tribe who invaded the country in 1146 A.D., and shortly afterwards ruled in the peninsula.

The last of them was driven out of Spain in the second half of the thirteenth century by the united efforts of St Ferdinand and the famous Yemenite Arab Mohammed I. of Granada, better known as Al Ahmar, who afterwards built the palace of the Alhambra. After the downfall of the Caliphate at Cordova the Abbadites, a federation of Yemenite Arabs, became rulers of more than half of Moslem Spain, and made their capital of Seville " as great a centre of civilization in the eleventh century as Cordova had been in the tenth."

The Arabs in Egypt—The Arabs began the conquest of Egypt in the year 639 A.D., and in 641 the country became a province of the Eastern Caliphate. Upon the capitulation of Alexandria the victorious general 'Amr wrote to the Caliph, " I have taken a city of which I can but say that it contains 4000 palaces, 4000 baths, 400 theatres, 12,000 sellers of vegetables, 40,000 tributary Jews." The numbers in this letter are obviously over-statements, no doubt due to later copyists of the letter, but the description serves to give some idea of the glories of the city of Alexander the Great. The Arabs let the splendid classic buildings fall into decay and founded a new capital not far north of the old Egyptian capital of Memphis, where 'Amr had pitched his tent before marching north upon Alexandria. This new city he called " El-Fustat " or " The Tent," and here 'Amr built his mosque. The Moslem rule in the valley was firmly established, and intermarriage between the Arabs and the Copts, or native Egyptians, took place.

From the years 868-969 A.D. Egypt was ruled by Turkish Governors appointed by the Caliphs. Tulun, the greatest of them, was appointed in 868, but when a year had passed he asserted his independence and had his head stamped upon the Egyptian coins.

The greatest period of Arab rule in Egypt was during the years 969-1171 A.D., when the Fatimides, who professed to be descendants of the Prophet, governed the land. They had previously established a kingdom in North Africa, but not content with this, they turned their thoughts to the country of the Nile. They not only conquered Egypt, but they established an independent Caliphate at El Kahira or Cairo, the great suburb which they built near El-Fustat. Here they erected splendid palaces and mosques, and it is during this period that some of the finest examples of Arab art were produced.

In the year 1171 A.D. Saladin reconquered Egypt for the Caliphate of Baghdad. Members of his House ruled until the year 1249 A.D., after which date Egypt passed under the rule of the Turkish Sultans.

The Fall of the Arab Empire—The caliphs of Baghdad were not able to hold their vast Empire together for long. We have seen how separate kingdoms were established in Spain, North Africa and Egypt, and in Asia Khorasan, Persia, Mesopotamia and Syria also detached themselves, although they set up no rival to the Caliphate. It was at this time that the Turks from Central Asia and the Mongols, who were a branch of the same race, began to leave their own districts and to start their long series of foreign invasions. The caliphs met the danger in the Near East by diverting the energies of the Turks, and appointing them as their governors. These men soon embraced Mohammedan religion and civilization, and were not long in wresting the power from their masters and bringing the Arabs under their own rule. In 1055 A.D. the Seljuk Turks, having subdued Persia, proceeded to Baghdad, where their leader, Turghril Bey, was recognized in Friday prayers as the lieutenant of the Caliph, which meant in reality that he was his master. The end of the Caliphate came in the year 1258, when Baghdad was sacked by Halaku, the Mongol (sometimes spoken of as Halaku the Tartar, Tartar being the name given to descendants of the Mongols), while in 1453 A.D. Byzantium also was captured, and was occupied by the Turks.

Art. General Characteristics—The Arabs had but slight creative artistic instinct and little imagination. The conquests that followed the birth of the Prophet with such amazing rapidity brought with them the necessity for the erection of numberless buildings, and the Arabs were content to adopt the current artistic ideals, together with the buildings, of each nation that they conquered, and to employ foreign workmen in the carrying out of their schemes. A more correct title for this lesson would have been "art produced under Arab rule." At the same time, however, the old name is a more convenient one, for wherever the Arab established his dominion certain artistic styles are to be found and the Arab is the connecting link between them.

In the words of Dr Martin, "Mohammedan art is only a natural development of the antique." Monuments that are now ruined were in a state of good preservation at the time of the Arab conquests and the new rulers of ancient civilizations found abundant material on which to model their art. The craftsmen of the conquered countries did what they could to please their new masters, and when the latter were Sunnites in belief (see page 265), the native artists represented only such motives as were approved of by those in power.

To understand the distribution of Arab art we must have some knowledge of Arab history, and it is for this reason that so many pages of this lesson have been devoted to a historical outline. When we turn again to the art of

the people we find that three main influences are
apparent in it.   They are those of Byzantium, the
Sassanids of Persia, and the Egyptian Copts.   The art
of China was also much valued by the Arabs, and an old
historian wrote that nothing was more fashionable for
wedding presents than "beautiful things from China."
Arab art was produced by the Arabs themselves as well as
by their foreign teachers and craftsmen, but their work
when it was finished was only touched with their own
personality, and reflected for the most part the inspiration
of other nations.

The historian Iln Khaldim wrote that "when a State
is composed of Arabs it needs people of another country
to build," and "people of another country" were also
needed for the production of Arab arts and crafts.
The Moslem troops incorporated men of many and
varied nationalities, and also a number of skilled
craftsmen from Persia, Syria and Egypt.   In this way
the arts of Asia and Africa were spread far and wide,
modified to suit the needs of the Mohammedan faith, and
stamped by the personality of the conquering Arab.   The
Arabs were no purists.   While certain buildings they
erected were simply Coptic, Syrian or Byzantine, others
were composed of a medley of styles, blended together
without any feeling for artistic unity.   Many Arab
buildings are full of a romantic charm and fascination, and
contain what Professor Lethaby describes as "elasticity,
intricacy, and glitter, a suggestion of fountain spray
and singing birds";[1] but when we look at many of
them more closely we become conscious of an inherent
weakness, and the lack of a dominating intellectual
conception.

Arab art reached its highest level at the Court of the

[1] *Architecture.*   Lethaby.   Williams & Norgate.

Fatimides. The work of this period is marked by rare delicacy and exquisite taste. Designs were bold and rhythmic, and technical execution reached an extremely high standard. With the fall of Baghdad, Arabic art based on the antique tradition came to an end. Later developments of Arabic art took place under the rule of the Turkish Sultans, but a good deal of the earlier simplicity of design was lost, and the art steadily declined. The Mohammedan art of the Persians, on the other hand, continued to flourish, and during the fifteenth, sixteenth, and seventeenth centuries Persian miniatures, textiles, and pottery attained very great beauty.

Ornament and Design — The belief has been generally held that Mohammed, in his hatred of idols, prohibited all representation of human and animal forms in art. In the *Sunna,* or written law of the Prophet, there is only one verse however into which this prohibition might be read. It runs as follows : " O believer, wine, games of chance, and idols are abominations, invented by Satan. Abstain from them and you will be happy." There was, however, a second book in which the Mohammedan found his creed. This was the *Hadith* or commentary on the law of the *Sunna,* said to contain words spoken by the Prophet and recorded by his disciples. In the *Hadith* the prohibition as to idols has been enlarged, either consciously or unconsciously, into the following dictums :—" Woe to him who has painted a living creature ! At the day of the last judgment the persons represented by him will come out of the tomb and join themselves to him to demand of him a soul. Then that man, unable to give life to his work, will burn in eternal flames." And again, " God has sent against them three kinds of men to crush and confound them. These are the proud, the polytheists, and the idolaters.

Refrain from representing either the Lord or man, and never paint anything but trees, flowers and inanimate objects."

There is no doubt that these verses greatly influenced Arab art and accounted for the fact that the Arabs had no schools of figure-sculpture and painting. But as far as the applied arts were concerned, the prohibitions were continually disregarded by certain sections of the Arab community. This has been amply proved by old Arab inventories of works of art that have been preserved, and also by the numberless existing specimens of Arab work containing conventionalized human and animal representations which are found in all parts of the ancient Arab kingdom. In the Alhambra, even portraits have been found, painted in fresco, and figure subjects, also in fresco, have been discovered in Arab buildings in the Near East. There is no doubt that the Persians and Copts were largely responsible for these designs containing animate forms, but such works of art when produced found a ready acceptance at both mosque and palace, except at the time when the Sunnite Arabs, who followed the law of the *Hadith*, were in power. The Arabs who belonged to the Shiite sect disregarded the prohibitions of the *Hadith*, and did not discourage the representation of animate forms in art. It is also a well-known fact that many of the caliphs were un-believers, taking little notice of any religious law.

The first contact of Islam upon the older civilizations proved to be a stimulating one. There is an intense vitality about early Mohammedan decorative design, and ancient motives lived again under Arab patronage. The history of these designs is often most interesting. For example, the winged bull or lion of ancient Babylonia was passed on by Assyria to Persia, from Persia to

Byzantium, and through the help of the Arab is found again in Sicily and Spain, from where it was copied by Romanesque sculptors.

The chief form of Sunnite Arab ornament was fanciful and intricate geometrical designs known as arabesques, which are found on every kind of Arab work, and which, when used architecturally, were carved in stone or moulded in plaster or stucco. Texts from the Koran in stone and plaster relief were also a characteristic of architectural ornament, and are frequently met with in the lesser arts also. The stalactite vaulting of Arab buildings is a special feature of Arab and Mohammedan architecture, and is found in the art of no other people. It was first introduced in the tomb of Zobeide, the favourite wife of Harun al-Raschid, which was built at the end of the eighth century at Baghdad. It was not until the later years of Arab rule that geometrical ornament began to run riot over all buildings, until the simplicity of surface, and feeling for dignity, were lost. The later mosques at Cairo and the decorations of the Alhambra are examples of this over-elaboration of detail. Another feature of Arab art is the lattice-work in wood and stone. The wooden lattice windows in particular were copied on every hand, and are still in use to-day in many parts of the East.

Byzantine Influence—The nomadic Arabs produced no works of art, but lived wandering lives in the desert. The Yemenite Arabs, on the other hand, were town dwellers, and developed a local school of art of their own. This school soon came under the influence of Byzantium, and we read that in the sixth century the Yemenite chief Abrahâ applied to the Emperor Justinian for aid in the building of a new church. So great was Abrahâ's interest in the building that it is recorded that

he lived and slept within its walls during the whole time
of its erection.   The Dome of the Rock at Jerusalem is
almost purely Byzantine work, and we are told by the
Arab historian Samhoudy that when the Caliph El Walid
wanted to build a great mosque at Medina he wrote to
the Greek Emperor, who sent him mosaics and eighty
workmen, forty of whom were Greeks and forty Copts.
The Arabs also learnt the art of gilding, enamelling and
wood carving from the Byzantines.

Coptic Influence—The Copts, or native Christian
population of Egypt, were the true descendants of the
ancient Egyptians.   The headquarters of the Coptic
School was at the Hellenistic city of Alexandria, and
both Greek art and the art of Byzantium exercised a
strong influence upon the Coptic craftsmen.   However
the ancient mystical strain which they had inherited from
their famous ancestors soon awoke in them, with the
result that the Coptic Church of Alexandria separated
itself from the Church of Byzantium to pursue a more
mystical creed of its own, one which recognized the
divine nature alone of Christ.   After this time Coptic
art became distinct and individual.   Its figure subjects
became more crude, but on the other hand the orna-
mental motives it produced grew in originality and
power.   The chief form of Coptic ornament took the
shape of conventionalized groupings of foliage, flowers
and birds, and delicate interlacing designs of knot-work
and scrolls, in part the result of Persian influence.   The
Copts also represented Biblical scenes, conventionalized
human figures, hunting scenes, and other such subjects,
until the time of the Arab rule, when, to please their
conquerors, who were Sunnite Arabs, the Coptic craftsmen confined their artistic energies to the representation
of inanimate forms.   With the accession of the Fatimides.

who were Arabs of the Shiite sect, the Copts regained their old freedom, and were once more able to continue their ancient traditions of work.

The Copts also delighted in representations of fantastic and hybrid figures, half animal, half bird, often part human and part flower. Many of these figures had symbolic meaning. The dragon-fly symbolized the Holy Spirit ; an eagle trampling upon a gazelle or lion stood for majesty rising above impurity and darkness ; force was represented by two winged lions affronted ; animals and birds in pairs signified the eternal principle of life, while eagles and lions alone were often introduced as the symbols of the ancient gods of Yemen. The lotus, sun, and royal serpent were also ancient Egyptian emblems used by the Copts.

Through the Arab employment of the Egyptian Christians, Coptic art was spread far and wide. In distant countries we find their favourite form of architecture, which was modelled on the design of the ancient Assyrian buildings, showing their pointed arches and the horizontal exterior lines which aimed at an architectural profile, where terrace after terrace would rise against the sky. According to M. Gayet, the Copts also made three-quarters of the damascened bronzes and enamelled crystals of the time " in which are seen garlands of flowers and inscriptions, hunters, birds, jackals and gazelles." They also taught to the Arabs the arts of blowing and making glass, the weaving of wool, linen and silk, and the arts of embroidery and lace-making, which they had carried to a high level of excellence.

Persian Influence—From the years 226-641 A.D. Persia and Mesopotamia were ruled by the Sassanids, a powerful and highly cultured Persian dynasty. Their art was founded on the ancient art of Persia, which had grown out of the art of Babylonia and Assyria, and was influenced by Hellenic art,with which thePersians had become familiar at the time when Alexander the Great, and later the Macedonian dynasty of the Seleucids, had ruled the country. Relations between Persia and China were well established during the Sassanid rule, and the artistic ideals of each country also acted and re-acted upon the other.

Arab art first came under the influence of Sassanid art in the second half of the sixth century, when Yemen was conquered by Chosroes I., one of the greatest of the Sassanian rulers. The ineradicable Persian strain in Egyptian and Spanish-Arab art can be traced to this time, when Persian and Yemenite Arabs dwelt side by side. Nearly a hundred years later the Arabs in their turn conquered Persia and brought the Sassanid dynasty to an end. They founded their new capital of Baghdad, only a few miles from the Sassanids' old winter capital of Ctesiphon, and erected their new buildings in very much the same style as that of the buildings of the late rulers of the country. The buildings of the Sassanids, with their barrel vaults, cupolas, and great doorways, were in this way perpetuated, in modified forms, and erected by the Arabs in different parts of their great empire. The Arabs also learnt the inlaying and chasing of metal from the Sassanian silversmiths of Mesopotamia, who had established a famous school for the industry at Mosul on the Tigris. These craftsmen had an instinctive feeling for mass and design, and their work had a great and beneficial influence upon the arts of Central Asia and Europe.

The Mosques—" Whosoever builds for God a place of worship, be it only as the nest of a grouse, God buildeth for him a place in Paradise." These words of the Prophet were no doubt responsible for the great number

of mosques or Mohammedan churches built by the Arabs.
As no images were permitted in the mosques, the main
thing that was required by the people was a large enclosure, where they could meet together for prayer and the
hearing of the word. The court, which was generally an
open one, contained fountains for ablution before prayer,
a pulpit, and a *mihrab* or niche in one of the walls,
indicating the direction of Mecca.   Arcades usually
surrounded the court, and were often enlarged on one
side of the enclosure and converted into a covered space
used as a prayer chamber. When the prayer chamber
contained a tomb it was the custom to surmount it with
a dome after the manner of the ancient Babylonian
sepulchral monuments, and this practice was sometimes
continued by the Copts and Greeks in Arab employ, even
when the mosque had no mortuary connection. Another
feature of the mosques were the tall and slender minarets
or prayer towers.

The earlier mosques, which were sometimes modelled
on the design of desert caravanserais, are distinguished by
the size of their courts, while those that were built in
succeeding centuries are generally designed with a smaller
court and have a number of elaborate surrounding
buildings.   Some of the most famous mosques are
those of Mecca, Medina, Cordova, Kairwan (in Tunisia),
Jerusalem, and Cairo.   The artistic development of the
buildings is well illustrated at Cairo, where the mosques
of 'Amr, Tulun, and the Sultan Hassan show the growth
of the Arab style.   The first of these, which was built in
the year 673 A.D., shows the simple, earlier Arab work,
in spite of the fact that it has been much restored and
enlarged, and that little if any of the original structure
remains.   The second, which is perhaps the most perfect
Arab monument in Egypt, was copied from the great

mosque at Samarra, near Baghdad, the residence of the
Caliphate during the years 836-861 A.D.   The Samarra
mosque, in its turn, had been built on the model of the
old Assyrian and Persian temples, and its curious tower,
with its winding outside staircase, was a faithful repetition
of the Persian fire tower, which was copied from the
Assyrian ziggurat (see Plate XXII.).   The third mosque,
which was erected during the years 1356-1359 A.D., is
a building of much magnificence, but shows the excessive
use of stucco decoration and the over-elaboration of
ornament common to late Arab art.   Its great dome fell
in the year 1660.   The famous tomb near Agra known
as the Taj Mahal is an example of Arabic art modified by
local influences.

The Art of the Eastern Caliphate—There is little
left of the art of the Eastern Caliphate either in Damascus
or Baghdad.   The great mosque of the former city, built
by the Caliph Walid I. in 705 A.D., was burnt in 1893,
and we have no witness of the glories of Baghdad under
the Caliphate but the old descriptions that have come
down to us.   The famous round city of Baghdad was
founded in 762 A.D. by Mansur, the Abbasid, one of the
greatest of the caliphs.   The town was finished in 766,
and a hundred and thirty years later was described by
the historian Ya'Kubi.   The architects who built it were
brought from Syria, Mesopotamia, Persia and Egypt, and
one of the number was said to be an Indian.   The plan
of the city was laid out in cinders, and balls of cotton,
saturated with naphtha, were placed at intervals along the
line.   When these were lighted a complete outline of the
city was burnt in the grass, and upon this the great
double walls were erected.   Outside, a deep ditch for
water was dug, and in the centre of the city a third wall
was erected, which enclosed the area of the mosque and

PLATE XXII

RUINS OF THE TOWER AND OUTER COURT WALLS OF THE MOSQUE AT SAMARRA, NEAR BAGHDAD

THE FOUNTAIN, COURT, AND TOWER OF THE MOSQUE OF TULUN, CAIRO

palace, while five great gateways gave entrance to the town. Unfortunately the entire town perished, and no building is left standing as a witness to its magnificence. We know that it was a great centre of learning, and that Harun al-Raschid discovered Algebra, and had Arabic translations made of Greek, Latin, Syrian, and Hebrew books ; but the glories of his Court, and the splendour of its art, can best be gathered from the enchanted pages of the *Arabian Nights*.

Arab Art in Spain — The greater part of the so-called Moorish art in Spain was produced, not by Moors, but by Arabs. Even when the Moors were fighting for power in the peninsula during the single century 1146-1248 A.D., they were chiefly represented by the troops which supported their uneasy rule, and the Arabs and their foreign craftsmen still continued to produce the greater part of contemporary Moslem art. The horse-shoe arch, which was an architectural form used by the Visigoths in Spain before the advent of Islam, became so popular that even the Yemenite Arabs adapted their favourite Coptic pointed arch to this popular design, and in this way the architecture of the Yemenite Arabs in Andalusia can almost always be distinguished from that of the Syrian Arabs, who used the ordinary rounded horse-shoe design. It was the Yemenite Arabs who placed their artistic projects in the hands of the Copts, and according to Mr and Mrs Whishaw, it was the Copts, and their pupils the Yemenite Arabs and Gothic Christians, who were responsible not only for a large number of the buildings of the day, but also for the lesser arts and crafts which were produced in such quantities, and were used not only at the Caliphate at Cordova, but also for Eastern trade. The art of the earliest dwellers in Spain, and of the Romans and Goths, was also an influence in

Spanish-Arabic art. These early traditions were preserved in Seville by the Gothic nobles, and helped to give
the town the artistic reputation which it held from the
eighth century until the end of the eleventh, when the
last Yemenite prince of Seville was dethroned.

Cordova and the Mosque

" O my beloved Cordova, when shall I see thee again !
  Thou art like an enchanted spot,
  Thy fields are luxurious gardens,
  Thy earth of various colours resembles a flock of rose-coloured
  amber."

" Do not talk of the court of Baghdad and its glittering magnificence ; do not praise Persia and China and their manifold
  advantages
For there is no spot on the earth like Cordova. . . ."

In these and similar strains the old Arab poets sang
the praises of Cordova, which was celebrated not only for
its natural beauties, but also for its magnificent buildings
and famous Court. Before the reign of Abderrahman III.
Cordova was subject to the Caliph of Damascus, but with
the accession of the great Omayyad, ruler in 891 A.D., its
independence and its fame were firmly established, and
the town took the title of the Caliphate of the West. It
was then that Cordova reached the height of its splendour
and prosperity. Old chronicles record that under the
rule of the great Caliph the town was said to measure ten
miles in diameter and to contain over 50,000 houses of
the aristocratic and official classes, and more than 100,000
dwellings of the common people, while there were hundreds
of mosques and public baths. Numberless palaces, bright
with marbles and inlay, and surrounded by lovely gardens,
lined the banks of the Guadalquivir and lay on the out-
skirts of the town. Among them were the Palace of
Contentment, the Palace of the Flowers, the Palace of

Novelties, the Palace of the Fortunate, the Palace of the
Lovers, and the Palace of the Diadem. Another palace,
known as the *Dimashk* (Damascus), was described in the
following words by a contemporary Arab poet :—

> "All the palaces in the world are as nothing when compared to
> that of Dimashk, for not only has it gardens filled with the
> most delicious fruits and sweet smelling flowers,
> Beautiful prospects and limpid running waters ; clouds, pregnant
> with aromatic dew and lofty buildings ;
> But its earth is always perfumed, for morning pours on it her
> grey amber and night her black musk."

Most famous of all the palaces, however, was the
Palace of Az-Zahra, founded in 936 A.D. by Abderrahman
III., for his favourite wife. It was built in the suburb of
the same name, but soon after the fall of the dynasty was
razed to the ground.

The great mosque of Cordova was begun by
Abderrahman I. in the year 784 A.D., and was built upon
the site of a Christian church which he pulled down in
order to make room for it. It was largely the work of
Byzantine and Syrian craftsmen, and was copied from
the mosque of Damascus, which would be well known to
the young Omayyad Caliph. Abderrahman did not live
to see his work finished, for he died in 788 A.D., and his
son completed the mosque in his stead. By the year
793 the structure was finished, but additions were made,
and further enlargements and decorations added, by each
succeeding Caliph until the fall of the dynasty. In later
years a high altar and cruciform choir were built in the
centre of the mosque by Charles V. ; a belfry took the
place of the minaret ; and a number of chapels were built
on to the sides of the great quadrangle. Otherwise, the
Arabic characters of the building were left unimpaired.

Granada and the Alhambra—The founder of the

Nasride dynasty of Granada was the Yemenite Arab
Mohammed ibn Yusuf ibn Al-Ahmar, known as Al-Ahmar,
or Mohammed I. (1232-1272). He established an extensive
kingdom in Andalusia, which included Granada, Almeria,
Malaga and Jaen, but as the power of the Christian kings
was growing fast in Spain, he wisely acknowledged as
his suzerain the Castilian king Ferdinand, known as
"The Saint." The two kings united to drive the last of
the Moors out of Seville, after which Al-Ahmar devoted
himself to the firm establishment of the Nasride dynasty
at Granada. So well did he succeed, that for nearly two
hundred and fifty years his descendants held sway at
Granada, until Boabdil, the last of the race, abdicated to
Ferdinand and Isabella, "the Catholic Kings," and so
brought to an end the history of the Moslems in Spain.

The brilliance of the kingdom of Granada was largely
the result of Al-Ahmar's wisdom. He was a good and
just man, who devoted his time to the cultivation of the
land, the erection of schools and hospitals, the improvement of horse-breeding, and the encouragement of all arts
and industries. Under his guidance the silk manufacture
of Granada became famous throughout Europe and the
East, the hill-sides blossomed like gardens in Spring, and
the Court of the Alhambra grew to be a brilliant centre
of culture, frequented by the greatest Arabian poets,
scholars and historians of the day. The town of Granada
was said to number half a million inhabitants during the
Nasride rule, and the surroundings were described by a
Moslem traveller in the year 1248 in the following words:—

> "Granada is the capital of Andalus, and the husband of its
> cities ; its environs are a delightful garden covering a space
> of forty miles, and have not their equal in the world. It
> is intersected by the well-known river Shenil and other
> considerable streams, and surrounded on every side by
> orchards, gardens, groves, palaces, and vineyards."

The Palace of the Alhambra, commenced by Al-Ahmar in 1248 A.D., was built within the walls of an ancient pre-Roman fortress, and the new Sultan set himself the task of turning it into a dwelling worthy of himself and his Court. He mingled with the workmen, superintended their labour, and filled the gardens with the choicest flowers and plants. After his death the work was carried on by his successors. Yusuf I. (1313-1354) finished the building, and Mohammed V. completed the decorations in 1354. Although the Arab interior of the Alhambra shows a certain romantic charm and delicate grace, it can never take high rank architecturally. It shows too much of the over-elaboration of detail and ornament, and lacks the essential strength and dominating intellectual conception of great architecture.

EXTRACTS

A

Description of one of the pavilions of the palace of the Caliph Harun al-Raschid.

"The Prince of Persia thought himself to be in one of those delicious palaces that are promised us in the other world. He had never seen anything come near the magnificence of the place he was in. The carpets, cushions, and other appendages of the sofa ; the furniture, ornaments and architecture were surprisingly rich and beautiful. . . . The slave . . . opened the door and conducted them into a large saloon of wonderful structure. It was a dome of the most agreeable form, supported by a hundred pillars of marble, white as alabaster. The bases and chapiters of the pillars were adorned with four-footed beasts and birds of various sorts, gilded. The carpets of this noble saloon consisted of one piece of cloth of gold embroidered with bunches of roses in red and white silk ; and the dome, painted in the same manner, after the Arabian fashion, presented to the mind one of the most charming objects. In every space between the columns was a little sofa, adorned in the same manner, and great vessels of china, crystal, jasper, jet, porphyry, agate and other precious materials, garnished with gold and jewels. In these spaces were also many large windows, with seats projecting breast-high, fitted up as the sofas, and looking out on the most delicious garden, the walks of which were of little pebbles of different colours, of the same pattern as the carpet of the saloon ; so that looking upon the carpet within and without, it seemed as if the dome and the garden with all its ornaments had been upon the same carpet."

> From "The History of Aboulhassen Ali Ebn Becap and Schemselnihar, Favourite of Caliph Haroun-al-Raschid."— *The Arabian Nights.* (According to the latest criticism *The Arabian Nights* was probably compiled during the ninth century, or at latest during the Fatimide period.)

B

From the Epilogue of *The Golden Journey to Samarkand.*[1]

At the Gate of the Sun, Bagdad, in the olden time.

The Merchants (together).

Away, for we are ready to a man !
  Our camels sniff the evening and are glad.
Lead on, O master of the caravan :
  Lead on the merchant-Princes of Bagdad.

The Chief Draper.

Have we not Indian carpets dark as wine,
  Turbans and sashes, gowns and bows and veils,
And broideries of intricate design,
  And printed hangings in enormous bales?

We have rose-candy, we have spikenard,
  Mastic and terebinth, and oil and spice,
And such sweet jams meticulously jarred,
  As God's own Prophet eats in Paradise.

---

[1] *The Golden Journey to Samarkand.* J. E. Flecker. Max Goschen, Ltd.

The Principal Jews.

And we have manuscripts in peacock styles
  By Ali of Damascus ; we have swords
Engraved with storks and apes and crocodiles,
  And heavy beaten necklaces, for Lords.

· · · · · · ·

The Chief Merchant.

We gnaw the nail of hurry, Master, away !

One of the Women.

O turn your eyes to where your children stand.
Is not Bagdad the beautiful ? O stay !

The Merchants (in chorus).

We take the Golden Road to Samarkand

· · · · · ·

A Pilgrim with a Beautiful Voice.

Sweet to ride forth at evening from the wells,
  When shadows pass gigantic on the sand,
And softly through the silence beat the bells,
  Along the golden road to Samarkand.

· · · · · · ·

The Master of the Caravan.

Open the gate, O watchman of the night !

Ho travellers I open.   For what land
Leave you the dim-moon city of delight?

The Merchants (with a shout).

We make the golden journey to Samarkand.
              [*The caravan passes through the gate.*]

LESSONS XII AND XIII

GOTHIC ART

PART I.—ELEMENTARY LESSONS IN STORY FORM

FIRST STORY—GOTHIC ART IN FRANCE. THE BUILDING OF CHARTRES CATHEDRAL

INTRODUCTION—What do you remember of Arab art? What other kind of art was flourishing in Europe at the same time? This is a story about Gothic art which grew up in Europe at the time when Byzantine and Arab art were dying away.

1. **The Devotion (A.D. 1144)**—In a little roughly built cottage in France, a father and mother and two children are sitting round the table at dinner-time. They are simply and poorly dressed in coarse home-spun clothes, and there is nothing on the table but a big loaf of bread, some goat's milk, and a few apples. The room is very bare, for it contains nothing but a couple of beds covered with straw, two forms, a chest, and a table, all of which have been made by the peasant himself, but in spite of poverty, the little group has happy and contented faces, and as they eat their supper they talk together eagerly. " What can we do to help to build the Church of Our Lady at Chartres? " asks the girl. " You can cut wood, father, and mother has spun fine linen, and so earned money to offer to the church, but we children must help too. Every one in the village is helping, what can we do? " The mother smiles at them. " I have an idea," she says ; " down in the valley the corn is being cut.

If you ask one of the servants of the rich lord who owns
the fields, perhaps he will let you follow behind the
reapers, and the corn that you can glean will help to
make bread for the workers who are labouring on the
great church for the glory of God and Our Lady."

The children clap their hands at the idea, and jumping
up from the table, run along the path, through the fields
until they come to the house where the noble owner of
the field lives. As they stand hesitating at the gates the
noble passes out. He sees the children and turns to
them, asking what they want. The boy tells him shyly,
and the face of the old man is full of kindness as he
answers the little bare-footed children. " You may glean
and welcome," he replies ; "and I would give you money
for the good cause, but this day I have given all my lands
and money to Our Lord and His Church. I am become
pauvre et peuple for His sake, and to-morrow I enter
a monastery to serve Him there until I die. I am too old
to fight for Him in the East : that chance I have lost,
but perhaps I am not too old to serve." He gazes before
him where the hills and valleys lie bathed in the warm
autumn sunlight. His face is lit up as if with some
inward vision, and the children, seeing that he has forgotten
them, and is talking to himself rather than to them, slip
away, and chase each other laughing down the hill-side to
the fields where the men and women, with gleaming
sickles, are cutting the corn and binding it into sheaves.

When the reapers hear the children's errand, they are very
willing to help them. " We also are going on pilgrimage
to-morrow," some of them say ; " we too are going to help
to draw the waggons and do what we can for the Church
of God and Our Lady at Chartres." When the children
have gleaned as much corn as they can stagger under
they turn homewards, and, reaching their village, they

pile the corn on one of the carts which is standing in the market-place in readiness for the next day.

Early next morning the children are up with the dawn. The whole village is astir, and the people are collecting round the carts, which are loaded with offerings of every kind for the great church that is being built at Chartres. Some are heaped up with enormous blocks of stone, some with big tree trunks, some with corn, some with wine, some with big jars of olive oil. The children pass from one cart to another watching the arrival of fresh gifts. Their father turns to their mother : " We have not done enough," he says. He goes back to their cottage, and taking an axe cuts down some trees that grow by the door. " The Church needs much wood. May the Lord bless these strong trunks to His use." He fastens ropes to the trunks and the mother and children help to drag them along the road and pile them on one of the carts.

The sun is high in the heavens and the autumn mists are rising from the valley. From the little grey church sounds of singing are heard ; the doors are thrown open, and the priest, followed by a number of the peasants, passes down the narrow street to the market-place. A hush falls upon the people, and they kneel down, and with bowed heads listen to the priest, who has climbed on one of the waggons. He urges them to start on the pilgrimage with free consciences and to forgive all wrongs and injuries, and ask for pardon of all their sins. No one may bring offerings to the Church who is not trying to lead a right life; only those with devotion and love for God may come on this holy errand. It is very still in the market-place. The swallows alone twitter and chatter while from the meadows beyond the fields of golden corn the cows are heard lowing by the river, waiting for milking time. The priest raises his hand and blesses the

PLATE *XXIII*

CHARTRES CATHEDRAL

people, who rise and in absolute silence harness themselves to the waggons. Slowly the big wheels begin to move, and one by one the waggons are drawn out of the village and along the rough road that leads to Chartres.

The children and the parents are prepared for the labour and fatigue, but it is even greater than they had imagined. The ropes seem to cut into their shoulders, and their backs ache almost unbearably, but no one complains, and the procession moves along in silence until a halt is made. The priest again mounts his waggon, and the people join in a hymn of praise and thanksgiving. The sound of singing floats away over the autumn woods and fields, and the labourers lay down their sickles and spades, and come to where the waggons are standing, and themselves make vows that they too will help the church at Chartres. A party of nobles and ladies on horseback pass. They dismount, and kneeling before the priest ask for his blessing. A lady takes a gold and jewelled chain from off her neck and places it reverently on one of the carts. As the people press forward again, drawing their heavy loads, they see in the distance other waggons, and as they draw nearer the town they are joined by many pilgrims, all bent on the same errand. They are dusty, foot-sore and weary, but on all their faces is the same expression of radiant happiness and trust.

Dusk is beginning to fall, and now in the distance the walls of the town are visible. A cry of joy rises from the people as they see standing high above them the great walls of the new church. They break into fresh songs of thanksgiving, and filled with enthusiasm and forgetting their weariness, they press on with their heavy loads until they reach the gates of the town. Passing through the narrow streets they see before them an open space, and looming dimly above it the two newly built towers of the

church of the Virgin.   The people find a place for their
wagons among the others which are waiting there, and
which form together a great circle round the shadowy
church, a spiritual camp with tired but happy pilgrims
resting in its shade.   Big wax candles are fastened to
the wagons, and the boy goes round with a light, until
a little uncertain flame flickers from each into the darkness.
Some of the people stretch themselves on the ground and
are soon lost in sleep ; others spend the night in prayer
and praise.   Overhead the friendly stars keep watch ; the
little bats give their shrill cries as they flutter past, while
in the grass the glow-worms light their tiny lamps among
the dew and leaves.

   2. The Crusades—Nearly a year passes.   The walls
of the great church are now strong and high, and hundreds
of workers are busy on the fabric, among them the boy
who gleaned the corn.   He is learning to be a mason
and lives in the shadow of the building.   One morning
when he is helping to put some blocks of stone in their
place, a man comes running up the hill.   "Bernard of
Clairvaux is coming," he cries out as soon as he is in
ear shot ; "even now he will be in the market place : he is
preaching the holy war.   Come and hear him."   Masons
and sculptors, glaziers and carpenters, throw down their
tools and hurry to the market-place, where a great crowd
is already assembled.   Bernard, in his monk's gown, is
preaching to the people.   His face is white and haggard,
but it lights up with fire and passionate faith, as he urges
his audience to give themselves to the service of Christ.
He tells them how Jerusalem, the city of Our Lord, is in
the hands of infidels and unbelievers, and he begs all who
are able to come on a fresh crusade, and fight and win
the city back again for the Christian faith.

   His words ring out into the summer air, and a low

murmur growing into a roar, rises from the people. " It
is the will of God! Crosses! Crosses!" The preacher un-
looses a great sheaf of them, cut out of red stuff or linen,
and in a frenzy of enthusiasm the people seize them as
they flutter down, and fasten the symbols of Christ upon
their breasts. The crowd breaks out into singing, and the
voices of the people echo back again from the grey walls
and towers of the Cathedral.

With banners flying and led by the clergy in their
gorgeous robes, Bernard is brought to the great church,
and there in its half-finished aisles he is elected general
of the army of Christ. "Oh! that I could go with him,"
thinks the boy; "if only I were older and could fight for Our
Lord in the East." Then he hears that Bernard is telling
the people that he cannot accept the honour that has
been offered to him, and that as he has never learnt the
science of war, he must spend his time instead in rousing
the people's enthusiasm and urging them to go on the
holy errand.

An old mason, who is standing by the boy, and has
read his eager thoughts, touches him on the arm. "Even
so for you and me," he whispers to him; "you are too
young for the crusade: I am too old; but we can serve,
for we can give our lives to the building of this church.
Our youth and our age, our hopes and our joys, our
sorrows and ecstasy we can build into these stones and
offer to Christ and His Mother. From this fire and
labour will spring our salvation, and that of all by whose
efforts the church is built." The boy is comforted, and
feels that in this way he too is in the army of Christ, even
though he will be left behind when so many of the men
of Chartres march out on the holy war.

The townspeople make their preparations, and by the
following year the great army that Bernard of Clairvaux

has raised is ready.   As the church grows daily in
beauty, the crusaders come to its shelter and dedicate
themselves to Christ's service in the East.   The night
before the army starts the boy returns late to the building
in search of a tool that he has left behind him.   Before
an altar where two candles burn, a knight keeps vigil.
He is dressed in chain armour ; on the breast of the
white tunic that covers it blazes a red cross, and on the
ground before him lie the sword and shield that he is to
use on the crusade.   He kneels in silence and with
bowed head.   As the boy passes him, stepping softly, he
thinks of the words of the old mason : " We are helping
too, we are helping too," he whispers to himself as he
creeps out into the moonlight again.

.   .   .   .   .   .

   3. A Hundred Years Later—Years passed and the
men who worked on the church passed away.   They
grew old in its service, and left behind them works of
unfading beauty ; figures in stone of kings, queens, and
saints, some with serious and intent faces, others with
smiling eyes and gentle gaiety in their glances.   The
sculptors never signed their names on the stones, for they
made statues for the glory of God and Our Lady, and
not for perpetuating their own fame.
   Then came a great fire and all the church was burnt
down except the towers and the west front with its great
windows, and the portals, with their wealth of sculpture.
What happened ?   The people undismayed, began to
build again.   The bishop and his Chapter gave up their
stipends for three years, in order that the money could
be expended on the fabric.   Men and women from all
parts of the Christain world came to Chartres on pilgrimage, bringing money and gifts to the church.   They
crowded into the newly rising aisles until they were full

to overflowing, and new-comers had to kneel on the steps outside, under the dreaming figures of saints and queens. Every year the church grew more beautiful. Carvings, stained glass, paintings, and embroideries gave it colour and added loveliness. As it grew it seemed full of a holy peace and joyfulness. All the devotion that had spent itself upon its upraising lived again in the lights and shadows of its aisles and vaulting, and in the wealth of the carvings and traceries. Men and women brought to it their joys and sorrows, and its beauty and serenity entered into their lives, and dwelt there.

Then one day when the building was all but finished, two kings came to see it. One was the King of France, Louis IX., called Saint Louis because of his goodness; the other was Henry III., King of England, who was travelling back to his own country, and had asked the French King if he might visit some of his chief towns, to see their most famous buildings. He loved beautiful pictures and buildings and carvings, and as he stood in the cathedral at Chartres, and looked around him, he thought of his own land, and determined that he would make his abbey at Westminster as wonderful as this great church and as all the others he had seen in the fair land of France. How he did it, the next story will tell.

SECOND STORY—GOTHIC ART IN ENGLAND.
THE BUILDING OF WESTMINSTER ABBEY

Introduction—Last Lesson.—Henry III. of England determined that he would pull down the old church at Westminster, and in its place build a splendid new one, modelled on the plan of the great French cathedrals which he had seen and had so much admired. This is a story about the building and opening of the new church, our present Westminster Abbey.

1. The Novice and the Apprentice—Two brothers are living in a deep gabled house in the City of London.

As they are fourteen and fifteen years years of age it is time to decide what must be done with them, and this is what has been arranged by their parents, after long and anxious discussion. The elder, who is the quieter and more studious of the two, shall be taken to the monastery at Westminster, to be trained as a monk, and the younger, who is never happy unless he is carving bits of stone into every manner of shape, shall be apprenticed to a mason, to learn how to build and carve.

The day comes when the boys must start on their new professions. Early one morning the mother ties her elder son's clothes up in a bundle, and leaving the town behind them, the boy and his parents walk through the flowering meadows until they see before them the group of grey stone buildings that constitutes Westminster. On one hand is the palace of the King, and round it cluster numberless small houses and buildings of every sort. The whole place hums with life. The boy watches with keen interest as people come and go through the great gates. There are troops of archers, their huge bows in their hands ; knights in armour on splendid horses, with pages running at their sides ; two men in green jerkins, one with a pole slung over his shoulder on which a row of hooded falcons perch, the other leading some big wolf hounds in a leash; and peasants and fishermen, carrying packed up hampers to the royal kitchens. Beyond the palace stands the monastery of St Peter, amongst orchards all pink and white with blossom, and gardens full of the gayest of flowers, while by its side towers the splendid Abbey church that the King is building, its beautiful grey walls half hidden by scaffolding. The boy has often seen it and has heard all about it many times, for is not every one in the city talking of the King's pleasure in it, how he thinks of nothing else, and how he even forces money from the people in order to pay for its building?

There is not time to linger, and nervous and excited, the boy is taken through the big doors into the monastery where he is to pass his life. There are monks everywhere with their long black habits and shaven heads, but to his relief there are also boys like himself, who look with curiosity at their future companion as he is ushered into the big hall where the abbot, the head of the monastery, is sitting writing. The boy and his parents bow low before the great personage, who is portly and full of dignity, and has a shrewd and kindly face. Then the boy is taken through the courtyard of the abbot's house, and along the cloisters to a door leading into the great new church. The nave is barricaded off with a big wooden partition at the choir. Transepts and side chapels are finished and are already bright with decorations. From beyond the partition comes the sound of distant hammering. The boy kneels down before the altar in the chapel to which he has been led. Everything seems dream-like and unreal. A priest comes forward and cuts off his long curls and lays them on the altar as an offering. Then he is presented to a second priest and vessels containing sacred symbols are put into his hands. Next he sees his parents advance and feels them wrap his hands in the pall of the altar, and he hears their words as they read a written promise, that they will never induce him to leave the monastery. Then the abbot himself blesses a hood and lays it on his head, after which he is taken back to the monastery, robed and shaved after the fashion of the order, and brought back again to the chapel, where he is received as a novice with many prayers. The service over, he says good-bye to his mother and father, and his life in the monastery is begun.

The next day the second brother is started in life as an apprentice to a master mason, or builder, and this is attended with a solemn ceremony. He is taken by his parents to the hall of the masons' guild in the city. There the heads of the guild, or company, are sitting, dressed in their special dress or livery. They are all clever builders, having served seven years as apprentices, and then worked as journeymen, and they are now honoured and respected, and rule the affairs of all the other builders in London. There are many other boys brought by their fathers and mothers, and, when their names have been read out, they stand in a row before the warden, or head of the guild, and are told about all the things that, as apprentices, they must, and must not, do. They must keep their hair short and dress tidily, be obedient and good workers, speak the truth, and be a credit to the guild. The boys stand very still, and are very well behaved while the warden is speaking to them, and they all determine to be good workmen, but they look at each other out of the corners of their eyes, and know that they will have plenty of fun and games together, as well as hard work, before their seven years' apprenticeship is over.

When the ceremony is finished the boy's parents put some money in a box for the funds of the guild, and sign their son's indenture, and our newly-made apprentice gives them a last hug, and, feeling very shy and a little homesick, is taken off by a bearded and kindly-faced master mason, with whom he is to live. They thread their way through the narrow twisting city streets, where the overhanging houses nearly touch each other, until the mason's house is reached. Here the boy is welcomed by the mason's wife, who introduces him to her sons and daughters, who are to become almost like brothers and sisters to him. He is shown the room which he is to share with the menkind of the family, and the big shed at the back of the house, where he is to be taught his new trade. After supper he is very glad to go off to bed, and falls asleep wondering how his brother is getting on at Westminster.

2. The Building of Westminster Abbey—Although they live such different lives, the two brothers are able to see a certain amount of each other, for many members of the masons' guild, and also a large number of the monks, are at work upon the Abbey church. Some or the most famous of the master masons are in the service of the King, and live in the palace enclosure with their assistants. The master of our apprentice is not of their number but he is a clever workman and is often employed upon the Abbey, and, when this is the case, brings the boy with him to hand him tools, mix mortar, and make himself generally useful. It sometimes happens that his brother the novice is allowed to wander about the church in his daily hour of free time, and it is then that the two boys may get an opportunity of seeing each other.

The first time the brothers meet there is much to talk about. The younger brother laughs at the shaven head and long black habit of the elder, who, in his turn, points at the thick leathern apron of the apprentice. "It's great fun being a mason," says the latter; "I am learning how to draw plans of buildings, and how to cut stone, and soon I am to be allowed to begin to carve figures. When I have served my time and grown famous perhaps I shall be a master mason and work for the King." "I draw and paint too," replies the elder brother, "but my drawings are made for books. There is an old monk in our monastery, who sits all day long in the cloister, working at a missal. I pick him flowers to copy, and apples and pears from the orchard, and once I caught a butterfly for

him in the abbot's garden. He copies them all and
makes his drawings into borders for the pages, and then
I grind his colours and he paints them, oh! so beautifully.
He is teaching me, and one day I too will make a missal.
I am going to learn to make stained-glass windows and
perhaps to carve too, for many of our monks can do these
things; they are helping to build this church just as much
as the townsfolk in the guilds."

The boys wander up and down the aisles, full of
interest in all that they see, and indeed what could be
more delightful than to watch the men in the choir, who
are putting finishing touches to the stalls, or those who
are fitting a stained glass window into place? The
sculptors are laughing together over some figures they
have just completed, a mermaid and a dolphin and some
wicked little grinning faces. The boys lean over their
shoulders and ask what the figures mean. "Never you
mind," replies one of the men with a chuckle. "Wait until
you are older, and then you can carve whatever you want.
If you would like to know, one is a scene out of an old
story my mother used to tell me, and one is a fish I saw
in the river or thought I did, and whose the faces are
it does not matter." The men fasten the carved pieces
of wood to the undersides of the seats where the monks
sit when they chant the *Miserere*, and the novice knows
the reason well. When the seats are turned back, and
the members of the choir have to stand intoning until
they nearly drop with fatigue, the projecting carvings give
them some support in their weariness.

The boys are next attracted by a member of the
painters' guild, who is working on the wall of a side
chapel. He is painting the slender figure of a saint, with
flowing robes, and eyes full of tenderness and peace. His
face is absorbed, and he hardly seems aware of the boys,

who watch him silently, as if the spirit of the saint were
holding them. They pass on to the new shrine of Saint
Edward, and hold their breath before its sumptuous richness. The King has given money for two great wax
candles to be kept there always, and in their light, the
shrine seems to glitter with gems. A foreign craftsman
is at work upon it, and near him a second Italian is
putting finishing touches to the mosaic pavement that
Abbot Ware has had transported from Rome. The boys
laugh and nudge each other at the sound of the foreign
language and then turn their attention to the men from
the glaziers' guild, who are fixing a window into place.
The bits of richly tinted glass are joined together with
thin lines of lead, and the boys make out the figures of
prophets and angels immersed in colour and sunlight.
Next a monk, mounted on a ladder, calls to the novice,
asking for a tool he has forgotten, and while waiting for
his brother who has run off on his errand, the apprentice
watches the sculptor's clever fingers fashioning some ivy
leaves in stone, after the likeness of a freshly cut green
spray that he has nailed up beside him. On every hand
there are workers, keen, gay, and interested, chatting as
they work, comparing notes, and joking with one another.

Suddenly a door opens, and a silence falls, as the King
is seen to enter by his private door that leads from the
palace. He is deep in talk with the master mason, who
follows him carrying a large roll of parchment under his
arm. The King passes from one group of workers to
another. All bow low as he approaches, and their faces
light up with pleasure if their work attracts his attention
and pleases him. He passes the shrine of St Edward,
and kneels for a moment in prayer. Then, crossing himself, he turns and gazes down the long aisles and with a
face full of content retraces his steps and returns to the

palace. The two brothers, whose hour of freedom is over, hurriedly slip back to their work, one to the mixing of his mortar, the other to the monastery, where the old monk awaits the grinding of his colours.

3. **The Opening of the Abbey, 13 October, 1269**—At last the day draws near when the first High Mass is to be celebrated in the newly finished Abbey. The King has decreed that the opening shall take place on St Edward the Confessor's day, which is an annual holiday. Every year a service is held in the saint's honour, in the church in which he is buried, and this year it is to be more solemn and beautiful than it has ever been before, for the golden coffin containing the saint's bones is to be publicly transferred to its new resting place. All London is on tiptoe with excitement, and pilgrims and visitors from every part of England crowd into the town, to hear the solemn service and to see the great new church, the fame of which has spread far and wide.

The night before the opening, the novice is wakened in the chill hour before dawn to take part in the *matins* in the Abbey. He creeps down the stairs with the monks, shivering in the cold air, and wraps his habit closer round him, as he enters the dim church. The building is lost in black shadow, except where the sanctuary lamps and the flickering tapers of the monks cast a pale and ghostly light upon carving and pillar, tracery and column. Only in one other spot is there a glimmer of light. Two great wax candles are burning in front of the shrine of St Edward and kneeling before it, with bowed head, the novice sees the King. He is clad in a long white robe, and his hands are clasped and his lips move in prayer. By his side kneel several nobles of the court, dressed in full armour, their swords at their sides, sharing the vigil of their master. The low intoning

PLATE *XXIV*

WESTMINSTER ABBEY FROM THE CHOIR

of the monks echoes through the vaults but the King is
as motionless as the ivory statue of the virgin, which
gleams palely in the dimness near him.   As he creeps
back into bed again the novice can hardly believe that
in a few hours the King's vigil will be over, and the
scene of midnight devotion will be changed to a blaze of
splendour and glory.

With the sunrise the boy is awake again.   The
monastery is humming like a hive.   The voice of Abbot
Ware is heard issuing orders, and the novice is sent to
empty the great chests of their store of wonderful copes
and vestments embroidered with saints and angels,
dragons and leaves, and coloured like flower-beds in
spring.   Next he is sent running to the store-rooms for
candles for the procession, and then there are the beautiful
illuminated books of the mass, which must be taken into
the choir and put in place for the abbot and bishops.
When this is done, he is sent with others to strew the
choir of the Abbey with rushes, mint, and sweet-smelling
herbs.

At last the preparations are done, and the priests,
monks, and novices form into a long procession, and pass
over to the palace.   On every side vast crowds are
collected.   Inside the church the people have waited
patiently since early morning, and are now counting the
minutes until the procession will arrive.   Outside the
great Abbey bells peal and clash to the blue sky overhead.
A soft autumn breeze stirs the trees in the orchard and
sends the leaves rustling down into the long damp grass,
while from over the wall of the abbot's garden comes the
scent of the stocks.   The gates of the palace are thrown
open at last, and a long procession issues forth.
Surrounded by the bishops and clergy in their magnificent
robes, the King, assisted by his brother and two eldest

sons, bears on his shoulder the new golden coffin
containing the bones of St Edward. The monks follow
in their long black habits, and the novice in his white
surplice swings a censer, and joins in the solemn chant
that the monks are singing. Behind the religious bodies
come the Knights Templar in chain armour, with sunburnt
faces, and crosses on their breasts, and after them walk
the Black Friars, the Knights of St John, the Mayor and
Corporation, and the representatives of all the city guilds
and companies, resplendent in hoods and surcoats,
embroidered with the arms of their crafts.

As the precious relic passes, the people fall on their
knees and cross themselves. The great doors of the
Abbey are thrown open, and slowly, and with steady
steps, the King and his sons, followed by the clergy, bear
the golden coffin round the aisles so that all may see it.
They then pass through the heavy curtains into the choir,
where the Queen and court are assembled. With
chanting and intoning the new shrine is reached, and
the coffin reverently placed in it. Mass is celebrated by
Abbot Ware, and then with a blast of music the curtains
are drawn aside, and the great Abbey is revealed to the
people in all its nobility and completeness. High in the
vaulting float the boys' voices, "Gloria, gloria in excelsis
Deo." The mellow autumn sunshine fills the great aisles
with a soft light. The windows glow and burn, some
sapphire and flame and cinnamon; some cool as sea
water and faint as mother-of-pearl. High in the shadowy
vaulting the sound of the music lingers and spreads.
The fragrance of the mint and the rushes mingles with the
scent of the incense. On every side candles are flickering,
and figures of grave-eyed saints and kings, and of mocking
grinning grotesques, gaze down upon the crowded aisles.
The gilded shrine of the confessor blazes with jewels, and

fresh treasures are added to its store as nobles and
knights, following the example of the King, one by one
lay their offerings before it. Richly wrought tapestries
hang round the choir, deep as forest greenery, and from
the walls the legends of the saints are blazoned forth.

The people gaze spellbound upon the beauty around
them. The novice from his stall searches among the
faces of the crowd for that of his brother, for he knows
the apprentice will be there. Among all that great
crowd there are none happier than the workers who have
helped in the building and decorating of the fabric, and
mason and sculptor, painter, glazier and goldsmith, feel
their hearts swell with joyfulness and pride.

The service over, the rest of the day is spent in
rejoicing and merriment, and the hour is late before the
novice and apprentice are in bed and asleep, dreaming of
lofty aisles, full of glowing colour and triumphant music,
and a great king bowing low before a jewelled and
gleaming shrine.

NOTES ON THE STORIES

First Story—To show how Gothic art was to a large extent the
result of waves of religious emotion and enthusiasm. The story is
imaginary. The details are chiefly taken from contemporary records
rranslated and published in *A Medieval Garner* by Coulton,
and *Chartres* by Cecil Headlam (Medieval Towns Series). The
description of St Bernard's preaching of the Crusade is taken from a
contemporary account of the same scene at Vezelay, which he visited
shortly before Chartres. The burning of the church took place in the
year 1194 A.D. Teachers who have not taken the story of the
destruction of Sancta Sophia (Lesson IX.) could give a description of
this fire, and if the second lesson on Gothic art should be omitted,
a more detailed account of the interior of the church should be given.
For particulars of building, etc., see *Chartres*, by Cecil Headlam.

Second Story—To show how the Church and Guild were largely
responsible in shaping Gothic art. The story is imaginary. The
details are largely taken from the books on Westminster by Dean

Stanley, Ridgeway, Professor Lethaby, and Sir Walter Besant, which
contain translations from many of the old Fabric Rolls, and from
contemporary chronicles, such as that by Matthew Paris, and the
Customary of Abbot Ware. The ceremony of receiving the novice,
as described in paragraph 1, dates from the end of the fourteenth
century, though it may have taken the same form in the thirteenth
also. There is no mention as to which chapel it took place in.
Although there is no proof, it is probable that the masons' guild
existed by the middle of the fourteenth century. There is no record
that a wooden barricade divided off the unfinished part of the church,
but something of the sort must have been provided, as the chapels
were in use before the nave was completed. For exact dates of work
in the Abbey, see Professor Lethaby's *Westminster Abbey and the
King's Craftsmen.*

PART II.—MATERIAL FOR ADVANCED LESSONS ONLY

History and General Characteristics—The passing
of the ancient world and the dawn of the Middle Ages
can be marked by no definite date. The Roman Empire
fell before the barbaric invasions from the north, and the
invaders, German people, speaking an Aryan tongue,
broke up the country into various kingdoms of their own.
The Franks and Burgundians settled in Gaul ; the
Jutes, Angles, and Saxons in Great Britain ; the Vandals
in North Africa ; the Visigoths in Spain ; and the
Ostrogoths and later the Lombards in Italy and the
Ostrogoths in South Russia. The imperial rule was
entirely destroyed in Europe, and after the year 470 A.D.
there were no more emperors in Rome. The new
kingdoms suffered many vicissitudes. Some were destroyed
and some absorbed ; but in each country a new nation
was formed, with its individual system of government
and an original and independent art and literature of its
own. The new nations soon forsook their northern gods,
and from Woden, Freya, Balder, and the visions of

Walhalla, turned instead to the teachings of Christianity. Centuries of wars and unrest followed, until at last Europe slowly settled down into a state of greater law and order. A gradual blending of old and new took place. Barbaric elements such as the Teutonic, Lombard, Celtic, and Anglo-Saxon came into contact with classic and oriental thought. Out of the confusion Gothic art emerged, created by the fierce energies of northern peoples, steadied by classical tradition and precedent, and embodying in every stone and beam and flaming window of its churches the triumph of Christianity.

The years 1150 to 1550 can be given to indicate broadly the period of Gothic art. It was the outcome of a new growth of emotion and action following the long period of comparative mental stagnation. Many of the superstitious minds of the day expected the end of the world to take place during the year 1000, and once the dreaded time was past, life began to blossom afresh. Great waves of religious enthusiasm swept over the land, resulting in the crusades and the reform of the numerous religious orders, while the latter, growing steadily in power and numbers, necessitated the erection of endless ecclesiastical buildings. As the foundations of liberty were laid in Europe, and the stirring and quickening of national life showed itself in ideals of romance and chivalry, and in the founding of Universities, and the establishment of merchant and craft guilds, Romanesque art, which had grown up during the latter half of the Middle Ages, developed almost imperceptibly into Romance or Gothic art. It reached its height about the year 1250, and after 1350 became gradually more flamboyant, until in the sixteenth century it slowly gave way before the incoming tide of the Renaissance. The *Isle de France*, or district round Paris, saw its birth, and it was there that it attained its highest expression, at a time when Paris was the centre of European learning.

From France, Gothic art quickly spread to England, where it developed on lines of almost equal beauty, and soon Germany, Flanders, and northern Spain and Portugal had welcomed it as their own. In Italy, however, it never became entirely indigenous and the style was often modified to suit the requirements of wall-paintings. It was a secular, no less than an ecclesiastical art. San Gimignano in Italy, Carcassonne in France, or Rothenburg in Germany are good examples of a medieval town, with their dominant features of wall and tower, and their narrow streets, flanked by gaunt-looking houses. Above all, Gothic art was the work of great medieval organisations, and the unity to which it attained was due to the co-operation of great communities of workmen, without which it would never have reached its splendid triumph.

Many old chronicles bear witness to the mystic reverence of medieval people for their works of art. Professor Lethaby gives two instances of this mysticism. This is how Dante describes images of the Virgin and Angel : " There, sculptured in a gracious attitude, he did not seem an image that is silent ; one would have sworn that he was saying ' Ave,' and in her mien this language was expressed ' Ecce ancilla Dei ' as distinctly as any figure stamps itself in wax." Hermann of Tournay, writing still earlier, says of the shrine of St Piat, that on it was represented the five wise and the five foolish virgins, " all who seemed to weep and be alive ; some wept tears like water, some like blood." [1] There is also the well-known account of the burning of the choir of Canterbury Cathedral in the thirteenth century. " The people were astonished that the Almighty should suffer such things,

[1] *Medieval Art*, Duckworth.

and maddened with excess of grief and perplexity, they
tore their hair and beat the walls and pavements of the
church with their heads and hands, blaspheming the
Lord and His Saints, the patrons of the Church; and
many both of the city and of the monks would rather
have laid down their lives than that the church should
have so miserably perished."

The Medieval Church—During the period of
Romanesque and early Gothic art the monasteries were
the great centres of artistic teaching. The most famous
of these early monastic schools of art in Europe were
those established by Eginhard for Charlemagne about the
year 800 A.D., and by De Siderius, Abbot of Mende,
towards the end of the eleventh century, while it is
recorded that by the end of the twelfth century there
were no less than eight hundred monk artists at Semur
alone.

In this way the Catholic Church was the most powerful artistic influence of the Middle Ages. Although
some of its greatest leaders, such as St Francis and St
Bernard, preached the gospel of simplicity, and denounced
all forms of rich and elaborate art, the whole trend of
its teaching led in the opposite direction. There were
few books and few people who could read. As early as
the year 600 A.D. St Gregory had written that "what
writing is for those who can read, painting is for
the uneducated who can only look," and the wise old
abbots and bishops were quick to realize that the
doctrines of the Church could be taught through eye and
ear, as well as by the spoken word (*Extract A*).

Religion was to be a joyous thing for the people, and
in their churches they were to find beauty, colour, and
mystery. How did the Apostle of old describe the heaven
that had been revealed to him? "Her light was like

unto a stone most precious, even like a jasper stone, clear as crystal—the first foundation was jasper ; the second sapphire ; the third a chalcedony ; the fourth an emerald —and the twelve gates were twelve pearls, every several gate was one pearl; and the street of the city was pure gold, as it were transparent glass." Even so was the beauty of the Church to express the hidden beauty of the faith in which it had its being. Nothing could be too beautiful to serve the faith, and neither money nor labour were spared in the enrichment of its shrines with forms of loveliness (*Extract B*). The craftsmen who laboured to this end had no thought of personal glory. Matthew Paris, a chronicler of the fourteenth century, wrote that a great work or building was always spoken of as the work of the abbot " for the glory of the office." It is true that there was another side to the picture, and that the dual nature of the Middle Ages was apparent in the Church services. Side by side with the beauty and the undoubted religious and emotional atmosphere went unbelievably irreverent scenes, but we are not concerned here with that side of the question.

A medieval church was to be a sermon in stone, a silent preaching of the word. During the early part of the Middle Ages, when Christianity and paganism flourished side by side, many pagan elements were unconsciously absorbed into Church doctrines. An element of magic and mystery was taken over from the East and with it a confusion of the symbol with the fact symbolized. This love of symbolism and allegory had, however, a very interesting side, and exercised a great influence upon art, which became absorbed in representing the inner meaning of things. This was what William Durandus, Bishop of Mende, wrote in the year 1220 : " Pictures and ornaments in churches are the true teachings and

PLATE *XXV*

HEAD OF A KNIGHT, XIIITH CENTURY
CATHEDRAL, BAMBERG

ETHELDREDA SUPERINTENDING THE BUILDING OF A CHURCH
ENGLISH SCHOOL OF THE XVTH CENTURY

scriptures of the laity. . . . The glass windows in a church are holy scriptures which expel the wind and the rain, that is all things hurtful, but transmit the light of the true sun, that is God, into the hearts of the faithful ; the silken coverings of the altar are the ornaments of divers virtues wherewith the soul is adorned ; the light of the candlesticks is the faith of the people ; the lamp burning saith ' I am the light of world ' ; the cock at the summit of the church is a type of preacher, for the cock ever watchful, even in the depth of the night, giveth notice how the hours pass, wakeneth the sleepers, predicteth the approach of day. There is a mystery concerned in each of these. The night is the world ; the sleepers are the children of this world who are asleep in their sins. The cock is the preacher who preacheth boldly and exciteth the sleepers to cast away the works of darkness, exclaiming ' Woe unto them that sleep ; awake him that sleepeth.' In churches sometimes flowers are portrayed and trees to represent the fruits of good works springing from the roots of virtue. On festivals, curtains are hung up in churches for the sake of the ornament they give ; and that by visible we may be led to invisible beauty."

As the thirteenth century advanced the number of lay artists and craftsmen increased, and the guilds into which they had formed themselves exercised a growing and powerful influence upon art.

The Craft Guilds (with special reference to those of London). The craft guilds were democratic brotherhoods of workmen composed of wardens, masters, journeymen, and apprentices. There had been guilds of a somewhat similar kind in Rome and Byzantium, but the forming of these later crafts guilds may be said to have been extended from the beginning of the twelfth century to the middle of the thirteenth, when they were officially incorporated into the national life, and brought into organized relationship with the municipalities. They soon attained a position of great power, and not only exercised complete control over their trades, but also were concerned with the governing of the towns.

During their early years the guilds had three main motives : first, the supplying of the material needs of members, which were provided for by large benefit funds, to be used in cases of sickness or distress ; second, the spiritual welfare of the community, for the furthering of which each guild was affiliated to a special church, where it often had its own chapel and attendant priest ; and third, the protection of the trade by means of strict rules regarding hours of work, pure material and skilled craftsmanship and laws for the prevention of foreign competition. Meetings and re-unions played an important part in guild life, and to the most important of these, all members were summoned. The Guild of St Catherine in Lynn had "four dayes of spekyngges tokedere for here comune profyte," and not only was every " broder and sistere " to pay a fine of a penny (about tenpence of our modern money) for non-attendance, but should any come "and thenne sit doune and grumble " a second penny had to be paid.

Many of the old guilds' articles and charters have come down to us and show what high ideals of workmanship were held by the medieval craftsmen. Here is an extract from the articles of the London Furbishers, written in 1350 : " No one of the said trade shall take any manner of work for working at from any great Lord or other person if he be not a man perfect and a man knowing his trade, by testimony of the good folks of the same trade, by reason of the perils which may befall the lords of this land and others among the people through false workmanship to the great scandal of the folks of the said trade." In the statutes of the Braders we read : " No one of the said trade shall be so daring as to work at this trade by night . . . seeing the sight is not so profitable or so certain as by day, to the profit of the community." And in another place : " No one shall work from the beginning of the day until curfew, nor at night by candle light." This rule, held by all the guilds, insured a certain amount of leisure. Here is another regulation taken from the Blacksmiths' articles of 1372 : "Because many of the trade . . . who dwell in foreign lanes, do sell their work in secret, to a secluded place, and not to a place that is open, by reason that the said work is not avowable and proper, so that the commonalty is deceived thereby, and greatly damaged ; it is ordained that no one of the said trade shall cause any false work to be taken through the streets for sale in the city, or shall go wandering about the said city . . . or suburb with false work." To prevent this there were certain places in London set apart for the erection of booths and the selling of wares, but for the most part the work was made and sold at the house of the craftsman, and the middleman was almost unknown. Competition in this way was regulated, for it was not considered right for a craftsman " for to have better sale than any other of the co-brethren."

There were no class distinctions in the guilds. Most of the members were of the labouring classes, but distinguished men also joined the fraternities, and younger sons of the noble families took their place with the ordinary apprentices. Only industry and proficiency brought highest honours, and no one was admitted to the guild whose conduct and honour were not stainless and who had not served as an apprentice. The usual term of apprenticeship was seven years, and although some crafts demanded a shorter period, others, such as the Parisian guild of painters and image makers, founded in 1391, fixed ten or eleven years as the required time of pupilage. In the Middle Ages the words "artist" and "architect" were unknown. There was no special privilege attached to the callings; the masons, painters, and sculptors took their place with the fishmongers, blacksmiths, bakers, and weavers. Why should a difference be made? They were all workers supplying the daily needs of a people who expected sound workmanship and good material in everything, and demanded beauty as a matter of course, wherever it could be combined with utility. Some crafts or trades allowed a fuller expression of it than others; that was the only difference.

The dates of the founding of the various guilds are unfortunately not known. In England it was not until the reign of Edward III. (1372-1377) that they first began to receive their royal warrants, but there are many evidences of their existence at a much earlier date. Stowe says that on the marriage of Edward I. to Queen Margaret in 1299 the Fraternities rode out to meet her to the number of six hundred, in one livery of red and white with the cognizances of their mysteries embroidered on their sleeves. Although there is no mention of the London guilds of masons until 1353 (owing to a disastrous fire in the hall of the company which destroyed all the earliest records), it is probable that the guild was started by the year 1200 at latest. The London guild of goldsmiths is mentioned in 1180, and the painters obtained a grant of ordinances from the mayor and barons of the town in 1283. As their chief work at that time was painting saddle bows, they were considered a subordinate branch of the saddlers' guild. The London weavers' guild existed in the reign of Henry I. (1100-1135).

As regards the apprenticeship system, witness is borne to its early date in England by an old document of 1274, which states that apprentices shall not be received for a less term than seven years "according to the ancient and established usage." It was not until the sixteenth century that a new regulation came into fashion, which required apprentices to produce a masterpiece before they were formally accepted as members of the guild.

It is easy to see how much Gothic art owed to the crafts' guilds and their splendid traditions of workmanship, which bore fruit until the rise of machinery destroyed the handicrafts, and introduced problems which are as yet unsolved. About eighty companies still exist in London as descendants of the old guilds, and Lord Mayor's day is the survival of the civic procession in which the fraternities marched on Midsummer's day.

The Development of Gothic Architecture—Early Christian architecture (see p. 234) contained the germs of both the Byzantine and Romanesque styles. The former of these styles developed in the Near East, according to the requirements of the Eastern Church, while the Romanesque style was slowly and gradually established in the West. It was born of the vigour and enthusiasm of Germanic tribes and was shaped by the traditions of classic art and of the art of the Hellenized East, and was still further moulded by the ritual of the Western Church. It was at first a tentative style, but by the beginning of the eleventh century we find it firmly established in Italy, France, Germany, and Northern Spain, and marked by distinctive and beautiful features of its own. It was essentially a transitional and experimental style, taking on fresh characteristics in each district where it developed, and as it spread, rapidly widening the departure from the old classic ideals and methods. In England the style was introduced at the time of William I. and is known as Norman architecture, while the work of Norman princes in Sicily dates from the same period. Romanesque churches being roofed with timber had in consequence narrow naves, while the massiveness of the construction was due to the Roman tradition and also to the fact that the western builder had not yet mastered the scientific methods of meeting strain and stress in architecture. As glass was rare, and oiled linen took its place, the windows were in consequence small and narrow. During the later part of the twelfth century, Romanesque art passed almost imperceptibly into Gothic art. In the words of Mr H. O. Taylor, " in Gothic, possibilities of Romanesque reach their logical conclusion. The Vault determines the rest of the structure. Downward stress and lateral thrust have been analyzed ; they have been gathered up and then distributed in currents of pressure exerted along the lines of the ribs of the vaulting. Each thrust or stress is met by separate support of pillar or colonette, or by directly counteracting pressure of pier or flying buttress." [1]

The monasteries at this time contained the wealthiest and largest assemblies of people. The order of the Cistercians, or reformed Benedictines, founded in 1098 at Citeaux in Burgundy, grew with such rapidity that within a hundred years of its foundation over three thousand monasteries were affiliated to the parent cloister. This gave a fresh impetus to architecture and the new churches were adapted to the new needs. The plans were enlarged and altered, and the choirs, which were occupied by a growing body of clergy, were in some cases nearly doubled in length. The timber roof was replaced by one of stone ; arches were pointed in form instead

[1] *The Classical Heritage of the Middle Ages.* The Macmillan Co., New York.

of rounded ; the building took the form of a Latin
Cross ; towers were multiplied, and the simple form
of the antique column was replaced by columns surrounded by detached shafts. Above all, the introduction
of the art of window glazing, which had been very little
practised in the West, exercised a far-reaching influence
upon Gothic architecture. The art was probably derived
from that of enamelling, and the windows were designed
as a means of teaching the people, and as an expression
of the faith, but they led eventually to the late Gothic
ideal of walls of glass connected by stone, as illustrated
by the *Sainte Chapelle* in Paris, and King's College
Chapel, Cambridge. The glass that was used was made
in small pieces, a few inches in width and slightly
irregular in surface, so that the minutely differing planes
caught the light at varying angles, and, aided by colour,
produced a wonderfully decorative effect. M. Huysmans
traces their decorative quality to the influence of the
carpets, brought by crusaders from the East. He
describes the windows as " diaphanous carpets, bouquets,
exhaling the odours of sandalwood and pepper, embalming
the subtle spices of Magian kings ; they are a perfumed
bloom of colours gathered—at what price of blood !—in
the plains of Palestine, which the West, which brought
them from thence, offers to the Madonna beneath these
colder skies, in memory of the sunny lands where she had
lived, and where her Son had chosen to be born."

Even as ancient architecture suggests control and
repose, so Gothic architecture shows fire and energy.
Ferguson describes its qualities in the following words :
" Not even the great Pharaonic era in Egypt, the age of
Pericles in Greece, nor the great period of the Roman
Empire will bear comparison with the thirteenth century
in Europe, whether we look to the extent of the build-

ings executed, their wonderful variety and constructive elegance, the daring imagination that conceived them or the power of poetry and of lofty religious feeling that is expressed in every feature and every part of them."[1]

Sculpture—During the early years of the Middle Ages figure sculpture was treated in a decorative and formal manner, due in part to the Oriental love of pattern, and influenced by the strong dislike of the Christian Church to all forms reminiscent of pagan worship. So strong were these influences that for many hundreds of years monumental sculpture was only used as an architectural adjunct. In Romanesque art, this decorative sculpture found its most splendid expression, and produced such figures as the " Ancestors of the Virgin " on the west front of Chartres Cathedral, figures remarkable for their dignity and rigid beauty, and for a certain spirit of delicate austerity which hangs about them like a fragrance.

Gothic sculpture developed out of Romanesque sculpture, and owing to the fire and energy of the Gothic spirit, coupled with a renewed observation of natural forms and a growing command over technique, attained a splendid expression. The bonds imposed by the Church were loosened and the craftsmen turned to nature for their inspiration. The medieval mind, simple and childlike, accepted all that it found there, and a dewy freshness and naïve simplicity lurk in late Romanesque and early Gothic work. A Runic inscription on a carved font in Bridekirk in Northumberland has been modernized by Mr Prior and Mr Gardner in the following words :—

> " He was Richard who me wrought
> And me to Grace with joy he brought."

---

[1] *History of Architecture.* Murray.

PLATE XXVI

THE RESURRECTION OF THE VIRGIN. SENLIS CATHEDRAL
ROMANESQUE SCULPTURE OF THE XIITH CENTURY

THE DEATH OF THE VIRGIN. STRASBURG CATHEDRAL
GOTHIC SCULPTURE OF THE XIIITH CENTURY
(The Apostles, in the background, are a later Gothic addition)

This unknown craftsman has chosen his words with
insight, for there could be no better description of the creation of the sculpture of this period than that of "bringing
to grace with joy." The same writers in describing the
architectural connection of Gothic figure-sculpture state,
firstly, that "Gothic architecture made an era of figure-
sculpture in the art history of the world—a creation of
style that was an event in the life of humanity; and
secondly, that as a corollary of this, the character of
Gothic figure work lay in its being carved of stone, as
distinguished from the metal and marble creations of the
classic and Italian arts." [1]

Sculpture, which was almost always coloured and gilded,
was constructionally, symbolically, and æsthetically a necessary part of Gothic churches, and a Gothic Cathedral
is a complete mirror of the life of the times. It is not
only the differing aspects of Christianity that are revealed
in its fabric, the ceremonial, the mystical, the emotional,
and all the joy, sorrow, and ecstasy of the faith; but
with a quaint and impish humour the episodes of
everyday life are also set forth, together with representations of the sins and faults that all must eschew, and
versions of the little histories and old fables that lingered
in the mind of the medieval craftsman. Pagan types
were altered to suit Christian themes. Hermes, carrying
his sheep, was changed into Christ with a lamb: Sibyls,
who prophesied the coming of the Saviour, took their
place by the side of the medieval saints; and old
abbots and bishops, who were preys to human foibles,
were slyly held up as examples to the discerning eye.
The vine, leaf, and blossom, that wreathed and clustered
so delicately in stone and wood, showed forth the

[1] *An Account of Medieval Figure Sculpture in England.* Gardner & Prior.
Cambridge University Press.

abundant beauties of the world of God's creation. The Gothic sepulchral effigy, in its remote serenity and utter peacefulness, was a new and unconscious expression of Christian faith, and differed from all classic monuments of a similar type.

The subject of the symbolism that underlies Gothic sculpture is too big to be entered upon here, but all who want a full and interesting account can find it in *Religious Art of the Thirteenth Century in France*, which is an English translation by Miss Dora Nussey of M. Emile Mâle's well-known work.

Gothic Painting—Gothic painting followed the same lines of development as Gothic sculpture. In the south, it found its greatest expression in the art of Giotto and the early Tuscan and Sienese painters, while in the north, the chief centre of Romanesque painting, situated in Germany, developed into the northern Gothic schools of Prague and Cologne. The school of the Netherlands, and that of Westminster in England, were offshoots of these northern schools, while fine schools were also established in France and Portugal.

EXTRACTS

A

From the " Treatise on Art" of the monk Thœophilus (Rugenus of Helmershausen), written about the year 1100 *A.D.*[1]

"Cheered by these supporting virtues, my beloved son, thou hast approached God's house in all faith, and adorned it with such abundant comeliness ; and having illuminated the vaults of the walls with divers works and divers colours, thou hast in a manner shown forth to the beholders a vision of God's paradise, bright as spring-tide, with flowers of every hue, and fresh with green grass and leaves, refreshing the souls of the Saints with crowns proportioned to their

---

[1] Published in the *Burlington Magazine*, October 1912.

divers merits, whereby thou makest them to preach His wonders in His works. For man's eyes knoweth not whereon first to gaze : if he looks up at the vaults, they are as mantles embroidered with spring flowers; if he regard the walls, there is a manner of paradise ; if he consider the light streaming through the windows, he marvelleth at the priceless beauty of the glass and the variety of this most precious work. Work, therefore, now good man—kindle thyself to a still ampler art, and set thyself with all the might of thy soul to complete that which is yet lacking in the gear of the Lord's house, without which the divine mysteries and the ministries of God's service may not stand."

B

From two old inventories of the embroideries of
(a) Ely Cathedral, (b) Lincoln Cathedral.

(a)

"A cope of blue bawdkin, with lions of gold and unicorns white."
"An altarpiece of blue velvet, embroidered with archangels."
"A great tappit of red to lie afore the high altar, with white roses and pomegranites."
"A front of old green bawdkin, with swans of gold."
"A suit of old white bawdkin, mixed with flowers."
"A single vestment of white damaske embroidered with lily pots."

(b)

A chesable of rede bawdkyn wt leopards powdered wt blake treyfoyles.
v coopes of Rede velvett wt kateryn wheels of gold.
An other coop of blew wt dolphins of gold.
ij clothes of bawdkyn wt magpyes and poppyn Jayes.
one old cloth powdered wt cocks and mullets in gold.
A rede coop wt birds more or lesse.
A red cope of satten wt two Angells singing in the hood.

C

Tax not the royal Saint with vain expense,
With ill-matched aims the architect who planned—
Albeit labouring for a scanty band
Of white-robed scholars only—this immense
And glorious work of fine intelligence !

Give all thou can'st ; high heaven rejects the lore
Of nicely calculated less or more ;
So deemed the man, who fashioned for the sense
These lofty pillars, spread the branching roof
Self poised, and scooped into ten thousand cells,
Where light and shade repose where music dwells
Lingering—and wandering on as loath to die ;
Like thoughts whose very sweetness yieldeth proof
That they were born for immortality.

Inside of King's College Chapel, Cambridge—WORDSWORTH.

D

A casement high and triple-arched there was,
All garlanded with carven imageries
Of fruits and flowers and bunches of knot grass,
And diamonded with panes of quaint device,
Innumerable of stains, and splendid dyes,
As are the tiger-moth's deep-damask'd wings ;
And in the midst 'mong thousand heraldries,
And twilight saints, and dim emblazonings,
A shielded scutcheon blush'd with blood of queens and kings.

The Eve of St Agnes—KEATS.

E

But let my due feet never fail
To walk the studious cloisters pale,
And love the high embowed roof
With antique pillars massy proof,
And storied windows richly dight,
Casting a dim religious light :
There let the pealing organ blow
To the full-voiced choir below,
In service high and anthem clear,
As may with sweetness, through mine ear
Dissolve me into extasies
And bring all heav'n before mine eyes.

Il Penseroso—MILTON.

BIBLIOGRAPHY

OWING to the limitation of space, it is unfortunately impossible to print the full list of authorities consulted in the compilation of this volume. A very great number of books and periodical publications on art, archæology, travel, history, and biography have been referred to, and the author is only sorry that full acknowledgments are not possible. The list given below, which has no pretensions to completeness, consists of English books and a few important foreign publications, which will be found useful by all who want further information in connection with each lesson. The author is indebted to the greater number of them. The books which have the best photographic illustrations are marked with a star, while those whose chief feature consists of a series of good illustrations are marked by a double one.

GENERAL

*A History of Art. Carotti. Vol. I., Ancient Art ; Vol. II., Medieval Art. Duckworth 1909
*Apollo. Reinach. Heinemann. 2nd ed. . . . 1907
*The Childhood of Art. Spearing. Kegan Paul . . 1912
The Dawn of Civilization. Maspero. Society for Promoting Christian Knowledge. 4th ed. . . . 1901
The Struggle of the Nations. Maspero. Society for Promoting Christian Knowledge. 1896
The Passing of the Empires. Maspero. Society for Promoting Christian Knowledge. 1900
*The Ancient History of the Near East. Hall. Methuen. 1913
*Histoire de l'Art Chrètien. Michel. Vols. I.-V. Paris . 1905, etc.

*Medieval Art. Lethaby. Duckworth. 3rd ed. . . 1912
The Classical Heritage of the Middle Ages. H. O. Taylor.
   The Macmillan Co., New York 1901
*A Short Critical History of Architecture. Statham.
   Batsford 1912
*Medieval Architecture. A. K. Porter. 2 vols. Batsford 1909
*A History of Architecture. Russell Sturgis. 4 vols.
   Batsford 1909
*A History of Architecture. Banister Fletcher. Batsford.
   5th ed. 1905
Architecture. Lethaby. Williams & Norgate (Home
   University Library) 1912
The Works of Man. L. March Phillipps. Duckworth.
   2nd ed. 1914
The Fine Arts. G. Baldwin Brown. Murray. 2nd ed. . 1902
The Works of Ruskin
History of Art. Elie Faure. 4 vols. Lane . . . 1921-4

Lesson I

The Beginnings of Art. Grosse. New York . . . 1897
Pre-historic Times. Lord Avebury. Williams & Norgate.
   7th ed. 1913
Pre-historic Man. Duckworth. Cambridge University
   Press 1912
*Ancient Hunters and their Modern Representatives.
   Sollas. Macmillan 1911
*Men of the Old Stone Age. Osborne. Bell . . . 1924
Guide to the Antiquities of the Stone Age. British
   Museum Trustees 1911
*La caverne d'Altamira à Santillane. Cartailhac et Breuil.
   Imprimerie de Monaco 1906
*La caverne de Font de Gaume. Capitan, Breuil et
   Peyrony. Monaco 1910
L'art Quartenaire. Reinach. Paris 1913
*Fossil Man in Spain. Obermaier. Milford . . . 1924

Lessons II and III

*A History of Egypt. Breasted. Scribner . . . 1906

A History of the Ancient Egyptians (abridged from the above). Breasted. Smith Elder 1908

A History of Egypt; Vols. I., II., and III. Petrie. Methuen 1899-1905

A History of Art in Ancient Egypt. 2 vols. Perrot and Chipiez. Chapman & Hall 1883

*The Arts and Crafts of Ancient Egypt. Petrie. Foulis . 1909

*Art in Egypt (Ars Una Series). Maspero. Heineman . 1912

The Life and Times of Akhnaton. Weigall. Blackwood 1910

*A Guide to the First and Second Egyptian Rooms. 2nd ed. British Museum Trustees 1904

*A Guide to the Third and Fourth Egyptian Rooms. British Museum Trustees 1904

*Die Plastik der Agypter. Fecheimer. Cassirer . .

Lesson IV

*Mesopotamian Archæology. Handcock. Lee Warner . 1912

A History of Art in Chaldea and Assyria. Perrot and Chipiez. Chapman & Hall 1884

*Exploration in Bible Lands. Hilprecht. Clark . . 1903

Nineveh. Layard. 2 vols. Murray 1849

*Guide to the Babylonian and Assyrian Antiquities. British Museum Trustees. 2nd ed. 1908

*Nippur. Peters. 2 vols. Putnam 1897

*Die Kunst des alten Persian. Sarre. Cassirer . . 1922

Lesson V

*Painting in the Far East. L. Binyon. Arnold. 2nd ed. 1913

*Epochs of Chinese and Japanese Art. Fenollosa. 2 vols. Heinemann 1913

*Chinese Art. Bushell. 2 vols. South Kensington Handbooks 1910

Introduction to the History of Chinese Pictorial Art. Giles. Quaritch 1905

The Ideals of the East. Okakura-Kakuso. Murray . 1905

*Les Peintres Chinois. R. Petrucci. Paris .   .   .   1910
*An Introduction to the Study of Chinese Painting.
    A. Waley. Benn   1923
*An Introduction to the Study of Chinese Sculpture. Leigh
    Ashton. Benn   1924
*Ruins of Desert Kathay. Stein. 2 vols. Macmillan .   1912

Lesson VI

Crete, the Fore-Runner of Greece. Hawes. Harper   .   1909
The Discoveries in Crete. Burrows. Murray .   .   .   1907
*Palaces of Crete. Mosso. Unwin   1907
Art in Primitive Greece. Perrot and Chipiez. Chapman
    & Hall   1894
Schliemann's Excavations. Schuchhardt. Macmillan .   1891
Troja. Schliemann. Murray   1884
*The Palace of Minos. Sir A. Evans. Macmillan .   .   1921

Lessons VII and VIII

A Companion to Greek Studies. Edited Whibley. Cam-
    bridge University Press   1905
*A History of Greek Sculpture. E. Gardner. Macmillan.
    2nd ed.   1896
*Six Greek Sculptors. E. Gardner. Duckworth   .   .   1911
Religion and Art in Ancient Greece. E. Gardner. Harper   1910
*Ancient Athens. E. Gardner. Macmillan   .   .   .   1902
*The Art of the Greeks. Walters. Methuen .   .   .   1906
*Greek Athletic Sports and Festivals. E. Norman
    Gardiner. Macmillan   1910
The Greek View of Life. Lowes Dickinson. Methuen.
    15th ed   1909
*The Architecture of Greece and Rome. Anderson &
    Spiers. Batsford. 2nd ed   1907
**Greek Architecture. E. Browne (Great Buildings and
    how to enjoy them Series). Black   1909
The Principles of Greek Art. P. Gardner. Macmillan .   1914
A Short History of Ancient Greek Sculptors. E. Legge.
    Unwin   1903
Essays on the Art of Phidias. Waldstein. Cambridge
    University Press   1885

**Antike Porträts. R. Delbrück. Bonn 1912
**Greek Art. Warrack. Schultz 1912
Life in Ancient Athens. Tucker. Macmillan . . 1907

LESSON IX

A Companion to Latin Studies. Edited Sandys. Cam-
    bridge University Press 1910
*Roman Art. E. Strong. Duckworth. 2nd ed. 2 vols. . 1912
*The Art of the Romans. Walters. Methuen . . . 1911
Roman Art. Wickhoff. Trans. E. Sellers. Heinemann 1900
*The Architecture of Greece and Rome. Anderson and
    Spiers. Batsford. 2 vols. 2nd ed. 1907
The Evolution of Art in Roman Portraiture. Wace.
    Journal of the British and American Archæological
    Society of Rome 1906
**Antike Porträts. R. Delbrück. Bonn 1912
Companion to Roman History. Stewart Jones. Oxford
    University Press 1912

LESSON X

*Byzantine Art and Archæology. Dalton. Clarendon
    Press 1912
The Church of Sancta Sophia, Constantinople. Lethaby
    and Swainson. Macmillan 1904
*Guide to the Early Christian and Byzantine Antiquities.
    British Museum Trustees 1903
*Christian Art and Archæology. Lowrie. Macmillan . 1906
*Byzantine and Romanesque Architecture. 2 vols. Jackson.
    Cambridge University Press 1913
The Age of Justinian and Theodora. 2 vols. Holmes.
    Bell 1907
Constantinople. W. E. Hutton (Medieval Towns Series).
    Dent. 3rd. ed. 1909
**Early Christian and Byzantine Architecture (Great
    Buildings and how to enjoy them Series). E. Browne.
    Black 1912
Justinian et la civilisation Byzantine au VIth Siècle. Diehl.
    Paris 1910

Lesson XI

Lessons XII and XIII

*An Account of Medieval Figure Sculpture in England.
Prior and Gardner. Cambridge University Press . 1912
*Religious Art of the Thirteenth Century in France. Mâle.
Translated D. Nussey. Dent 1913
**The Sculptures of Chartres Cathedral. Marriage. Cam-
bridge University Press 1909
Chartres (Medieval Towns Series). C. Headlam. Dent . 1902
**Documents de Sculpture Francaise. Vol. II. Le Moyen
Age. Vitry. Paris 1911
**Deutsche Plastik des Mittelalters. Sauerlandt. Düssel-
dorf. 2nd ed. 1911
English Guilds. Toulmin Smith. Early English Text
Society 1870
The Symbolism of Churches and Church Ornaments.
(Translation of first book of William Durandus.)
Edited Neale and Webb. Gibbings 1893

INDEX

(Referring to Part II. of each Lesson only.)

323